Overcoming Body Image Problems Including Body Dysmorphic Disorder

A Self-help Guide Using Cognitive Behavioral Techniques

David Veale

Rob Willson

Alex Clarke

16

EasyRead Large

Copyright Page from the Original Book

Constable & Robinson Ltd
3 The Lanchesters
162 Fulham Palace Road
London W6 9ER
www.constablerobinson.com

First published in the UK by Robinson,
an imprint of Constable & Robinson Ltd 2009

A copy of the British Library Cataloguing in
Publication Data is available from the British Library.

Important Note

This book is not intended as a substitute for medical advice or treatment.
Any person with a condition requiring medical attention should consult
a qualified medical practitioner or suitable therapist.

ISBN 978-1-84529-279-9

Printed and bound in the EU

1 3 5 7 9 10 8 6 4 2

ReadHowYouWant partners with publishers to provide books for ALL Kinds of Readers. For more information about Becoming A (RHYW) Registered Reader and to find more titles in your preferred format, visit:

<u>www.readhowyouwant.com</u>

TABLE OF CONTENTS

DR DAVID VEALE is a Consultant Psychiatrist in cognitive behavior therapy at the South London and Maudsley Trust and The Priory Hospital North London. He is an Honorary Senior Lecturer at the Institute of Psychiatry, King's College London. He is an accredited cognitive behavior therapist and was President of the British Association for Behavioural and Cognitive Psychotherapies from 2006 to 2008. He sat on the National Institute for Health and Clinical Excellence (NICE) working group that provided guidelines for treating Obsessive Compulsive Disorder (OCD) and Body Dysmorphic Disorder (BDD) in the UK. He has about 70 publications to his name, and his own website: www.veale.co.uk. He runs a national specialist service for BDD at the Maudsley Hospital, London.

ROB WILLSON is a cognitive behavior therapist in private practice. He is a tutor at Goldsmiths College, University of London. He holds an honours degree in Psychology, an MSc in Rational Emotive Behavior Therapy, and a Postgraduate Diploma in Social and Behavioral Health Studies. He has been involved in treating individuals with body image problems for the past 13 years. David Veale and Rob Willson are authors of *Overcoming Obsessive Compulsive Disorder* and *Manage Your Mood,* also published by Robinson.

DR ALEX CLARKE is a consultant clinical psychologist in plastic and reconstructive surgery at the Royal Free Hospital, Honorary Lecturer in the Department of Mental Health Sciences at the Royal Free and University College London Medical Schools, and Visiting Professor at the Centre for Appearance Research at the University of the West of England. She has acted as consultant to the organization Changing Faces, a charity for individuals with disfigurement, and she has a particular interest in the psychological aspects of disfigurement and reconstructive surgery.

The aim of the **Overcoming** series is to enable people with a range of common problems and disorders to take control of their own recovery program. Each title, with its specially tailored program, is devised by a practising clinician using the latest techniques of cognitive behavioral therapy – techniques which have been shown to be highly effective in changing the way patients think about themselves and their problems. The series was initiated in 1993 by Peter Cooper, Professor of Psychology at Reading University and Research Fellow at the University of Cambridge in the UK, whose original volume on overcoming bulimia nervosa and binge-eating continues to help many people in the USA, the UK and Europe.

Titles in the series include:

All titles in the series are available by mail
order.
Please see the order form at the back of this
book.
www.overcoming.co.uk

Acknowledgements

We would like to acknowledge the host of individuals who have inspired or taught us and who have done most of the research into body image. We have not included full references in this book but most of the research findings are taken from the publications of Tom Cash, Christina Lambrou, Fugen Neziroglu, Sandra Mulkens, Katharine Phillips, Nichola Rumsey, Roz Shafran, Sabine Wilhelm, and many other researchers too numerous to mention. Lastly, we thank all our patients, from whom we have learnt so much. We recognize the struggle they face every day, and hope that this book will be helpful to them and others.

Why a cognitive behavioral approach?

The approach this book takes in attempting to help you overcome your body image problems is a 'cognitive behavioral' one. A brief account of the history of this form of intervention might be useful and encouraging. In the 1950s and 1960s a set of therapeutic techniques was developed, collectively termed 'behavior therapy'. These techniques shared two basic features. First, they aimed to remove symptoms (such as anxiety) by dealing with those symptoms themselves, rather than their deep-seated underlying historical causes (traditionally the focus of psychoanalysis, the approach developed by Sigmund Freud and his associates). Second, they were scientifically based, in the sense that they used techniques derived from what laboratory psychologists were finding out about the mechanisms of learning, and they put these techniques to scientific test. The area where behavior therapy initially proved to be of most value was in the treatment of anxiety disorders, especially specific phobias (such as extreme fear of animals or heights) and agoraphobia, both notoriously difficult to treat using conventional psychotherapies.

After an initial flush of enthusiasm, discontent with behavior therapy grew. There were a number of reasons for this, an important one of which was the fact that behavior therapy did not deal with the internal thoughts which were so obviously central to the distress that many patients were experiencing. In particular, behavior therapy proved inadequate when it came to the treatment of depression. In the late 1960s and early 1970s a treatment for depression was developed called 'cognitive therapy'. The pioneer in this enterprise was an American psychiatrist, Professor Aaron T. Beck. He developed a theory of depression which emphasized the importance of people's depressed styles of thinking, and, on the basis of this theory, he specified a new form of therapy. It would not be an exaggeration to say that Beck's work has changed the nature of psychotherapy, not just for depression but for a range of psychological problems.

The techniques introduced by Beck have been merged with the techniques developed earlier by the behavior therapists to produce a therapeutic approach which has come to be known as 'cognitive behavioral therapy' (or CBT). This therapy has been subjected to the strictest scientific testing and has been found to be highly successful for a significant proportion of cases of depression. It has now become clear that specific patterns of disturbed thinking are associated with a wide range of psychological problems, not just depression, and that the treatments which deal with these are highly effective. So, effective cognitive behavioral treatments have been developed for a range of anxiety disorders, such as panic disorder, generalized anxiety disorder, specific phobias, social phobia, obsessive compulsive disorders, and hypochondriasis (health anxiety), as well as for other conditions such as drug addictions, and eating disorders like bulimia nervosa. Indeed, cognitive behavioral techniques have been found to have an application beyond the narrow categories of psychological disorders. They have been applied effectively, for example, to helping people with weight problems, couples with marital difficulties, as well as those who wish to give up smoking or deal with drinking problems. They have also been effectively applied to dealing with low self-esteem. In relation to the current self-help manual, over several years effective CBT techniques have been developed for helping people overcome their problems with their body image.

The starting-point for CBT is the realization that the way we think, feel and behave are all intimately linked, and changing the way we think about ourselves, our experiences, and the world around us changes the way we feel and what we are able to do. So, for example, by helping a depressed person identify and challenge their automatic depressive thoughts, a route out of the cycle of depressive thoughts and feelings can be found. Similarly, habitual behavioral responses are driven by a complex set of thoughts and feelings, and CBT, as you will discover from this book, by providing a means for the behavior, thoughts and feelings to be brought under control, enables these responses to be undermined and a different kind of life to be possible.

Although effective CBT treatments have been developed for a wide range of disorders and problems, these treatments are not currently widely available; and, when people try on their own to help themselves, they often, inadvertently, do things which make matters worse. In recent years the community of cognitive behavioral therapists has responded to this situation. What they have done is to take the principles and techniques of specific cognitive behavioral therapies for particular problems and present them in manuals which people can read and apply themselves. These manuals specify a systematic programme of treatment which the person works through to overcome their difficulties. In this way, cognitive behavioral therapeutic techniques of proven value are being made available on the widest possible basis.

The use of self-help manuals is never going to replace the need for therapists. Many people with emotional and behavioral problems will need the help of a qualified therapist. It is also the case that, despite the widespread success of cognitive behavioral therapy, some people will not respond to it and will need one of the other treatments available. Nevertheless, although research on the use of these self-help manuals is at an early stage, the work done to date indicates that for a great many people such a manual is sufficient for them to overcome their problems without professional help. Sadly, many people suffer on their own for years. Sometimes they feel reluctant to seek help without first making a serious effort to manage on their own. Sometimes they feel too awkward or even ashamed to ask for help. Sometimes appropriate help is not forthcoming despite their efforts to find it. For many of these people the cognitive behavioral self-help manual will provide a lifeline to a better future.

Peter J Cooper
The University of Reading, 2009

1

Appearance matters

First impressions

Appearance is important. First impressions depend partly on what we look like and partly on how we behave. Faces, in particular, have a number of functions. Our faces allow us to express ourselves and communicate. Our emotions – such as happiness and sadness, disgust and anger – are all conveyed through our facial expressions. When we communicate with someone, we are constantly noting (whether consciously or not) what their eyes, mouth and stance are telling us, as well as what we are hearing in their words and tone. Is the other person interested in what we are saying? Or are they bored? Faces communicate vital information as we find our way through a conversation, showing that we are listening, indicating questions or taking turns to speak. Faces also indicate age and attractiveness, ethnicity, gender, and familial or racial characteristics. There are many reasons, therefore, why faces are important in human behavior, and this is why it can be particularly difficult if something about your own face worries or disturbs you.

Similarly, we all pay attention to 'body language' (meaning the way we use our bodies and behave to convey additional information to other people). If you are excessively concerned or anxious about your appearance, changing the way that you look may seem the obvious or only way of changing how you feel. But you can also manage your concern about your appearance by thinking and behaving differently. So the goal in this book is for you to become less preoccupied with your appearance rather than to radically change your appearance in itself. It also means being able to get on with what is important in life, despite what your mind is telling you. This will be explored in later chapters. First we will discuss appearance and body image in more detail. What is a normal appearance? And what is normal in terms of how much we think about it and try to change it?

What is body image?

Psychologists use the term 'body image' to describe our internalized sense of what we look like. This can be thought of as a mental representation or map of our body, against which we judge our external appearance. The idea of body image was first developed by neurologists, who were investigating how the brain interprets information that it receives from different parts of the body. For example, after people lose a limb they often experience phantom pain or sensation – as if the limb were still there. For this to occur, the brain must have some kind of internalized representation of the limb. This mental image takes time to adjust once the external appearance has been altered. The body image of people with eating disorders has also been studied, and their perception of their body size may differ greatly from their actual size. People with anorexia may feel normal or fat even though, in reality, they are very thin. Once again, their internal body image is providing inaccurate information about what they look like.

For most of us, there is a relatively good match between what we think we look like (subjective appearance) and how we appear to other people (objective appearance), although it is interesting how often people dislike photographs of themselves. To some extent, our body image is idealized (based on how we would like to look). It is also based on a mirror image of our actual appearance. Other people see animated or moving images, whereas we view our own image mainly through photographs or mirrors where expression is still. Body image also changes slowly as we get older. We recognize our image as 'our self' when we are children and as we grow into adults.

However, when our appearance changes suddenly, perhaps after an accident or as a result of disease, it can be very disconcerting, and it can take quite a long time before we 'see ourselves' once more when looking in the mirror. Even a dramatically different haircut can be quite shocking when we catch sight of an unexpected reflection, for example in a shop window.

Body image can also be studied in terms of what we look like in the eyes of an observer. What other people see and what we think they can see – the outside and inside view of body image – are like two sides of a coin, as they both contribute to how we feel about our looks. For example, we might receive positive or negative feedback about our appearance that might influence the way we think and feel. Equally, the way we act and feel about our appearance will have an impact on others. For example, if you keep your head down, don't make eye contact and say very little then others will think you are not interested in them. They could be critical and reject you, not because of your appearance but because of your actions.

Body image can therefore be positive or negative and can vary over time. It is just one aspect of the way you feel about yourself. For instance, you might have a negative body image and a high sense of worth about other aspects of yourself or vice versa. Ideas about body image overlap with feelings of high or low self-esteem. If low self-esteem is a problem then it may take longer to overcome your body image problems, and we will discuss this in Chapter 2.

Body image changes as we get older

Attractiveness is difficult to define but there are several common factors across different cultures. For instance, someone with a very symmetrical, balanced face is usually rated attractive. More symmetrical features may be a sign of good health and fertility, as an infection at a young age can interfere with facial symmetry. One theory is that the human brain has a built-in mechanism for detecting symmetry because it demonstrates to others that the person has good genes and does not have any serious illness. Even babies are born with a tendency to pay attention to attractive faces. Studies have found that a baby's attention is held for slightly longer by images of faces that that have been rated as very attractive compared to images of unattractive faces. Older children also play for slightly longer with attractive dolls.

Very young children show little awareness of their own appearance, and they don't make value judgements about other people based on the way they look. However, from the age of about seven, children become more aware of their own appearance, and may begin to discriminate between 'good' and bad' appearance and ascribe characteristics to other people based on what they look like. Children's literature reinforces this development by linking the ideas of beauty and goodness. Fairytales such as 'Cinderella' or 'Beauty and the Beast' (variations of which can be found in all cultures) reinforce the idea that beauty is rewarded and is therefore to be prized, and ugliness is associated with evil. This assumption appears even in films where the hero is generally strong and good-looking and the villain characterized with a scar or disfigurement. One of the few 'plain' heroines in literature is Jane Eyre, but she is not married to Mr Rochester until he has been blinded in a fire and has acquired additional disabilities! Media images from publications such as *Hello!* and *OK!* magazine increasingly link physical attractiveness with exceptional success and celebrity, although in reality the celebrities featured often seem to find that their fame brings them problems rather than happiness.

Adolescence is the period when people's appearance changes most noticeably, and over a very short period of time, as they reach puberty. Before puberty, male and female children have very similar body shapes. After puberty, girls develop breasts and curvier hips. For boys, the trunk slims, the shoulders broaden, facial features become more masculine, and facial hair starts to grow. Although breast development is characteristic of girls, some boys also experience breast changes. 'Man boobs', as they are sometimes called, can be very worrying for teenage boys and may lead to teasing but they usually disappear as puberty continues.

Most importantly, appearance becomes linked with sexuality during puberty. The way people look affects their attractiveness in the eyes of other people. It also influences the way they see themselves. Whilst girls are usually thought to worry most about their physical appearance, young men are also very concerned with how they look. However, whilst girls aspire to an ideal weight and shape, boys focus more on fitness and bulging muscles.

The hormonal surge that occurs at puberty not only triggers the physical changes mentioned earlier; it can also impact on other very visible aspects of appearance, such as people's skin. For example, acne (caused by excessive production of sebum in the skin) can cause very visible and painful pimples across the face and shoulders in particular. Although associated with adolescence, acne can continue throughout someone's life and often causes considerable unhappiness and anxiety about appearance. Fortunately, this condition can usually be well controlled with a combination of medications, which reduce the production of sebum and combat infection. Acne is a good example of a condition that is common but often misunderstood. Although it is usually seen as a minor issue or a 'normal' part of growing up, the level of distress experienced by some acne sufferers may be highly significant. While it may be assumed that someone with severe facial burns will experience more distress than someone with acne, this is not necessarily true. Any form of altered appearance may cause distress if the individual feels that it makes them different from their peer group, and puts them at a disadvantage compared with other people.

The self-consciousness associated with these rapid changes in appearance is perfectly normal. Adolescence is a time when people can become acutely aware of body changes, particularly if they are either first or last in their peer group to, for example, develop breasts. Whilst some people enjoy the sense of being different or exceptional, it is far more common to want to 'fit in' or to be 'unremarkable'. Therefore comments about appearance can make people feel acutely uncomfortable. Unfortunately, adolescence is also a time when bullying is most common. And, since appearance is the most immediately obvious thing about people, bully-ing remarks will often concern their appearance. Thus weight, shape, hair or skin colour, height, obvious scars or birthmarks, and skin conditions such as acne, can all become the focus of bullying.

However, it is important that the problem here is recognized as the bullies' behavior rather than the young person's appearance. Bullies pick on the things about which people feel vulnerable, and schools should therefore take measures to prevent bullying about appear-ance in the same way as they try to prevent the expression of racism and sexism. Bullying is not a good reason for seeking to make changes in your appearance, particularly during adolescence. But it is a good reason to develop some strategies for managing intrusive or bullying behavior from other people. Further-more, 'ghosts from the past' can influence us in the present. People who have been bullied or abused when they were younger often feel, in adulthood, that they are still being humiliated by others (when they are not) and may become excessively preoccupied with their appearance.

Body image is often assumed to be less important for older people. Look at the vast and lucrative industry devoted to helping people slow down or prevent the obvious signs of ageing, however, and a different picture emerges. Many older people are clearly still very interested in their appearance. Likewise, younger people often anticipate that they will be more relaxed about their appearance once they 'reach 40' but people whose sense of self-worth is largely determined by their appearance are unlikely to change as they grow older. In some work settings, particularly those in the media, such as television, personal appearance has great importance and an attractive individual is likely to do better when competing for a high-status job. This has led many older employees to worry about the effects of ageism and pursue a more youthful appearance in order to protect their employment.

Cultural factors and changes in the body image ideal

Some body image 'ideals' have remained relatively unchanged over the centuries. For example, a smooth and unblemished skin has been prized in women across all the cultures that have been studied throughout history. Thus smallpox, which left the skin very pockmarked in previous centuries, led to women wearing veils and being considered less attractive as potential wives. In modern times women in some developing countries are sometimes attacked with acid in order to cause facial burns that may result in them being unable to find a husband. Unblemished skin is thought to be prized because it is associated with youth and therefore fertility; ageing is most visible in the skin, compared with other organs. Disease is also very apparent in skin appearance, so smooth, healthy skin is likely to have a strong evolutionary advantage and to be prized in all cultures.

Other aspects of appearance may vary with socioeconomic conditions. Weight is a good example. In cultures or at times when food is short, plumpness becomes a sign of wealth and is valued. However, with the advent of cheaper mass-marketed food in the West, obesity is becoming prevalent, and a slimmer, more muscular, 'physically fit' ideal has developed. Tanned skin, associated with wealth in European populations before the advent of cheap travel, is becoming less desirable as it becomes more easily achievable for all, although this may also be a result of the negative link between sun exposure and skin cancer and premature age-ing. This particular change in ideal body image therefore associates appearance with wealth and status.

Promotion of unattainable ideals

Playboy magazine centrefolds, as well as images of models used in fashion advertising, from different decades of the twentieth century show that our idealized female body shape has become increasingly androgynous, and in some ways more male than female. Over the years, models' hips have become slimmer and their waist-to-hip ratios have been reduced. (However, well-defined breasts are still widely valued, leading some women to opt for cosmetic surgery.) This change in the ideal female body shape is probably partly due to the require-ments of the fashion industry, clothes being easier to drape and photograph on a thinner form. However, an idealized female form that is unattainable (or only attainable by means of extreme dieting) is a potential problem for all of us. If we compare ourselves to the ideal and find ourselves wanting, we are more likely to become anxious about our appearance.

Those who are influential in fashion are now being asked to select models from a wider range of body shapes and sizes in order to help reduce the pressure felt by vulnerable young women. However, there is much that still needs to be done to redress this balance. Another related problem arises from the increased use of modified photographic images, in which a perceived defect can be airbrushed out, or the image can be created by combining images from a variety of sources. For the average person, it is impossible to tell a real image from a fabricated one, and this is an additional concern for those working in the field of body image research where images are still idealized and sought after by some people even when they are impossible to achieve. Different racial characteristics may also be idealized. Thus fairer or whiter skin is prized and promoted by manufacturers of skin-whitening creams in Asia; while plastic surgeons may be asked to modify Chinese eyelids to provide wider, more characteristically Western-looking eyes.

'Normal' body image

How can we define a normal body image, if it is clear from research and from the vast amounts spent on clothes and make-up that most of us attempt to modify or change our appearance to some extent on a regular basis? Even without knowing the cultural history of body image, most of us recognize that there is a certain pressure on women, and increasingly on men, to look good. Magazines that promote celebrity status and unachievable body images also carry critical articles that mock popular figures for their appearance, weight and choice of clothing. Whilst this does help to show that no one looks like a magazine photo all the time, it is very similar to the bullying experienced in the school or workplace by those whose appearance is unusual. Most people respond to this pressure, for example, by dressing in an appropriate way for work.

In the Western world, the majority of us shower or bath regularly. We have more than one set of clothing, and whilst most of us have a certain 'style' that we adhere to, there is a tendency to take more time and trouble over our appearance in situations where we are meeting people for the first time. This is perhaps because we know that, whilst some judgements about us will be made on the basis of our appearance in an initial meeting, subsequent meetings will focus much more on our behavior, personality, and competence (in a work setting). Appearance therefore becomes less important in longer established relationships.

Use of make-up, removal of some body hair, colouring of hair, body piercing and tattooing are all regarded as normal in modern western society. Using surgery to enhance our appearance is much more accepted than it used to be, although someone who undergoes multiple or repeated procedures may be excessively concerned with his or her appearance.

The factors that distinguish someone with a normal body image from someone who has a body image problem are linked with the way they think and act. Different kinds of body image problems will be described more fully in Chapter 2. However, it is important to realize that you don't have a body image problem simply because you dislike certain parts of your body, think that you would like to lose a few pounds, regularly wear make-up or love clothes. Nor do you have a body image problem if you have a significant disfigurement or an unusual appearance. Many people whose appearance falls outside the 'norm' live perfectly happy lives and celebrate the things that make them exceptional. Body image disorders are much more to do with thinking about your appearance to the exclusion of other activities, and avoiding social situations, workplaces or relationships because of the way you look. Believing that you can only feel confident or be happy if you change the way you look or that your appearance is preventing you from participating in certain activities are also typical of body image disorders. Excessive worry, repeatedly checking your appearance, consistent use of very heavy make-up or refusal to leave the house without make-up are all extremes of normal behavior, though they tend to reinforce the idea that your appearance is abnormal, thus increasing body image anxiety.

Why does being attractive matter?

Being attractive might have a 'halo effect'; in other words others might believe that 'what is beautiful is good'. For instance, all things being equal, a very attractive person might have a very slight advantage in getting a particular job. Attractiveness is important in the first encounter and influences initial impressions; other qualities, such as social skills and self-confidence, are then more important in the long term. However, being attractive is about much more than just your physical appearance. For example it includes:

- *Your body language and posture.* For example, are you playful and do you flirt appropriately? (Or do you keep your head down, make little eye contact and hope that others will go away?)
- *Your sense of style.* Do you dress well in clothes that suit you? (Or do you wear worn-out, badly fitting clothes?)

• *Your manner.* Do you act as if you have charisma and enthusiasm? (Or are you someone with little to say and not much interest in others?)

There are many couples in which one partner is much less physically attractive than the other. In such cases, the less attractive partner may be valued highly because of their other qualities. Being very attractive can also have disadvantages such as attracting unwanted attention, or inhibiting others who feel that they can't match such a high standard.

Research has shown that the way someone *feels* about their appearance has far more influence on their quality of life than how physically attractive they are to others. Thus an individual who is extremely disfigured can have a good quality of life and an individual who is generally considered attractive may be deeply distressed and have a poor quality of life. The examples of Katherine and Tom, described below, illustrate either end of this spectrum.

KATHERINE

Katherine's face was severely disfigured from burns in a road traffic accident. Most people would rate her appearance as unusual and would not have come across some-

one who looks so visibly different in their everyday experience. To start with, after the accident, Katherine was shocked by her appearance, and failed to recognize herself in the mirror. After a period of rehabilitation, she is now familiar with her new looks, accepts that no amount of surgery is going to restore her previous appearance, and has rebuilt her self-esteem by acknowledging all her talents, abilities and skills. She is a good partner and parent and a full member of the community, functioning well in society. Sometimes the questions and curiosity about her story get her down, but generally she has learned to manage other people's curiosity and is confident and at ease in social situations.

TOM

Tom is someone who most people would agree now has a reasonably attractive appearance. However, he was teased and bullied as a child about his acne and has carried the feeling of being insecure and conspicuous into adult life. He believes that others will be critical of him and blames his appearance for his lack of confidence. He repeatedly checks his facial appearance in mirrors and avoids a wide *range of social situations and intimacy because of his fear of being humiliated. Like many people with body image problems, he believes that if he could change what he looks like he would feel more confident and be more successful, both in his social life and in close relationships.*

We are not saying that individuals who are disfigured do not experience problems or that an attractive person does not have an advantage in life – but we are saying that people's quality of life does not depend on their objective appearance. What makes the difference is how you think and act about your appearance. For instance, Katherine knows that she has a disfigured appearance but she also recognizes that this is only a small part of how she is perceived by other people – particularly those who know her best. Tom, however, sees his appearance as the major factor defining who he is and how he relates to others. But rather than changing his appearance, the key to changing his quality of life lies in changing the way he thinks and acts. This is the key to understanding and changing all body image problems. We understand this is not going to be easy, as these patterns of thinking and behaving have often built up over many years, but many people have succeeded in overcoming body image problems using this approach.

Making the most of life

Appearance is important. It influences how people view us, particularly when they meet us for the first time. Beauty has always been and remains highly prized, though most of us aim to fit in rather than stand out. This may lead us to modify our appearance to some extent to fit in with our job, lifestyle and peer group. Feeling happy with our appearance may make us feel positive about ourselves, as well as giving us the sense of others being attracted to us and being positively regarded.

If we don't keep this in proportion, however, we can become excessively preoccupied with appearance in a way that is very unhelpful. Far from working to our advantage, this will increase any beliefs about being abnormal and viewed negatively by others. If we check our features excessively or avoid certain situations, we end up not only limiting our own lives severely, but also affecting those around us, and this in turn has an effect on how attractive we are to others.

In the following chapters we will help you to assess the way you think and act. We will also help you to make changes that will allow you to enjoy taking an interest in your appearance without this limiting your life and opportunities.

2

Have you got a body image problem?

This book will discuss a whole range of problems that are broadly described as body image problems. We will cover body dysmorphic disorder (including compulsive skin-picking), eating disorders and certain medical disorders. For example, skin problems (such as acne and eczema) and disfigurements, such as burns, sometimes cause difficulties that are the same as those caused by other body image problems, in terms of the resulting preoccupation and distress interfering with people's day-to-day lives. For this reason, we are including these conditions within the scope of this book, although we recognize that not everyone who has a visible difference in appearance is distressed or worried by it.

We will start by describing each of these problems and how they affect body image.

Body dysmorphic disorder (BDD)

Body dysmorphic disorder (BDD) involves an extreme preoccupation with one or more features that are not that noticeable or abnormal to others. People with BDD usually feel they are ugly, that they are 'not right' and are very self-conscious. They usually have compulsive behaviors such as mirror checking that are difficult to resist. They may resort to needless cosmetic and dermatological procedures with which they are either dissatisfied or that have little impact on their preoccupation and distress. People with BDD also tend to be very secretive and reluctant to seek help because they are afraid that others will think them vain or narcissistic. (Of course they are **not** vain at all, as their goal is to fit in rather than to stand out and they usually hate their appearance.)

The older term for BDD, 'dysmorphophobia', is sometimes still used. The media sometimes refer to BDD as 'Imagined Ugliness Syndrome'. This isn't particularly helpful, as the ugliness is very real to the individual concerned.

Some people with BDD acknowledge that they may be blowing things up out of proportion. At the other extreme, others are firmly convinced of the reality of their supposed abnormality. Whatever the person's degree of insight into their own condition, someone with BDD usually knows that others believe their appearance to be 'normal' and will have been told so many times.

The degree of disability caused by BDD varies from slight to very severe. Many people with BDD are either single or divorced, which suggests that they find it difficult to form relationships. It can make regular employment and family life impossible. Those who are in regular employment or who have family responsibilities would almost certainly find life more productive and satisfying if they did not have the symptoms of BDD. Their partners may also become involved and suffer greatly.

The questionnaire below highlights the key characteristics of BDD and your answers should indicate whether or not you have the condition.

QUESTIONNAIRE 2.1: HAVE I GOT BDD?

1. Do you feel that you have one or more features that are very noticeable, abnormal, ugly or 'not right'?

Yes _ No _

2. Have others close to you or a health professional said that the feature(s) are not that noticeable, abnormal or ugly or look 'OK'?

Yes _ No _

3. If you add up all the time your feature(s) is/are at the forefront of your mind and make the best estimate for a typical day, do you worry (or brood) about it/them for an hour or more a day?

Yes _ No _

If you answered 'yes' to all the first three questions, proceed to question 4. If you did not answer 'yes' to all these questions, then you don't have BDD and there is no need to finish the questionnaire.

4. Does your worry about your feature(s) cause you marked distress?

Yes _ No _

5. Does your worry about your feature(s) significantly interfere with your ability to work or study, or in your role as a homemaker?

Yes No

6. Does your worry about your feature(s) significantly interfere with your social life? Or do you try to avoid social situations because of your feature(s)?

Yes _ No _

7. If you have no current partner: Has your worry about your feature(s) had a significant effect on dating or interfered with your ability to form an intimate relationship?

If you have a regular partner: Has your worry about your feature(s) significantly interfered in the relationship with your partner?

Yes _ No _

If you answered 'yes' to the first three questions and to one or more of questions 4 to 7 then you *may* have BDD. However, only a health professional can give you a firm diagnosis, as there could be another problem (such as an eating disorder) that may account better for your body image concerns. Thus if you are mainly preoccupied about being 'too fat' or overweight and are significantly restricting your food or binge eating, then this is probably not BDD. However, some individuals with an eating disorder may also have a form of BDD, which does not involve their weight or shape. (For example, a person with anorexia and BDD may also be preoccupied by their weight and shape as well as feeling ugly and scarred on their face.)

Up to 1 per cent of the world's population may have BDD, and it may be more frequent in some cultures where cosmetic surgery is more common. It is recognized to be a hidden disorder, as many people with BDD are too ashamed to reveal their problem.

Both sexes are equally affected by BDD. People with BDD are most commonly concerned with their skin, followed by concerns about their nose, hair, eyes, chin, lips or overall body build. People with BDD may complain of a lack of symmetry, or feel that something is too big or too small, or that it is out of proportion to the rest of the body. Any part of the body may be involved in BDD, including the breasts or genitals. Although women are more likely to have hair concerns (e.g. that hair is the wrong colour, or it lacks body, or there is excessive body hair), men are significantly more concerned with hair thinning or baldness.

The sex differences also occur with body size and shape. Women are more likely to be preoccupied by their breasts, hips, weight and legs, usually believing that they are too large or fat. In contrast, men tend to be preoccupied with their body build, which has also been described as muscle dysmorphia (described below). Another significant sex difference is that men are more likely to report preoccupation with their genitals (usually a concern that their penis is too small), or be concerned about breast development, which they see as too feminine. Women may also feel that their genitalia or labia are too large and seek cosmetic surgery to reduce their size.

Muscle dysmorphia is a variation of BDD in which a man is usually worried about being too small or too skinny or not muscular enough. Despite such concerns, many such men are unusually muscular and large. Many of them spend hours lifting weights and pay great attention to nutrition. Others may abuse steroids. In our experience, such individuals are less likely to seek help than other people with BDD and may be less disabled by the condition.

BDD usually begins in adolescence, a time when people are generally most sensitive about their appearance. However, many people wait for years before seeking help. They may repeatedly consult dermatologists or cosmetic surgeons but often get little satisfaction from these treatments. When they do finally seek help from mental health professionals, they often ask about other symptoms such as depression, social anxiety or obsessive compulsive disorder (OCD) and do not reveal their real concerns. However, people with BDD are often also depressed with a high rate of attempted suicide.

Treatments for body dysmorphic disorder

In the UK, the body responsible for producing treatment guidelines is the National Institute for Health and Clinical Excellence (NICE), which is highly regarded throughout the world. Experts in BDD, including doctors, therapists, and individuals who have experienced BDD, have got together to review the evidence and produce the guidelines, based on published research into BDD. At present, unfortunately, there is very little research into BDD – compared with, say, depression. Furthermore, the published research is only a snapshot of current evidence, which will be updated as new evidence becomes available.

The treatment guidelines on OCD and BDD can be downloaded from the NICE website (see Appendix 1).

The guidelines are based on scientific 'evidence' – that is, studies in which people with BDD are randomly selected to receive one or more different treatments or to remain on a waiting list. One group might be given a placebo (or dummy) treatment so that researchers can see to what extent the attention of a doctor or therapist and the passage of time affects the outcome. At the end of the study the researchers then re-test participants to see which treatments are more effective.

In all the guidelines, there is particular emphasis on patient choice and on the patient's experience with previous treatment. However, treatment options partly depend on the availability of therapists and local resources. If you are seeing a doctor or therapist, he or she will advise you as to what is best for you given the resources available. It isn't always obvious which treatment is most effective for a particular person. Sometimes you may have to try two or three different approaches before you find one that works for you. The core message is that there is evidence that BDD *is treatable and you can get back to a normal life.*

COGNITIVE BEHAVIOR THERAPY (CBT) FOR BDD

CBT was initially described by Aaron T. Beck, who revolutionized the psychological treatment of depression in the early 1970s. It has been adapted for BDD and has been shown to be effective for adults in a few small studies. CBT is therefore recommended by NICE for treating BDD. This book is based upon the principles of CBT and is ideally used with the support of an accredited therapist (see Chapter 15). However, change *is* possible with the support of a friend, family member, or even alone. Many people with body image problems find that they may have to wait many months to see a thera-pist, so getting started with self-help can be a really good first step.

MEDICATION FOR BDD

Anti-obsessional medication (a seroton-ergic reuptake inhibitor) is not recommend-ed for mild symptoms of BDD. However, it may be recommended if a patient's doctor believes that the BDD symptoms are likely to get worse (or if the symptoms have lasted for a long time). Anti-obsessional medication is also a recommended option in treating moderate to severe symptoms of BDD. We discuss the use of medication in both adolescents and adults in more de-tail in Chapter 14.

COMBINING MEDICATION WITH CBT

In general, we do not recommend using medication alone because there is usually a higher rate of relapse when a person stops taking his or her medication. Results tend to be better when the medication is combined with CBT (and for relapse preven-tion purposes most people need to take medication for at least a year, which may be beyond the course of therapy). However, a few people can do fine on medication alone – the difficulty lies in identifying such individuals.

If you are seeking treatment for BDD, you need to think about the function of medication for you. If you have tried more than one course of medication and you are hoping that your doctor will come up with a drug that will get rid of your bad feelings, you are not really helping yourself. As we will show in Chapter 4, trying to escape from a bad feeling actually becomes part of the problem and maintains the problem. The main goal of medication is to stop you feeling distressed, whereas the psychological approaches described in this book are generally geared to helping you do the things you value in life, despite the way you feel. We have no evidence that one approach interferes with the other. People with more severe problems may do better on a combination of medication and CBT.

It's worth being aware, though, that more research is needed on the long-term effects of combining medication and effective psychological therapies. Mental disorder is complex and there are no easy answers. Whatever approach you take, make sure you monitor your progress with the rating scales in this book so you can decide (with your therapist or doctor) what is helping and whether to try something else.

INEQUALITIES IN FUNDING FOR MEDICATION AND PSYCHOLOGICAL TREATMENTS

After you recover from your body image problem, we hope that you will think seriously about campaigning for better access to evidence-based psychological treatments so that there is a real choice for everyone. For this to happen, there needs to be better funding for research into the use of psychological treatments in BDD. For example, we need to measure the effectiveness of combining CBT and medication and compare it with the effectiveness of using either treatment alone for severe BDD in the long term.

We also need to measure the relative cost-effectiveness of each treatment. For example, medication may seem a cheaper option in the short term, but if there is a high rate of relapse it can, in the long term, become a more expensive option, as patients have to take the medication for many years. Proving this can be difficult and expensive because researchers need to recruit a very large number of participants. Pharmaceutical companies have plenty of money for research, whereas scientists who want to investigate psychological treatments have great difficulty in obtaining grants because the pot of money available is much smaller. This is partly related to the stigma of mental disorder – scientists studying cancer or heart diseases have a relatively easier time raising funds for research.

Psychogenic excoriation

Psychogenic excoriation is popularly known as 'compulsive skin-picking'. However, it includes a broader range of behaviors such as excessive scratching, picking, gouging, lancing, digging, rubbing or squeezing of the skin. 'Psychogenic' implies a psychological factor for the excoriation. Psychogenic excoriation is not yet recognized as a formal diagnosis but is sometimes referred to as a habit disorder or compulsive skin-picking.

People with compulsive skin-picking (CSP) often have body image problems and feel ashamed about the damage they have caused. A minority of patients may pick skin only in response to sensations such as a feeling of itchiness or an underlying dermatological condition. CSP may be a symptom of BDD, as a way of coping with minor irregularities in the skin that are hardly noticeable to others. However, once the skin-picking has started, then it may develop into an automatic or impulsive behavior and the original reason for picking may be forgotten. CSP can also be a symptom of other mental health problems such as borderline personality disorder or obsessive compulsive disorder.

There are treatments for compulsive skin-picking, whether it is part of BDD or not. This is a very under-researched area so the relative effectiveness of medication and psychological therapies is not well known. Expert opinion is that the best psychological therapy for overcoming CSP is a method called 'habit reversal' and this is discussed in Chapter 11.

QUESTIONNAIRE 2.2: DO I HAVE COMPULSIVE SKIN-PICKING?

1. Do you repeatedly scratch, pick, gouge, dig, rub or squeeze your skin and does it lead to noticeable skin damage?
Yes _ No _
2. Are you preoccupied with scratching, picking, gouging, digging, rubbing or squeezing your skin and are the urges intrusive or irresistible?
Yes _ No _

If you answered 'yes' to both questions, then proceed to question 3. If you did not answer 'yes' to both questions then you do not need to complete this questionnaire.

3. Do the urges or behaviors associated with skin-picking cause you marked distress?

Yes _ No _

4. Are the urges or behaviors associated with skin-picking significantly time-consuming or do they interfere with your social life or work?

Yes _ No _

5. Do the behaviors result in medical problems (e.g. infections or significant scarring)?

Yes _ No _

If you answered 'yes' to the first two questions and to one or more of the questions 3 to 5 then you probably have compulsive skin-picking. However, only a health professional can diagnose you as suffering from psychogenic excoriation or tell you if there is an underlying problem such as BDD. Sometimes a medical condition can account better for your behavior.

Skin disorders and disfigurement

Individuals with disfigurement can have many or all of the body image problems related to preoccupation, shame and worry about appearance. They may also have to cope with social problems such as intense curiosity from others, teasing and bullying, staring, comments and questions. Disfigurements can be caused by a congenital disorder (people are born with them) or they may be acquired at any stage in life as a result of injury or disease.

Because severe disfiguring conditions are relatively rare, most people seldom come across someone who looks visibly different. This means that when they do, they tend to notice, do a 'double take' or even ask the person how their condition was caused. This response to anything out of the ordinary is a natural human reaction; our brains are 'hard wired' to take notice of the unique or unusual. But for someone who is constantly being stared at or asked questions, life can become frustrating and annoying. It can then be easy to slip into a pattern of avoiding social situations, particularly when there are likely to be lots of new people present.

Medical and surgical solutions are not always possible. Therefore treatment is based on understanding the responses of others, learning to pre-empt problems by taking the initiative in social situations, and building on the research evidence that people respond to behavior as much as to appearance in building relationships. These issues are explored more fully in Chapter 12.

As yet, there have not been any controlled trials comparing one psychological treatment with another for people with disfigurement or physical defect. However, there have been a number of small studies in which CBT has produced promising results, both when delivered to individuals and in group settings. There is also evidence that CBT methods are much more effective than no treatment at all, and that written programmes – such as this book – are also effective.

This book uses the principles of CBT, which can be applied to body image problems involving disfigurement, and the specific problems of disfigurement are discussed in more detail in Chapter 12. The charity Changing Faces (See Appendix 1) has also recently funded a study, which has developed and tested a computerized program for treating disfigurement. The results of this study are looking very promising and this development will enable people to access treatment from their own homes.

Trichotillomania

Trichotillomania involves repeated hair-pulling. The hair pulled is commonly on the scalp or eyebrows but may also be pulled from under one's armpit or pubic area. Having pulled the hair, people often feel less tense and sometimes have a sense of gratification. They may then become ashamed of the consequences of hair-pulling and will strenuously try to cover any resulting patches of baldness. People with trichotillomania often have body image problems as a result of bald patches on their scalp. Like compulsive skin-picking, hair-pulling can sometimes occur in BDD when an individual pulls hair from themselves as a way of coping with a 'defect' to improve their appearance. The principles of overcoming skin-picking can also be used to overcome trichotillomania and these principles are discussed in Chapter 11.

Anorexia nervosa

Anorexia nervosa is a condition in which a person keeps their body weight low by restricting what they eat. Someone with anorexia is severely underweight, with a body mass index (BMI) of 17.5 or under. The best way to find out whether or not you are underweight is to calculate your BMI. To do this, you need to divide your weight (in kg) by your height (in metres) squared. For example, if you weigh 46 kg and you are 1.72 metres tall, then your BMI is $46 \div (1.72 \times 1.72) = 15.5$, which is underweight. An even easier way to calculate your BMI (for which you can also use old-fashioned feet and inches and stones and pounds) is to use the automatic calculator on the website http://www.globalrph.com/bmi.cgi

Anorexia is more common in girls and young women but can also occur in boys and men. People with anorexia are preoccupied with their shape and weight. At one level, people with anorexia nervosa 'feel' fat. They fear losing control and becoming overweight. However, at another level, they may know that they are underweight and that others do not view them as 'fat'. Some people with anorexia may vomit food or exercise excessively after binge eating. They often wear baggy clothes and may avoid looking at their own bodies, even in the shower or bath or in the mirror. Or they may constantly check their features in their own mirrors or feel the feature that worries them with their fingers (e.g. pinching any fat on their bodies).

If your preoccupation with your appearance is predominantly focused on being 'too fat' or overweight, then this is not BDD. However, about 20 per cent of individuals with anorexia nervosa may also have a form of BDD, which does not involve their weight or shape. (For example, a person with anorexia and BDD may be preoccupied by their weight and shape but also feeling ugly and scarred on their face.)

If you have anorexia, we would not recommend trying to overcome a body image problem without also tackling the anorexia. The priority is to get back to a normal body weight and to stop trying to control your thoughts and feelings. Recommended psychological treatments for anorexia include CBT and, for adolescents, family therapy. However, work on body image in this book might be helpful during recovery from anorexia. A whole range of psychological therapies, including CBT, may be considered for anorexia nervosa, and treatment must also take into account the person's physical state. We recommend reading the book *Overcoming Anorexia Nervosa* by Chris Freeman in this series.

Bulimia nervosa

Bulimia nervosa is an eating disorder in which a person goes through cycles of binge eating, followed by vomiting, taking laxatives or diuretics, or exercising excessively and then restricting their diet in order to avoid gaining weight. In contrast to anorexia, people with bulimia usually have a normal weight and shape but 'feel' fat and fear becoming fatter. They may excessively check their body by pinching the skin around their tummy and avoid revealing their body to others. They might hide their tummy behind a bag or make sure their thighs do not rest on a chair if they are sitting down.

Like anorexia, bulimia nervosa is more common in young women but can also occur in men and at any age. People with bulimia nervosa often have mood swings and low self-esteem.

CBT is the most effective psychological treatment for bulimia nervosa. As with anorexia, we would not recommend trying to overcome a body image problem on its own if you have bulimia. Working on your body image may, however, be helpful as part of an overall CBT package. You can also get help from reading *Bulimia Nervosa and Binge-Eating* by Peter Cooper in this series and *Overcoming Binge-Eating* by Chris Fairburn.

People with bulimia nervosa are commonly preoccupied by concerns about becoming too fat or being the wrong shape. If you are mainly preoccupied with being 'too fat' or overweight and have other symptoms of bulimia, then you don't have BDD. BDD and bulimia nervosa can, however, occur together when someone is preoccupied by feeling ugly or by perceived 'defects' in their appearance which are unrelated to weight, shape or being 'too fat' (e.g. the appearance of their nose, skin or hair). More attention needs to be focused on BDD in people who are in eating disorder units in order to find out what happens to the symptoms of BDD when anorexia or bulimia is effectively treated.

Other eating disorders

Most people with an eating disorder do not fulfil all the diagnostic criteria for anorexia or bulimia. They might have some of the symptoms of these disorders, such as dieting, binge eating, vomiting, and a preoccupation with food, but not all; or they might move from one set of problems to another over time. Another common pattern is of disordered eating and a preoccupation with weight and shape. A woman may have normal weight and shape but feel fat. She will do everything she can to camouflage her body and will probably be fearful of intimacy.

QUESTIONNAIRE 2.3: HAVE I GOT AN EATING DISORDER?

Only a health professional can diagnose you as having an eating disorder but the key issues are covered in this questionnaire. (Reproduced with kind permission of Dr Morgan.)

1) Do you make yourself sick because you feel uncomfortably full?

Yes _ No _

2) Do you worry that you have lost control over how much you eat?

Yes _ No _

3) Have you recently lost more than one stone in a three-month period?

Yes _ No _

4) Do you believe yourself to be fat when others say you are too thin?

Yes _ No _

5) Would you say that food dominates your life?

Yes _ No _

If you tick two or more of the 'yes' boxes, you may have an eating disorder and may benefit from being assessed by a health professional.

Amputee identity disorder (AID)

BDD is sometimes confused with 'amputee identity disorder' (AID) or 'body integrity identity disorder' (BIID). These are conditions in which people want one or more of their fingers, toes or limbs to be amputated. Individuals with AID feel that one or more limbs are not part of their 'self' and that amputation will lead to them becoming more able-bodied. This preoccupation is based not so much on a feeling of being defective as on a feeling that they would be so much more comfortable if one or more of their limbs or digits were amputated. Prior to amputation, people with AID may live *as if* they had a disability and are known as 'pretenders'. For example, they may live with a wheelchair, crutches or leg braces. When surgeons refuse to operate, some individuals hasten amputation (e.g. by chainsaw wound or shooting) or carry out self-amputation (e.g. on railway lines).

Although such people are preoccupied with becoming disabled, they do not believe their limbs to be defective or ugly (as in BDD), nor do they wish to alter their limbs cosmetically. AID is therefore more akin to a gender identity disorder in which an individual feels that he or she is trapped in a body of the wrong gender. AID is a strange condition but people who have it are suffering a great deal, and there are some reports that they may benefit from amputation. Fortunately, this condition is rare and it should not be confused with BDD.

Body modification or self-mutilation

There is a group of individuals, some-times mistakenly thought to have body im-age problems, who modify or mutilate their bodies as a form of art. Alternatively, some of them may transform their body so that it resembles a particular animal. Self-muti-lation commonly occurs in young women – for instance, they may cut themselves on the forearms with razors or other sharp im-plements. A number of studies have linked childhood abuse with subsequent self-muti-lation, especially in people with borderline personality disorder. In the 1990s, body piercing and tattooing became increasingly popular, partly because of the rise of punk fashion, which has now become mainstream. (The growth of gay sadomasochism may also have been a factor in these trends.) Decora-tive implants of various sorts are also popu-lar, including some inserted under the skin. These include lobe stretching, ear scalpelling, tongue piercing, and various modifications of the genitalia. For most people, body modification appears to be simply a lifestyle choice. However, a few people who have modified their bodies might have BDD and be using the modification as a way of camouflaging their 'defect' or distracting attention from it.

Additional problems that may coexist with a body image problem

People with body image issues often have other problems as well. This can make the body image problem harder to treat, and it might be difficult to separate the problems from each other.

Depression

The most common additional condition to that of body shame is depression, especially in individuals with BDD. Everybody feels down from time to time but the feeling usually passes fairly quickly and doesn't interfere too much with the way we live our lives. When most people say 'I'm depressed' they mean that they are feeling low or sad, or perhaps stressed, which are normal human experiences. However, when health professionals talk of depression, they are using the term in a different way. They are referring to a condition that is different from the normal ups and downs of everyday life. This is the type of depression we shall be discussing: it is more painful than a normal low, lasts longer and interferes with life in all sorts of ways.

Depression nearly always occurs after the onset of a body image problem. This suggests that the feeling of depression comes on as a result of the frustration caused by body shame. Often, individuals with body shame do not necessarily have a full-blown clinical depression but experience mood swings, irritability and a sense of frustration. If you suffer from depression, you might also find it helpful to read our book called *Manage Your Mood* in this series, and Paul Gilbert's *Overcoming Depression.* After years of social isolation, individuals with body image problems often have low self-esteem relating to areas other than their appearance. If this is a problem, then we would also recommend the book in this series on *Overcoming Low Self-Esteem* by Melanie Fennell.

A good way to rate the severity of depression and anxiety is to use the Hospital Anxiety and Depression scale, reproduced in Appendix 2 by permission of Dr Phillip Snaith.

HAVE I GOT DEPRESSION?

So how do you know if you are experiencing depression or you are just going through a period of feeling low? Depression can be diagnosed only by a health professional, but to meet the criteria for a diagnosis you must have been feeling persistently down or lost your ability to enjoy your normal pleasures or interests for at least two weeks. The symptoms should be sufficiently distressing or seriously interfere with your normal activities. The lowered mood should vary little from day to day, and not usually change according to circumstances. However, it's not unusual for people who have depression to find that their mood is worse in the morning. There is a lot of variation from one individual with depression to another, especially among adolescents. In some cases, anxiety and agitation can be more prominent than the depression, or the depression might be masked by irritability, excessive use of alcohol, or a preoccupation with your health. Typical symptoms of depression include feeling tearful or irritable; being socially withdrawn or inactive; having poor concentration; experiencing disturbed sleep or appetite; and being very negative in your thinking and brooding a lot on the past.

Social phobia

Most people with BDD or body shame have varying degrees of social anxiety and worry what others think about them. Social phobia (or social anxiety disorder) consists of excessive anxiety in situations where you feel you might be scrutinized or judged by others. People with social phobia fear they will do or say something that will be humiliating or embarrassing. They may fear that other people will see them blush, sweat, tremble or look anxious. They try to avoid participating in meetings, talking to strangers or people in authority, eating or drinking in public, dating, or being the centre of attention.

Social phobia is diagnosed when social anxiety significantly interferes with a person's life and stops him or her from doing things that he or she would like to do. When it is persistent and chronic, it is often linked to low self-esteem and depression. It may be diagnosed in addition to BDD or an eating disorder, when the concerns are not only about appearance. For example, the person is not only worried about how they look to others but also about their performance and how they come across (for example, if they are being funny enough or if their hands are shaking).

Effective treatment of social phobia often helps reduce body image problems, although some people will require specific treatment of body image disorder. For more information and advice, read *Overcoming Social Anxiety and Shyness* by Gillian Butler.

Obsessive compulsive disorder (OCD)

OCD is a condition involving recurrent intrusive thoughts, images or urges that the person finds distressing or disabling. These typically include thoughts about contamination; harm (for example, that a gas explosion will occur); aggression or sexual thoughts; and an excessive need for order. The person often becomes very concerned with avoiding thoughts and situations that might trigger the obsession or compulsion. Actions such as obsessive washing or checking might have to be repeated over and over again until the person feels comfortable or certain that nothing bad will happen. For more details see our book in this series, *Overcoming Obsessive Compulsive Disorder,* which contains a useful questionnaire, devised by Professors Foa and

Salkovskis, that may help establish whether you may have OCD.

Sometimes the symptoms of OCD and BDD overlap – for example, a person may believe that their skin is contaminated and this may lead to washing compulsions or compulsive skin-picking. Others who are preoccupied with perfection and symmetry in their home extend this to their appearance and their clothing. Such people do not believe their feature to be defective or ugly, but might feel a need for their hair to be exactly symmetrical or their make-up to be perfect or 'just right'.

Generalized anxiety disorder (GAD)

Generalized anxiety disorder (GAD) is a condition characterized by persistent worry that is difficult to control. However, people with GAD often describe themselves as 'having been a worrier' all their life and seek help only when their condition has become severe and uncontrollable. For a diagnosis of GAD to be made, the anxiety should occur most of the time and not be focused only on body image. In most people with GAD, the worries are most commonly about relationships or health or money. People usually experience some of the following feelings most of the time:

• restlessness or feeling keyed up or on edge
• being easily fatigued
• difficulty concentrating or mind going blank
• irritability
• muscle tension (for example, headaches)
• sleep disturbance

GAD can also cause a number of physical symptoms and interfere with your ability to function normally. It is a very common problem either alone or in combination with depression and body image problems. For more information, see *Overcoming Worry* by Mark Freeston and Kevin Meares in this series.

You can use the Hospital Anxiety and Depression scale in Appendix 2 to monitor your anxiety levels.

Health anxiety

Health anxiety, or hypochondriasis, consists of a preoccupation with a fear that you have a serious disease. Some people have both BDD and health anxiety: these individuals have usually misinterpreted normal blemishes or sensations as evidence of an illness. They may compulsively check the relevant feature, follow a special diet or take measures to protect the particular area on their body. They will have a lasting suspicion or belief that not only is the feature ugly or defective but that they must be suffering from an illness despite repeated medical investigations and reassurance. However, the degree of illness (in a condition such as acne) will often be very mild and will not require the measures that are being used. The principles described in this book can also be used for health anxiety.

Alcohol and substance misuse

Sometimes people 'cope' with body image problems by excessive use of alcohol or illegal drugs such as cannabis or stimulants like cocaine. However, the alcohol or drugs then become the problem, as cannabis or stimulants increase paranoia and depressed mood and decrease motivation. Individuals will usually need to stop drinking or using illegal drugs first, as they interfere with therapy. Regular use of substances such as cannabis or ecstasy may also trigger the onset of BDD.

Consuming excessive amounts of alcohol or binge-drinking are another form of avoidance – they make you emotionally numb and reduce unpleasant thoughts and feelings about the way you look in the short term.

QUESTIONNAIRE 2.4: HAVE I GOT A DRINK PROBLEM?

One way of helping you decide whether you have a drink problem is the CAGE questionnaire for your current drinking.

- Have you ever felt you should **C**ut down on your drinking?
- Have people **A**nnoyed you by criticizing your drinking?
- Have you ever felt **G**uilty about your drinking?
- Have you **E**ver had a drink first thing in the morning to steady your nerves or to get rid of a hangover?

If you answer 'yes' to two or more of these questions (or have more than 21 units a week if you are a man, or 14 a week if you are a woman), you need to reduce your drinking.

Olfactory Reference Syndrome (ORS)

Olfactory Reference Syndrome (ORS) is a condition in which an individual is preoccupied by body odour or bad breath or farting, which is not noticeable to others. It is sometimes regarded as part of BDD. Such individuals may be using perfume to hide the presumed odour. They frequently shower, brush their teeth, change their clothes and ultimately avoid public and social situations where they think their body odour will be noticed. Some people seek frequent reassurance about their body odour. Others go to great lengths to avoid being around people and may become housebound. We have seen some people with BDD who are also preoccupied with their body odour. This blended easily with their preoccupation with aspects of their appearance. For example, if you believe you look hideous, it is not surprising if you also believe that you smell disgusting.

Schizophrenia

People with schizophrenia may have a distorted body image and may make dramatic changes in their appearance (for example, bizarre use of make-up, sun-glasses or unnecessary clothes). They may 'hear' voices commanding them to act in a particular way or have other unusual experiences. They may be inaccurate in their body size estimations, feeling that parts of their body are unusually small or that their body size has changed. They may also feel that they are no longer at home in part of their body or that their body is torn apart.

Borderline personality disorder (BPD)

People with borderline personality disorder (BPD) usually have unstable and intense relationships. They have great difficulty being alone and fear being abandoned. They have a poor sense of their own identity, with a feeling of worthlessness and emptiness. They have frequent mood swings and have difficulty tolerating unpleasant feelings. They can be easily hurt and this leads to frequent expressions of anger. They may cut or harm themselves (e.g. take an overdose) or carry out other impulsive behaviors (e.g. spending excessively, binge-eating, drinking or taking illegal substances). They may lead chaotic lives and have had a background of abuse or neglect. Being ashamed of your body or having BDD is a very common feature of borderline personality and is often regarded as part of the disorder.

Celebrities with body image problems

Many celebrities have been ashamed of their bodies or may have had BDD. Note that in most of these examples there is a discrepancy between how others rate their appearance (or whether it is important to them) and how the person rates themselves.

Andy Warhol, who died in 1987, probably had BDD. The pop artist, who became famous for his paintings of Campbell soup cans and coloured photographs of Marilyn Monroe, was very self-conscious and preoccupied by 'redness' on his nose. In his autobiography he reveals:

I believe in low lights and trick mirrors. A person is entitled to the lighting they need ... At one time, the way my nose looked really bothered me – it's always red – and I decided that I wanted to have it sanded ... I went to see the doctor and I think he thought he'd humour me, so he sanded it and when I walked out of St Luke's Hospital, I was the same underneath but had a bandage on ... If I didn't want to look so bad, I would want to look 'plain'. That would be my next choice.

Carl Withers, who became his lover in 1952, confirmed in a magazine interview that Warhol 'was incredibly self-conscious and had such a low opinion of his looks, it was a serious psychological block with him.'

Shirley Manson, the lead singer in the pop group Garbage, has said in a magazine interview that she had symptoms of BDD:

I always turned up five hours late be-cause I'd be fussing about my hair and make-up. I would change into a million different outfits, and make them change the lighting a million times, I would spend two hours crying in the toilet – and whatev-er the result, I always thought I looked disgusting. I would look in the mirror every morning and be upset. I would get dressed and look in the mirror again, and be upset. It could be anything; I could be too fat, too thin, too flat-chested. My hands were not long enough, my neck was too long. My tummy stuck out, my bum was too big ... It was driving me crazy and I was wasting energy – precious energy – that I should have been putting into my music or my family or friends.

Uma Thurman, whose beauty is recognized worldwide, has stated in interviews that:

I spent the first 14 years of my life convinced that my looks were hideous. I was tall, with big feet and bony knees. I felt quite ugly. I had a big nose, big mouth and those kind of far-apart eyes that looked like I had two fish swimming between my ears. Even today, when people tell me I'm beautiful, I do not believe a word of it.

She is an attractive six-foot blonde and has admitted to 'being troubled about her weight' ever since giving birth to her daughter, Maya, in July 1998.

3

How body image problems develop

This chapter summarizes what is known about the 'causes' of body image problems and what makes a person vulnerable to experiencing one. Although it can be important and useful to have some understanding of how you have come to develop a problem, we do not want to encourage you to look endlessly for reasons or causes. When you fall down a hole, you don't need to know the exact route by which you arrived at the bottom in order to climb out again. Usually there are fairly obvious triggers for body image problems (for example, being teased during adolescence) or vulnerability (for example, being abused as a child). If there is a family history of a mental disorder such as depression or anxiety, genetic inheritance could also be a factor.

Possible causes

When considering possible causes for your symptoms of body image problem, it is usually helpful to think of three groups of factors, those that:

(a) have made you vulnerable to developing symptoms (for example, childhood abuse, trauma, genetic inheritance and unknown factors)

(b) have triggered your symptoms (such as experiencing acne or being disfigured, or living or working in an environment that places exceptional pressure to 'look' a certain way)

(c) have helped maintain your symptoms (for example, the way you react, with particular patterns of thinking and acting).

We will discuss the third group – that is, the patterns that maintain your body image problem – in Chapter 4. It is not only within your ability to change them but doing so is the cornerstone of self-help and CBT. In this chapter, we will examine the first two factors.

As we outlined in the previous chapter, there are many different types of body image problems, and no one can be sure exactly what causes them. What we *can* safely say is that a body image problem is usually the result of a mixture of psychological and biological factors and life experiences since birth. In some cases long-term parental neglect, and a deep sense of being unloved from childhood, may be important factors. Likewise, a person might be teased by their peers over a long period, or a trauma such as a car crash occurs and the person is left with a disfigurement.

Bullying is not uncommon in schools, particularly during adolescence. Bullies tend to pick on the thing that singles someone out or makes them different from their peer group. Unfortunately, appearance is the thing that is most apparent to others. Many people who have body image problems can recall being picked on in a way that made them feel vulnerable and alone.

Bullying also occurs in relationships, and this can be more subtle. Someone who knows another well tends to know about their insecurities, and may pick on things that they know to be the most hurtful. Unfortunately, this can sometimes be taken as confirming evidence – for example, that the person is fat, or ugly, or has a big nose – when in fact they look perfectly normal.

Bullying does not have to be sustained, or a hurtful remark be made intentionally. One very thoughtless comment can haunt someone for years – a ghost from the past – and sustain a body image problem many years later. Often, when challenged, the person who said it will have had no idea of the lasting preoccupation that this comment has triggered, and will be amazed at the upset caused by something that to them seemed inconsequential.

When you consider possible causes of body image problems, it's important to remember that life experiences all interact with each other. Imagine that the cause of a body image problem is like a cocktail in a glass. The ingredients of the cocktail will be different for each individual and they will also mix and interact in different ways.

What makes a person vulnerable to a body image problem?

Vulnerability to a body image problem could be due to three types of factors, which may overlap:

- physical conditions, including medical, biological and genetic causes
- personality or psychological traits, and
- life experiences

Genetic factors

A mental health problem can sometimes run in families. For instance, if you have a close relative who has had BDD, depression, an eating disorder or obsessive compulsive disorder, you could be at increased risk of experiencing a body image problem at some time in your life. However, having a genetic factor does not mean that you will inevitably develop a body image problem. Similarly, it is possible to develop a body image problem without any evidence of genetic risk, so there is no point in worrying that you may be at greater risk than other people.

Psychological factors

Certain aspects of your personality can make you more vulnerable to developing a body image problem. For example, you might be a perfectionist or excessively shy and reserved. Such traits, in combination with one or more triggers, can make you more vulnerable to developing a body image problem.

People with body image problems might also be more aesthetically sensitive than the average person. According to a small study that compared people with BDD with people suffering from post-traumatic stress disorder, depression or obsessive compulsive disorder, people with

BDD were much more likely than the other three groups to have had an education, training or occupation in art and design. At present, it is unclear whether being more aesthetically sensitive makes you more vulnerable to developing BDD or is a consequence of developing BDD.

Other studies suggest that healthy people might be slightly positively biased (or 'wearing rose-tinted glasses') when it comes to rating their own attractiveness, compared with how others rate them. This tendency can be beneficial, as such individuals are more likely to have happy relationships and to be working successfully and doing the things in life that are important to them. In contrast, people with a body image problem seem to have lost their 'rose-tinted glasses' and have no positive bias when rating their own attractiveness. People with body image problems can *appear* to have problems with their perception – for example, in perceiving their body size to be larger than it really is in anorexia – but the problem lies more in their emotional reaction to their appearance, the degree of importance they attach to appearance and the way they judge themselves. We shall discuss these psychological factors in Chapter 4.

Life experiences that may make you vulnerable during childhood or adolescence include emotional neglect, rejection, bullying or sexual abuse, which can all lead to a sense of being worthless or unloved. Traumatic experiences, such as accidents resulting in scars or a skin condition such as acne or eczema, can lead to a lot of attention being focused on appearance. For others, the importance of appearance might be positively linked with success during childhood (e.g. comments such as 'You were wonderful on stage and you looked so good,' rather than 'Your performance was excellent'). Alternatively, a particular body part, or a person's height or weight, might have been highlighted. Early dating success, and other adolescent experiences where the importance of appearance is at a premium, could also play their part.

Social factors

Most cultures value appearance. Less attractive leading female television or movie stars are in the minority, and several recent TV reality shows have focused on unattractive women who undergo a radical transformation. In addition, we are bombarded by advertisements telling us that physical attractiveness is necessary for success and that we need cosmetic products and surgery to achieve the appearance we want.

Some cultures seem to put a greater emphasis on the importance of looking attractive. For example, cosmetic surgery in Brazil is very common and out of proportion to the wealth of the country. Equally, in western culture gay men seem to feel that they are under increased pressure to look attractive. Other cultural aspects can be relevant in individual cases. For example, a Puerto Rican woman was intensely distressed by a small facial scar that she received in an accident. This was because, in her community, a scar was inflicted as a punishment for adultery.

Apart from cultural factors, immediate peers and family can have a big influence on the importance of appearance to an individual. For example, research has shown links between a daughter's recollection of her mother's earlier attitudes to her own body and the daughter's own current body image. In addition, having a more attractive sibling may encourage a person to rate their own attractiveness unfavourably.

Medical conditions

There are many medical conditions that can alter someone's appearance, such as polycystic ovary syndrome (which leads to weight gain and excessive hair growth), or an under-active thyroid (which might lead to weight gain, forgetfulness, excessive tiredness, a hoarse voice, slow speech, constipation, feeling cold, hair loss, dry rough skin, irregular periods and infertility as well as symptoms of anxiety and depression). There are also many medical treatments that alter personal appearance (for example, there may be facial wasting after anti-retroviral treatments for HIV, or 'moon face', altered body shape and skin thinning after use of steroids).

However, a change in appearance does not inevitably lead to a body image problem. Body image problems are more closely related to how much you believe that others will notice your abnormality, the importance you attach to appearance and the unfavourable comparisons you might draw with a former self.

Biological causes of BDD

There are a very few medical conditions that might aggravate or mimic BDD. If your medical history suggests a possible physical cause or if you are not getting better with conventional treatments, such causes should perhaps be investigated despite their relative rarity. For example, a thyroid problem could be linked to BDD.

Some theories are based on biological explanations – for example, that a 'defect' in brain chemicals or an 'illness in the brain' causes BDD. This sort of explanation may reduce the stigma and blame attached to individuals with BDD by ignorant people who think that they should just 'pull themselves together'. However, biological factors alone do not fully explain the symptoms of BDD, and the social stigma will not necessarily be reduced by this approach. Furthermore, such explanations don't place enough emphasis on the social context and psychological factors involved in BDD and therefore underplay the importance of psychological treatments for the condition.

Trying to unravel the biology of BDD or depression is a complex business, and statements that BDD (or any other mental disorder) is caused by an imbalance of serotonin or other chemicals in the brain are simplistic nonsense. Unfortunately, some pharmaceutical companies have placed far too much emphasis on this aspect and have thus spread misinformation.

In general, any biological changes observed in the brain of a person with BDD can be reversed by psychological treatment or physical therapy. Permanent structural damage in someone who recovers from BDD is unlikely, and the use of medication does not tell us anything about the cause of BDD.

What can trigger a body image problem?

A body image problem usually occurs as an understandable response to specific events and in a particular context. Many of the triggers in a body image problem are long-term difficulties that may drain someone emotionally and psychologically over time. The most common triggers for a body image problem are:

> • being teased or bullied about being different, for example your height, being chubby or your legs being thin
> • being aware of a change in your appearance such as being found attractive and then developing acne or a skin condition
> • being involved in an accident and developing a scar.

Sometimes a body image problem such as BDD seems to occur out of the blue, without any identifiable trigger or social factors. In this case there could be more biological factors at work.

Understanding the psychological causes of a body image problem

Even when there are strong biological influences in your body image problem, the way you react to the problem still influences the severity of the symptoms. For example, if there is a significant genetic component you may be ashamed both of having a family history of mental disorder and of your body image disorder. The way you respond (for example, by being withdrawn and inactive and brooding on how awful you are for having a body image problem) could determine the severity of your symptoms and the speed of your recovery.

Even if a health professional recommends that you take medication for BDD or another problem such as depression or an eating disorder, there is nothing to stop you easing your symptoms by also using the approaches described in this book. This will involve developing a more compassionate and caring view of yourself, acting as if you truly believe you have nothing to be ashamed of in your appearance, and doing more of the activities you are avoiding.

One way of thinking about your mind is that it consists of a large number of modules, each designed to do certain jobs. For example, there is a module for fear, another for memory, and so on. In some mental disorders, there may be damage to a particular module. In conditions like dementia, for instance, there may be damage to the module for memory. In other disorders, certain modules are trying too hard or shutting down because there is an excessive load on the system.

A body image problem can be regarded as a failure in the brain's system because it is overloaded and is trying too hard to solve a problem with the way you feel about your appearance. In such a case, the mind's solutions become a problem. The system is overloaded because of the way you try to escape from unpleasant thoughts, images and feelings, or control your feelings by brooding about the past or worrying about all the bad things that could occur. The mind normally tries to fix unpleasant thoughts and feelings by escaping from them or finding ways of controlling them, and it copes the best way it can. This process can be seen in abnormal brain scans and serotonin activity. In our opinion, these biological changes do not cause the body image problem but are more of a reaction to it – the consequence of the mind desperately trying to escape from and control the way you feel.

This is not to say that the biology is not important, as it does become part of the process. For example, when you are stressed, your cortisol goes up, and over time this will reduce your serotonin levels. As your serotonin goes down, you may feel more tired. This will affect your sleep and the next day this will affect the way you cope with everyday events. Your body and your mind work together and one has an effect on the other. However, you can switch off these biological responses by acting *against* the way you feel about your appearance, and this will lead to better feelings. We shall develop this psychological understanding of body image problems in Chapter 4.

Each of us is a product of our genes and what we have learnt since we were born. The way we think and act is shaped by our experiences. Throughout this book, we emphasize the importance of the context. For instance, lots of 'bad' events may occur, especially in childhood, from emotional and physical abuse and neglect to lack of boundaries or learning about the importance of appearance. If we experienced unpleasant events when we were younger, we tend to avoid anything similar and anything that reminds us of them when we are older. If you were teased or not loved during childhood or adolescence, it would not be surprising if you grew up believing yourself to be ugly.

Much of our development occurs without our being aware of it, and we are exposed to literally millions of moments of learning. It is utterly impossible to unravel or organize them into a causal order. This is why therapies that promise to 'get to the bottom of it all' and discover the cause of your body image problem in childhood are often unhelpful. In fact, such therapies may sometimes make things worse by encouraging you to brood on the past.

If you do have very low self-esteem and are very self-critical, you may justify your actions as a way of protecting yourself (or even punishing yourself before others can punish you) and making sure you are not hurt or not criticized by others. In this book, we will be examining if this really prevents bad things from happening or whether it makes it more difficult to achieve what you really want to achieve in life.

Identifying your triggers and vulnerability

In the following drawing, we use the metaphor of a flower to identify areas of vulnerability to, and triggers for, body image problems. You will see that the roots represent the biological causes of vulnerability, such as your genes. Your psychological make-up and life experiences (the other two factors that lead to vulnerability) form the stem and leaves. Triggers (bad things that have happened recently and have triggered the body image problem) are shown by clouds and lightning – as life is never going to be all sunlight and warmth.

Now try this exercise for yourself on a blank flower with its stem and roots (see above). You can consider the risk factors under the following headings.

BIOLOGICAL FACTORS (THESE FORM THE ROOTS OF YOUR FLOWER)

Are there any possible genetic or biological risks? For example, do you have a family history of mental disorder? Did you have a persistent skin problem like eczema or acne? Were you born with a visible difference in your appearance? Have you regularly taken an illegal substance?

PSYCHOLOGICAL FACTORS (THESE FORM THE STEM AND LEAVES OF YOUR FLOWER)

Are there aspects of your personality that make you vulnerable? For example, have you always had low self-esteem, been a perfectionist, had an anxious temperament, or been someone with a particular appreciation of art and beauty?

LIFE EXPERIENCES (THESE ALSO HELP TO FORM STEM AND LEAVES OF YOUR FLOWER)

Did you have any bad experiences like bullying or neglect when you were younger that might have made you more vulnerable and less able to cope well with stress now? Did your parents or culture emphasize the importance of appearance? Does success in your work depend on what you look like (e.g. modelling or acting)?

TRIGGERS (THESE FORM THE CLOUDS AND THUNDER IN YOUR FLOWER)

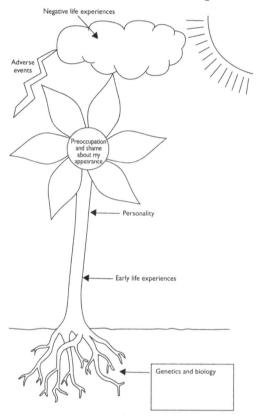

Have there been social or personal problems in your life, like the break-up of a relationship or an accident such as a car crash? Have been there any major changes in your role in life?

By writing down the factors that might have made you vulnerable to your body image problem and inserting labels on the roots, leaves and thunderstorms in your picture, you are building an understanding view of the 'history' behind your body image problem. This will help you to be less critical of yourself for having a body image problem, and will help put your problem in context.

I CAN'T IDENTIFY ANY FACTORS IN THE CAUSE OF MY BODY IMAGE PROBLEM

Don't worry if you can't identify particular factors that make you vulnerable to developing a body image problem. It can sometimes be difficult to be certain of the causes, especially if a problem developed from a young age. As yet, we do not fully understand all the causes of body image problems. Constantly searching for a reason might seem like a good idea if you think that you need to find the reason before you can fix the problem. This approach usually works with physical problems: if you have a chest pain caused by a lack of oxygen to your heart because of a blockage in an artery, then a doctor can do the right investigations to find the blockage and bypass the blocked artery with a graft. However, this approach does not work if you have an emotional problem, be- cause – the more you try to stop feeling bad by searching for an elusive 'root cause', the more you focus on how bad you are feeling. As a result, you are likely to end up making yourself feel worse.

Inevitably, you will read or be told different things by different therapists or doctors. The more opinions you seek and the more books and websites you read, the more your doubts will increase. Some experts may emphasize the role of brain chemicals, while others may empathize with your childhood experiences. Change involves learning to tolerate uncertainty and accepting that you will never know the 'exact' combination of factors that might be relevant for you. Some of the 'causes' are probably in the unknown category and, even if you knew the exact order of events, you probably can't do anything effective about them. Just say no to any therapy that offers to find the route you took into the hole. Instead, insist on a proven psychological treatment for a body image problem that helps you get out of the hole!

4

What keeps a body image problem going?

Any attempt to solve a problem is only as good as the definition of what the problem is. Imagine that the light-bulb in a room stopped working. Naturally you might assume that the problem is that the light-bulb has broken, and go ahead and change it. However this would not be an effective solution if a fuse on the light circuit had blown. The light will never work if you make the wrong assessment about what the problem is and therefore use the wrong solution. In the same way, if you have a body image problem, then you probably see your appearance as the problem. However, in this chapter we can start to build a more accurate explanation of the problem and of how it is being maintained. Only when we have agreed on the true nature of the problem can we find helpful solutions to it.

Body image is a thinking and emotional problem

How many hours a day do you spend thinking about the feature you dislike? For many people with a body image problem, the feature they dislike is at the forefront of their mind for between one and several hours a day. (For some people, it is on their mind all day and sometimes they dream about it as well.) Can you recall the last time anything else in your life occupied that much time? Being preoccupied with or thinking about your features is at the very heart of body image problems. Anything that brings your feature to the forefront of your mind is part of the problem. This includes even positive feedback on your appearance or 'helpful' suggestions about how you could improve your looks.

How will it ever be possible to put your worries about your appearance to the back of your mind, and get on with what is important in your life, if your actions keep bringing your appearance back to the forefront of your mind? Even if some of things you do (such as checking in a mirror) temporarily reduce your doubt and help you to stop feeling bad, they are very much part of the problem because they serve to prime your attention and re-train your brain that appearance is highly important. In this chapter, we shall therefore discuss the different ways we maintain body image problems, often without realizing that we are doing so.

Perception in body image

Perception is the way we make sense of what we see or hear or smell. In the previous chapter, we saw that many people with a body image problem have lost their 'rose-tinted glasses' and in some ways have a heightened sense of awareness of particular aspects of their appearance.

Imagine, for a moment, that a pair of identical twins have been brought up separately. One of them has a body image problem and the other does not. The one without a problem has a positive slant and rates herself as slightly more attractive than others would rate her. When she is in front of a mirror she focuses her attention on those features that are more attractive and less time on those features that are less attractive. The other twin (who has a body image problem) tends to focus on the features that she considers ugly and ignore the features that are more attractive. In addition, she rates the features that she hates as being important in defining who she is. For example if she is preoccupied and distressed by her hips and tummy, she tends to see herself as a walking pair of hips and wobbly tummy and not much else. This twin has a different way of rating her appearance because she has lost the positive slant used by the twin without a body image problem. She focuses her attention on those features that are less attractive and bases her rating of herself on those features. For these reasons and others, the effects of a cosmetic procedure would be unpredictable, as the surgery might not alter her heightened sense of awareness of her appearance or give her back a positive slant. Neither would a cosmetic procedure affect some of the emotional links with 'ghosts from the past' that are still influencing her in the present.

The twin with the body image problem might say she does not want to be 'deluded' into thinking that she looks 'OK' when she does not, as she fears that she will then be humiliated or rejected when she is not expecting it. However, this reaction is not surprising, as being over-aware of your features fuels the fear of being humiliated.

EXERCISE 4.1: WHICH FEATURES DO YOU VIEW AS ATTRACTIVE AND UNATTRACTIVE?

Complete the following statements. Describe each feature that you view as ugly or unattractive and say what you think is wrong with it.

I focus my attention on the following features that I view as ugly or 'not right':

1. _____
2. _____
3. _____
4. _____

I focus less attention on these features, which others view as being attractive:

1. _____
2. _____
3. _____
4. _____

Mental images

Intrusive images are pictures or felt impressions that just pop into your mind, especially when you are more anxious in social situations or in front of a mirror. Images are not just pictures in your mind but can also be felt sensations or impressions you have of how you appear to others.

People with body image problems often experience such images from an observer's perspective – that is, as if they are looking back at themselves. They believe that the picture in their mind is an accurate representation of how

EXERCISE 4.2: SELF-PORTRAIT

Can you draw yourself based on the picture in your mind or how you think you appear to others? Once you have drawn your self-portrait, discuss it with someone you trust and ask whether they view you in the same way?

they appear to others. However, this is questionable, as such pictures might be linked to bad experiences and are like ghosts from the past, which have not been updated. Thus if you have been teased or bullied, and learnt from your tormentors that you were ugly or defective, then that memory becomes ingrained and influences you in the present.

Pictures often reflect and reinforce your mood. For example, if you are very anxious, you might have mental pictures of being humiliated in the future. However, treating images as reality can create many problems. Change involves recognizing that you are just seeing a picture in your mind and that this is not current reality.

Intrusive thoughts

When you are ashamed of your body, you may think negatively about your appearance by comparing and rating yourself against others unfavourably. You might judge yourself as 'ugly', 'abnormal', 'not right', 'too fat', 'too masculine' or 'too feminine' or 'not muscular enough'. You may think that others will view you as inferior, flawed or defective. You probably believe that you are extremely noticeable and that others are looking down at you. It might be just your features that you think others are looking down on; or you might assume that the whole of you is being condemned or humiliated.

For some people, their appearance becomes the single most important aspect in defining them as individuals and they hold attitudes such as 'I am my nose' or 'My skin defines who I am'. If you hold such an attitude, and are satisfied with your appearance, then you may be worried and anxious about losing your looks. If you are dissatisfied with your appearance, then you are more likely to brood on how helpless you are to do anything to change it.

We hope to show you that your appearance is only part of who you are, and that, even if you are visibly very different from other people, this does not mean you can or should define yourself by your defect.

EXERCISE 4.3: SELF-DEFINITION PIE CHART

The amount of importance someone attaches to their appearance in defining their 'self' identity can be represented by a pie chart. In the following example, Amy has filled in a pie chart to show how she defines herself. The divisions in the chart show the relative importance she gives to her appearance and to her roles as partner, friend, parent, member of the community and student. Below the sample, there is an empty pie chart for you to complete.

1. Amy's completed pie chart

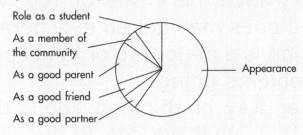

2. Empty pie chart for completion. Indicate how much of the pie is focused on your appearance and how much on all your other roles.

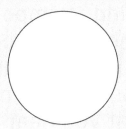

Fusion of thoughts and reality

One of the problems in body image disorders is that your thoughts become fused with reality and accepted as facts. As a consequence, you develop a pattern of thinking that is like holding a prejudice against yourself. The same process may occur with the picture in your mind or the felt impression of how you appear to others; your brain fuses the mental picture or impression with reality (the reality that has already lost its positive slant). So what you 'see' in a mirror is what you feel (and not what others see or feel and why your loved ones may get so exasperated with you). Fusion is a major factor in keeping body image problems going.

Another way of thinking about this is to consider that what we see in our surroundings is based upon a process that is a bit like waving a torch in the dark. Your mind is constantly creating a picture of the world around you in order to make sense of the world. If your mind is important in creating what you see, then it is not surprising that ghosts from the past and other experiences will influence your body image. From this point of view, what you hear is probably more accurate than what you see. Your mind is less likely to influence what you hear – unless of course you have been conditioned to associate a particular sound with panic.

Later in this book, you will learn how to deal with these thoughts by prefacing them with 'I am having a thought that I am ugly', thus underlining that it's just your thought or a mental event and not reality. Learning to accept these negative thoughts and images willingly as 'just thoughts' and not buying into them has been shown to be an important part of overcoming body shame.

EXERCISE 4.4: INTRUSIVE THOUGHTS AND REALITY

What intrusive thoughts do you experience that fuse with reality? List four of them. Then ask yourself: how believable are your thoughts about your appearance? Which of them seems most real to you?

1. _____
2. _____
3. _____
4. _____

Self-focused attention

When you are ashamed of your body, you become more focused on your own thoughts and feelings. This makes you more likely to assume that your view of the way you look and the picture in your mind are reality. This in turn interferes with your ability to make simple decisions, pay attention or concentrate on your normal tasks or what people around you are saying. When this problem is severe, it may make you feel more paranoid. Your view of the world now depends on your thoughts and how they chatter away, rather than your experience. In other situations, you may be so focused on comparing yourself with others that you fail to take in the context and find it difficult to concentrate on what people are saying or their body language.

When you have a picture in your mind of the features that you feel look ugly you become self-focused, as you have to monitor exactly how you look when you don't have a mirror. It's as if your features are like a dangerous tiger that has to be watched very carefully. Once a threat is on your mind, you will find that this has an impact on what you notice in the world; you develop a bias in your attention and you become more aware of the way you look. In contrast, someone without a body image problem tends to be focused on what they see in their surroundings or on a task (like talking to the person in front of them), rather than looking back at themselves and constantly monitoring how they think they are coming across.

An attentional bias happens all the time in everyday life. For example, when a woman becomes pregnant, she starts to notice other pregnant women and babies everywhere. It is not that there are more pregnant women and babies – just that she is just more aware of them. Another common example occurs when you or someone you know is about to buy a certain type of car. Suddenly it seems as if there are many more of that type of car on the roads. If you were to concentrate now on how your big toes feel, after a minute or so you might start to feel a sensation that you were not aware of before. A person with a spider phobia will notice a spider in a room far more readily than someone without that kind of fear.

People with body image problems are a lot more aware of a feature (or any changes that occur in their appearance) than someone without a body image problem. This 'attentional bias' is a result of their over-concern about their appearance, and also contributes to its maintenance, since their personal world can seem flooded with information about the importance of appearance, reinforcing their own sense of the exaggerated importance of appearance. If you have experienced this, you will know that, because your own fears are related to threats about certain features, you are very likely to want to focus on those features. In this way, a vicious circle is set up, whereby the more preoccupied you are with your features, the more you focus your attention on them, further fuelling your preoccupation and so on. We discuss how to overcome self-focused attention in Chapter 6.

EXERCISE 4.5: WHAT DO YOU 'OVER-NOTICE'?

Take a moment to consider the past day or past week, and complete the following statements. Try to identify the things about yourself that you tend to notice too much. (These are things that your imaginary twin without a body image problem would hardly notice, if at all.)

I'm over-aware of:

[Space left intentionally blank in the original book]

The unintended consequences, for myself, of being over-aware of certain features are:

[Space left intentionally blank in the original book]

The unintended consequences, for others, of my being overaware of certain features are:

[Space left intentionally blank in the original book]

To tackle this aspect of a body image problem, start by recognizing that biased attention will very probably lead to biased conclusions. For example, if you constantly monitor your feature, you are more likely to rate it as ugly. Once you recognize this, you can correct for this bias in your mind.

Imagine riding a bicycle that tends to veer to the right when you point the handlebars straight ahead. What would you do to make the bicycle go straight? You would correct for the bias by steering slightly towards the left. You can do exactly the same in your mind. So, if you tend to over-assume ugliness, you can correct your thinking by deliberately assuming that most people, most of the time, do not hold the same view as you and do not notice what you are aware of.

However, it is also important to realize that trying not to notice something, in an attempt to correct this bias, is doomed to failure. This is because it is impossible *not* to think of something – by telling yourself not to think of something, you inevitably focus your thoughts on that very thing! However, later on we will be teaching you how to practise being absorbed in your surroundings, rather than your own thoughts.

Body shame

Body shame usually consists of a mixture of different emotions. Typically, someone experiences disgust (directed against the self) and anxiety or depression. Disgust is an emotion that means literally 'something offensive to the taste'. Objects of disgust may include waste products, injuries and wounds to the body, and moral disgust. With disgust, there is a reflex closing up of the muscles around the mouth. When disgust is directed against the self it is called shame, and when it is directed specifically against your own body, it is called body shame.

Shame about your appearance can be broken down into 'external' and 'internal' body shame. External shame means believing that others think you are unattractive or ugly; this may lead you to feel anxious in social or public situations. People have learnt that it is humiliating or painful to be rejected and therefore try to avoid it. Human beings are social animals. We want to be part of a group, even if we feel under constant scrutiny. External shame is therefore based on what you worry other people think about you.

Internal shame is what you think about yourself. It occurs if you rate yourself negatively, sometimes even feeling a sense of disgust about all or part of yourself. You feel unattractive or ugly to yourself and feel you have to limit the damage to yourself either by avoiding or giving in to others. However, what matters is the sense of not meeting your own standard and being something less than you want to be. Often people continue to feel damaged and spoiled in some way long after the specific events that caused the shame have passed.

Internal and external shame often go together but not always. Thus, someone may rate himself or herself as ugly according to their own standards but know that others are not bothered by it. Equally, someone may believe that others think they are ugly but not care about their opinions.

Shame is not something that we are born with. It is something we probably learn over time. Positive feelings about ourselves usually come from parents and peers when we are loved and given compliments. Thus, from a young age, children develop a sense of pride when they know others feel positively about them and this enables them to feel positive about themselves. We discussed some of these issues in Chapter 3 on how a body image problem develops.

EXERCISE 4.6: INTERNAL OR EXTERNAL SHAME?

How much is your problem driven by concern about what you think others think (external shame)? And how much is it driven by your own standards (internal shame)? For example, would you still have a body image problem if you had a guarantee that no one was thinking negatively about your features? Or would you still have a body image problem if you were completely alone on a desert island and knew that you were not going to be rescued?

Write down one or two thoughts based on external shame, then estimate what percentage of your shame is external.

External:

[Space left intentionally blank in the original book]

Now write down one or two thoughts based on internal shame, then estimate what percentage of your shame is internal.

Internal:

[Space left intentionally blank in the original book]

Effect of mood

You might feel anxious in social situations, or before checking in the mirror, hoping you might see something different from how you think you look in your mind's eye. However, after you look in a mirror you may feel worse. You might feel disgust as you rate your feature as ugly. During a long session in front of a mirror, some people might experience feeling disconnected from their bodies and a sense of being very unreal. Some might become angry or feel more shame for wasting so much time.

Anxiety is usually triggered by a sense that you are in danger. The threat might be real or imagined and may be from the past (for example, a memory), present or future. When anxiety dominates the picture, your mind will tend to think of all the possible bad things that could occur ('catastrophizing') and will want to know for certain that nothing bad will happen in the future. This leads to people worrying about how to solve non-existent problems. The natural desire is to escape or avoid situations that are anxiety-provoking. Anxiety can produce a variety of physical sensations, including feeling hot and sweaty, having a racing heart, feeling faint, wobbly or shaky, muscle tension (for example, headaches), upset stomach or diarrhoea.

If, however, you are becoming despondent about the future, you may feel down or emotionally 'numb' or feel that life has lost its fun. These are core symptoms of depression.

Others may frequently feel hurt and angry because they feel they are being unfairly treated and humiliated when they don't deserve it, or don't deserve to be born the way they are. They may become irritable or lash out.

If you are feeling stressed by a conflict in a relationship or you have been depressed, withdrawn, inactive and brooding on the past, it will probably make you more self-focused and more preoccupied with how you look, creating a further vicious circle. Anything that improves your mood and decreases other stresses is likely to improve your body image.

EXERCISE 4.7: THE EFFECT OF YOUR MOOD ON YOUR BODY IMAGE

Completing the following statements will help you assess the effect of your mood on your body image.

I feel _____

When (in what context)?

[Space left intentionally blank in the original book]

The unintended consequences of such feelings on my preoccupation with my feature(s) are:

[Space left intentionally blank in the original book]

The unintended consequences of such feelings on others are:

[Space left intentionally blank in the original book]

Thought suppression

Many people with body image problems experience negative thoughts, images, or doubts relating to their appearance. One way of coping is to try to push them out of your mind or to suppress them. Unfortunately, the main effect of suppressing intrusive thoughts is to increase the frequency of the upsetting thoughts and make the person feel worse. This is quite normal, since your brain will keep putting them back into your mind while it is trying to sort them out.

To understand how trying not to think of something increases rather than decreases its intrusiveness, try the following experiment. Close your eyes and try really hard not to think of a pink elephant. For a minute, try and push any image of a pink elephant out of your mind. Every time you think of a pink elephant, try to get rid of it from your mind.

What did you notice? Most people find that, when told not to think of a pink elephant, all they can think of is a pink elephant. Understanding this apparent paradox is the key to understanding and overcoming a body image problem. Many people with this problem are caught in the trap of trying too hard to rid themselves of thoughts and doubts, and in fact this brings about the very opposite of what they want.

If you are still not convinced that trying to get rid of intrusive thoughts, images, or doubts makes them worse, try an experiment. Spend one day dealing with your thoughts in the usual way, and record their frequency and the distress they cause you. Spend the next day trying to get rid of your thoughts or images, and record their frequency and your distress levels. The following day, repeat the first step, and then the next day the second step.

What happened? Most people discover that the harder they try to get rid of their thoughts and images, the more frequent and disturbing they become. If you don't try so hard not to have the thought or image that's bothering you, it will bother you much less! After all, a thought is intrusive only if you don't let it in and recognize it for what it is. Embrace such thoughts, fully accept them and carry them as part of you. You will learn later not to engage with them, as they are, after all, just thoughts.

Trying to avoid or escape from difficult situations is a very natural response and can be the right thing to do in certain situations. For example, it may sometimes be helpful to keep your distance from a bully but at other times you may have to engage with them. It's all about finding the appropriate response for a particular problem and not avoiding your thoughts and feelings about what seem like bad events. Escaping from difficult thoughts and images is always unworkable.

If you have fused your thoughts with reality and believe them to be true, it's not surprising that you want to escape from them. In order to escape unpleasant thoughts and feelings, you might start to:

• avoid activities and people that you have previously enjoyed, and become more focused on yourself

• withdraw from friends or family

• spend more time in bed

• use alcohol or drugs to numb your feelings

• brood about the past and try to work out reasons for the way you feel

• avoid calling friends because you think you may be humiliated or rejected

• try to distract yourself with the Internet or DVDs

• 'put your head in the sand' and pretend that the problems around you will go away if you ignore them

• ignore the door bell or telephone

Such behaviors become habitual so you may not even be aware of why you are doing them. In many ways, escape is a natural response to try to avoid bad feelings. However, it merely digs you deeper into your hole.

EXERCISE 4.8: CONSEQUENCES OF THOUGHT SUPPRESSION

What thoughts and pictures in my mind related to my appearance am I trying to suppress or escape from?

[Space left intentionally blank in the original book]

What are the unintended consequences of trying to suppress or avoid these thoughts and pictures?

[Space left intentionally blank in the original book]

Brooding and worrying

Some people cope by trying to 'put right' or make sense of past events or their appearance by brooding, constantly mulling the problem over. If this sounds familiar, you are probably trying to solve problems that cannot be solved or analyse a question that cannot be answered. This usually consists of lot of 'why?' questions. 'Why am I so ugly?' or 'Why did I get that surgery?'. Another favourite is the 'if only...' fantasies, as in 'If only I looked better...'. Alternatively, you may be constantly comparing yourself unfavourably with others and making judgements and criticizing yourself. Brooding invariably makes you feel worse, as you never resolve the existing questions and may even generate new questions that cannot be answered.

The process of worrying is a variation on the same theme, in which you try to solve non-existent problems. These usually take the form of 'What if...?' questions. Examples include 'What if my partner leaves me?' and 'What if I get called names in front of others? Chapter 6 will help you 'think about thinking' in more detail and explain how you can best cope with your mind's tendency to try to solve such worries.

You may also find yourself brooding on why you look the way you do, or why you had a particular cosmetic procedure. This brooding process may reduce your distress for a brief period so you get a payoff because brooding seems to 'work'. Then the next time you feel bad, you will have trained yourself to brood or avoid activity again. Unfortunately, in the long term this will make you feel more depressed.

All the time spent alone means that you miss out on what is important to you in life and prevents you from having any positive experiences. The belief that you are ugly or unlovable is therefore strengthened, as you are unable to test out or disprove your negative expectations.

EXERCISE 4.9: WHAT DO I BROOD OR WORRY ABOUT?

Write down the three things that you most often brood or worry about. For each one, write down the main 'Why?', 'If only' or 'What if?' question.

[Space left intentionally blank in the original book]

Avoidance and safety behaviors

As well as ways of thinking, people with body image problems use a variety of different behaviors to cope with their condition. However, these strategies usually make the situation worse in the long term. For example, if you have a body image problem you may try to escape from or avoid social or public situations – in severe cases you may become housebound or only go out at night or when you are heavily madeup. This is an example of a 'safety behavior', which is intended to prevent harm and reduce anxiety but usually leaves people feeling worse and prevents them from testing out their fears. For instance, you might be:

- repeatedly checking your appearance in a mirror
- seeking reassurance about your feature
- feeling your skin with your fingers
- cutting or combing your hair to make it 'just so'
- picking your skin to make it smooth
- comparing your feature against models in magazines or people in the street
- measuring body parts to see 'how bad they are'
- covering up or altering the shape (padding out) body parts using clothing
- styling hair to cover up a flaw, draw attention away from a flaw, or until hair is 'just so'
- re-touching your hairstyle throughout the day
- using make-up to conceal flaws, or applying it until it is 'just so'
- re-touching make-up repeatedly throughout the day

- looking for and trying out new beauty products
- researching or seeking cosmetic surgery
- collecting magazines for photographs and appearance-related articles
- making frequent trips to beauty salons or hairdressers
- doing 'DIY' cosmetic surgery, having dermatological treatments, and dental procedures
- changing posture or covering a feature with your hand
- avoiding social situations
- avoiding 'attractive' people
- being careful about the choice of lighting
- being careful about choice of certain mirrors
- using alcohol or drugs to alter your mood
- using 'mental' cosmetic procedures in your imagination
- brooding about the past

It's worth reflecting on what you think might happen to someone with a relatively healthy body image who practised a number of these activities on a regular basis. We tried this once for just a few hours, and we soon started to become preoccupied and dissatisfied with our own appearance. Thus a further vicious circle has been set up, as the unintended conse-quence of safety behaviors is to increase preoccupation and distress.

All methods of escaping from a situation or checking how you look are safety behaviors. A message we shall return to over and over again is that safety behaviors maintain your worry. They prevent you from testing out your fears, allow the worry to persist and make the prob-lem worse in the long term. Clearly, you have to stop all your safety behaviors if you are to overcome your body image problems success-fully.

Effects of safety behaviors on others

Many of these safety behaviors therefore also have an effect on others around you. Examples include:

• Frequently seeking reassurance. This can leave another person feeling frustrated and impotent when they are unable to have a lasting effect (if any) on how you feel.
• Other people thinking you are obsessed with yourself and finding this boring or unattractive.

- Your worries placing restrictions on socializing, reducing your friends' or partner's pleasure at seeing you, and increasing your sense of isolation and conflict.
- Your worries about your looks increasing feelings of jealousy, placing strain on a relationship.
- Your worries about your looks restricting physical intimacy.
- Wearing particular types of clothes to hide a feature, which might provoke comments.
- Keeping your head down and avoiding eye contact, leading others to assume that you are not interested in them. They will then back off and you are more likely to think there is something wrong with you
- Being distracted by your worries about your looks causing you to seem aloof or uninterested. This in turn may lead people to be less warm towards you than they would otherwise be.

All these examples show how a safety behavior can leave you trapped in a cycle, where the behavior you have put in place to protect you becomes the problem in two different ways. First, it preoccupies you and prevents you attending to what is really happening.

Second, it stops you developing a positive and helpful way of behaving with other people.

When your solutions are the problem

The US psychologist Steve Hayes uses a metaphor to describe people who are trying to cope with a body image problem through no fault of their own. Imagine you're blindfolded and placed in a field with a tool bag. You're told that this is what life is all about and that your job is to run around this field, with the blindfold on. Now, what you don't know is that there are some deep holes in this field. So you start running around and enjoying life. However, sooner or later you fall into a deep hole. You can't climb out and you cannot find an escape route. So you feel inside your tool bag for something you can use to get you out. The only tool is a shovel. So what do you do? You start digging. It's seems so obvious because you are stuck and can't get out. Soon you notice you're not out of your hole, so you try digging faster; but you're still in the hole. So you try big shovelfuls, you try throwing the dirt far away from you and so on, but you're still in the hole.

Does this relate to your experience of trying to solve your body image problem? You might be seeking help from this book or going to a therapist in the hope that you can find a bigger or better shovel to help you feel better. Well, the fact is that you can't dig your way out. However, if you let go of the shovel, you can feel around to see whether there is anything else to help you out – a ladder, for example. Remember, you are blindfolded and you won't be able to find the ladder or anything else until you drop the shovel. From the perspective of this book, your shovel represents the attempts you are making to control or escape from the way you feel about your appearance.

Looking at your actions compassionately

It is important to remember that, like falling down a hole in the example above, having a body image problem is completely understandable. Yes, life is unfair but it's not your fault – you've fallen down a hole. You have the ability to get out but, before you started to read this book, you did not know what to do, and you did what you did because it seemed natural. We are not saying that the situation is hopeless but, and this is very important, your solutions –

trying to avoid or control the way you feel about your appearance – are not working. All they do is make the situation worse and make you feel more stressed and depressed. Remember, working out how you fell into your hole is not going to get you out of it. Some therapies unintentionally provide you with a bigger shovel.

Only when you stop shovelling can you feel around for something to help you out – like a ladder or rope. This may seem like a leap of faith but if you don't accept the uncertainty, it's guaranteed to get worse.

Building alternative explanations: Theory A versus Theory B

The essence of overcoming a body image problem using the various techniques outlined throughout this book is to gather evidence to see 'which theory fits the facts'. Doing the various tasks will allow you:

1. to find out whether what you fear will happen does in fact happen, and
2. to learn new ways of behaving by acting against the way you feel.

You will also be finding out whether the results of your experiment best fit your existing explanation for your body image problem or an alternative. In body image problems there are two broad alternatives to be tested:

Theory A: *I have a problem with the way my hair looks. My solution is to take every possible step to avoid being humiliated and rejected. This has led me to avoid people, hide my hair, and repeatedly check in mirrors.*

Theory B: *I have a problem with being excessively preoccupied by my hair and am worried about being humiliated and rejected; my 'solutions' (driven by theory A) have become my problem and feed my preoccupation.*

Try thinking of your own body image problem in terms of two competing theories. Remember that only one theory can be correct – they can't both be true. In the space below, write under 'Theory A' how you have viewed the problem, and how it has led to you using avoidance and safety behaviors. Then write against 'Theory B' another way of looking at your experience that would enable to test out your alternative.

Theory A:

[Space left intentionally blank in the original book]
Theory B:
[Space left intentionally blank in the original book]

If you have a body image problem, you will probably have been following Theory A for many years. However, in order to determine whether Theory B might be the correct explanation for your problems, you will have to act as if it were correct, at least for a time while you collect the evidence.

This may seem rather scary. But think of it like this: if, after, say, three months, you remain unconvinced, you can always go back to Theory A and carry on with your current solutions. Remember the image of the hole and the spade? You might believe that the risk of being humiliated or being rejected through testing out Theory B is too high to risk dropping your spade to see if there is in fact a ladder there. However, if you don't let go of the spade, then you won't ever know if there is anything else there to take hold of. If there's nothing there, you can always go back to your spade; but if you don't test out the alternative theory, all you will ever have is your spade – and all you will do is dig yourself further into the hole, causing yourself more distress and limiting your life even more.

When problematic solutions seem to work

It may seem to you that digging your way out of a hole works because you are doing something with the tools you have and stopping bad events from happening. It is therefore likely that you will avoid or escape from unpleasant thoughts and situations in the future because such behavior has been 'reinforced'; it has apparently been successful. However, as we have already pointed out, if you cope by avoiding or escaping from unpleasant thoughts or situations, the technique becomes unworkable for a number of reasons:

1. Your 'solutions' of avoidance and escape will make you feel worse and more depressed as you come to realize that they are not going to work and you begin to worry more about problems.

2. Avoidance often prevents you from finding out whether something is true or not. For example, if you never ask a person why he appeared to ignore you, you will never find out if it was because he dislikes you or

whether, for instance, he was not wearing his contact lenses or was busy worrying about a problem of his own.

3. Avoidance and escape have unintended effects on the people around you. Your friends and family might stop trusting you and end up taking on your responsibilities. This in turn could create a vicious circle in which you feel incapable of doing certain things.

4. Avoidance stops you from doing what is important to you. For example, you want to be a person to whom your friends and family can turn for support or to be a good parent. When you can't do these things you will inevitably feel more depressed. You might spend more time focusing on yourself and beating yourself up. Your behavior then has an effect on the people around you. Others may be critical or unsupportive and you will probably become more depressed, in a vicious circle.

While you focus on your negativity, you totally buy into the content of your thoughts as if they were facts. These thoughts are just mental chatter, not objective evidence. In general, the aim should be to 'understand' these thoughts, not so that you can question whether they are true or not, but to consider how you react to them.

Perfectionism and high standards

Many people have their first taste of being really worried about their appearance when they are teenagers. This is not only a time of considerable change in appearance, but also a time when humans are biologically programmed to become more aware of being physically attracted to others and wanting others to be physically attracted to them. For some people with body image problems it seems as if their attitude to their appearance has not been updated since they were much younger. Many still treat their appearance every day as if looking their best is as important as it would be on a special occasion, TV appearance, or first date. Part of recovery is becoming more flexible in the standards you set for your appearance, and on most days prioritizing other aspects of your life.

The way you've trained your brain

One way of thinking about the way your actions might be maintaining your problem is to think about the message they send your brain. The more you act as though an aspect of your appearance is something shameful, or has potential for you to be humiliated, the more your brain understands that a flaw (or flaws) in your appearance is an important problem. Because of this, your brain will frequently send you thoughts about your appearance so that you don't forget to solve the problem. It will also keep your nervous system on 'red alert' in situations you have trained it to believe are threatening. It will do this by, for example, over-preparing for the situations, using safety behaviors or avoiding them, or escaping from them. This 'red alert' means anxiety, and a tendency to jump to the conclusion that something threatening is happening. This just makes your life more difficult and less enjoyable, as you can't relax and fully engage in experiences that you would otherwise find rewarding.

Building connections between your coping strategies and their results

Really understanding how your solutions are the problem is a crucial step in overcoming a body image problem. Here are some examples of how coping strategies and 'safety behaviors' backfire and in fact fuel a body image problem:

My preoccupation	Example of safety behavior	Unintended consequence
Nose too big	Change posture to avoid being seen side-on	Increases self-conscious-ness, strengthens belief that people will notice and think negatively
Nose too big	Pressing nose with hand to try and re-shape	Increases focus of atten-tion, nose feels red and sore (swollen and bigger)
Lines on face	Checking	Become too aware of them
Hair might be get-ting thin	Researching hair products	Fuels my preoccupation, as I spend yet more hours thinking about it
My face doesn't fit together properly	Avoiding social situ-ations	I never find out whether my fears of being humiliat-ed come true, I feel lone-ly. People assume I don't want to see them

Use the blank table provided in Appendix 2 to monitor your safety behaviors and their consequences over a period of time.

You can use what you have written in this table to build up your own 'vicious flower', diagram, as described in the next section.

Building your own vicious flower

A vicious flower is a model you can use to help think through the effects of your current methods of coping. There are several completed vicious flowers in Chapter 9 and we have provided an example below. This visual illustration of how a body-image problem is being maintained can be very striking. Many people are surprised to see just how much is 'going on' in the maintenance of their body image problem.

We have also provided a blank vicious flower for you to fill in yourself, though it's sometimes easier to draw your own on a blank sheet of paper so that you can have as many 'petals' as you wish. Once you have filled in or drawn your own vicious flower, you can return to it as you progress through the rest of this book. You might add a new petal if you identify a new safety behavior, but we hope that most of your time will be spent pulling the petals off your flower by facing things you have been avoiding, re-training your attention, and dropping unhelpful safety behaviors.

Vicious flower of body image problems

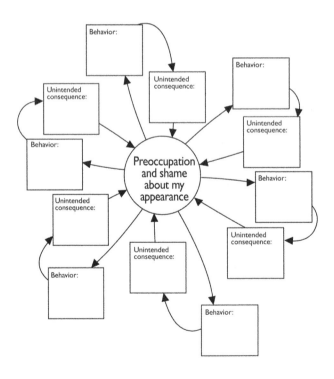

5

Setting yourself on the right course

This chapter is designed to help you define your problem and monitor the severity of your body image problems and their impact on your life. Identifying and rating the current severity of your body image problem at the outset will give you a reference point against which you can measure your progress. You may find it helpful to make additional copies of these questionnaires to help you to measure your progress. They are designed to help you define the nature of the problem and its effect on your life. Some of them can be completed weekly to determine whether you are making progress or not.

Identifying the problem feature

Please study this example before completing Questionnaire 5.1. In a moment, we shall ask you to describe the feature(s) of your body that you dislike or would like to improve. If you want to improve more than one feature, please list all the features. The example is based on a woman whose main worry was her nose and

124

who was concerned to a lesser extent by her skin and bottom. She is currently seeking cosmetic surgery for her nose.

SAMPLE QUESTIONNAIRE

Features causing concern

Please describe the feature(s) of your body that you dislike or would like to improve and tick the box if you are seeking a cosmetic or dermatological procedure for the feature either now or in the future.

Please tick the appropriate box.

	Now	In the future
First feature		
Nose is too crooked with a bump	☐	☐
Second feature		
Blemishes and acne scars on face	☐	☐
Third feature		
Bottom is too big	☐	☐

We will then ask you to draw a pie chart and estimate the percentage of concern allocated to each feature. The person above completed her pie chart like this.

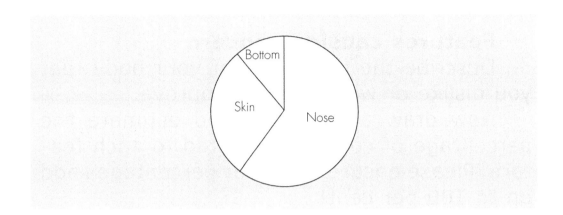

QUESTIONNAIRE 5.1: IDENTIFYING THE PROBLEM FEATURE

	Now	In the future
First feature	☐	☐
Second feature	☐	☐
Third feature	☐	☐
Fourth feature	☐	☐
Fifth feature	☐	☐

Features causing concern

Describe the feature(s) of your body that you dislike or would like to improve.

Now draw a pie chart and estimate the percentage of concern allocated to each feature. Please ensure that your percentages add up to 100 per cent!

From now on, we will refer to these concerns as your 'feature(s)'

Noticeability of your feature

The next set of questions relates to how noticeable you think your feature is. You may find it helpful to discuss this aspect of the problem with a trusted friend or therapist. You could ask this person to rate the features using the same scale without him or her knowing how you rated yourself.

QUESTIONNAIRE 5.2: RATING THE NOTICEABILITY OF YOUR PROBLEM FEATURE

1. How noticeable do you feel your feature is to other people (if you do not camouflage yourself, e.g. with clothes, padding and/or makeup, and the feature has not been pointed out to them)?

a. Please specify the first feature you are rating

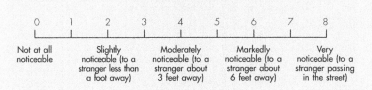

b. Please specify the second feature you are rating (if applicable)

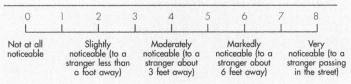

c. Please specify the third feature you are rating (if applicable)

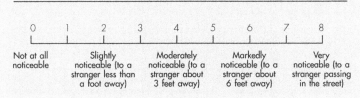

d. Please specify the fourth feature you are rating (if applicable)

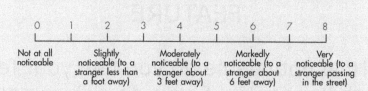

2. How do you feel your feature compares to the same feature possessed by other people of the same age, sex, and ethnic group?

a. Please specify the first feature you are rating

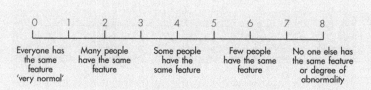

b. Please specify the second feature you are rating (if applicable)

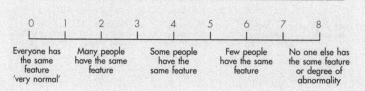

c. Please specify the third feature you are rating (if applicable)

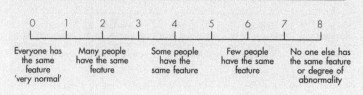

d. Please specify the fourth feature you are rating (if applicable)

_____

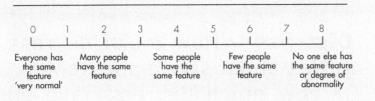

| 0 | 1 | 2 | 3 | 4 | 5 | 6 | 7 | 8 |

Everyone has the same feature 'very normal'

Many people have the same feature

Some people have the same feature

Few people have the same feature

No one else has the same feature or degree of abnormality

Severity of your body image symptoms

The following questionnaire has been designed for you to use weekly or fortnightly to monitor your progress in overcoming your body image problems.

QUESTIONNAIRE 5.3: RATING THE SEVERITY OF YOUR BODY IMAGE SYMPTOMS

Answer the following questions by circling a number that best describes the **past week.**

1. **Frequency** – How much of your time on an average day has been occupied by worries about your appearance and related behaviors (e.g. checking, comparing) **over the past week?**

130

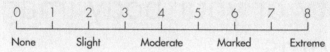

2. Distress – How much distress have your worries about your appearance caused you? Or how much distress have you felt when confronted with a situation you wanted to avoid?

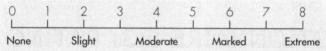

3. Handicap – How much have worries about your appearance and related behaviors (e.g. checking, avoiding) interfered with friendships, relationships, family life or your ability to perform at work or study?

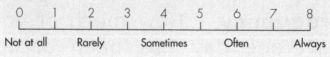

4. Avoidance – How much have you avoided situations or activities or thoughts that are related to your worries about your appearance?

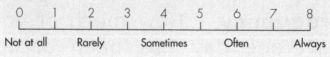

Avoidance of situations because of your preoccupation

The next questionnaire focuses on the extent to which you avoid situations, people, or activities because of your preoccupation with your appearance. You can use a number of the items you avoid in order to test out your fears in Chapter 7 (Taking action).

QUESTIONNAIRE 5.4: AVOIDING SITUATIONS

What do you avoid because of the way you feel about your feature(s)? Please read the situations below and in the second column rate the degree of anxiety that you anticipate in each of the situations on a scale between 0 and 100 where '0' is no anxiety at all and '100' is total panic. In the third column, rate the degree to which you currently avoid each of these situations on the following scale:

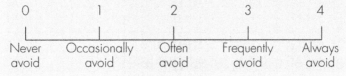

Please add other situations or activities that you avoid at the end of the list.

Situation or activity	Degree of anxiety (0–100)	Frequency (0–4)
I avoid going to a party or social gathering because of my feature(s).		
I avoid having a medical examination or treatment because of my feature(s).		
I avoid going to a public changing room because of my feature(s).		
I avoid exercising in a gym or playing a sport because of my feature(s).		
I avoid wearing a swimming costume on a beach because of my feature(s).		
I avoid being physically close to someone because of my feature(s).		
I avoid making love or intimacy because of my features (or only under certain conditions e.g. lights off or wearing make-up).		
I avoid certain types of clothes because of my features (please specify).		
I avoid certain types of lighting because of my features (please specify).		
I avoid looking at pictures in magazines or on television because of my feature(s).		
I avoid all or certain mirrors that are unsafe because of my features (please specify).		
I avoid having a photo or video taken by someone else because of my feature(s).		

Situation or activity	Degree of anxiety (0–100)	Frequency (0–4)
I avoid looking at old photographs because of my feature(s). (Please say if you have destroyed them.)		
I avoid having my hair cut at all.		
I avoid having my hair cut at a hairdresser's.		
I avoid looking at my features in mirrors or reflective surfaces.		
Others (please specify).		

Rituals and safety behaviors

The following questionnaire focuses upon the things you may be doing excessively or more precisely because of your preoccupation with your appearance. You can use this checklist to help identify the rituals and safety behaviors that you are going to target for change in Chapter 7.

QUESTIONNAIRE 5.5: PERFORMING RITUALS AND SAFETY BEHAVIORS

Please read the list of actions below that you might perform because of the way you feel about your feature(s). In the second column, rate the frequency with which you use each of the behaviors on the following scale:

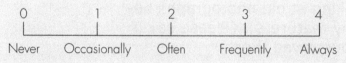

Behavior	Frequency
I check my feature(s) in mirrors.	
I use a particular light to check my feature(s) in a mirror (please specify).	
I check my feature(s) in other reflective surfaces, e.g. cutlery, windows, CDs (please specify).	
I check my feature(s) directly by looking at it/them without a mirror.	
I check my feature(s) by taking photographs of myself.	
I check my feature(s) by feeling it/them with my finger(s).	
I compare my feature(s) with others in magazines or on television and film.	
I compare my feature(s) with those of other people I meet.	
I compare my feature(s) with old pictures of myself.	
I pinch the fat on my skin.	
I wear something to distract attention from my feature, e.g. jewellery, a tattoo (please specify).	
I change my posture to avoid my feature being seen at a certain angle (please specify).	
I hide my feature(s) with something, e.g. my hand, a baseball cap, hat, scarf, baggy clothing, newspaper (please specify).	
I use padding in my clothes to camouflage or increase the size of a feature (please specify).	

Behavior	Frequency
I try to convince others about how unattractive my feature(s) is/are.	
I ask others to confirm the existence of a defect in my feature(s).	
I seek reassurance about whether my feature(s) has/have got worse.	
I seek reassurance about whether my feature(s) is/are camouflaged, e.g. by make-up.	
I keep changing my clothes before I go out.	
I get my partner or family member to 'help' me in camouflaging or checking my appearance (please specify).	
I keep measuring my feature(s).	
Hair: I wear a wig because of my feature(s).	
I grow or arrange my hair to hide certain features (please specify).	
I comb or groom (smooth/straighten) or adjust my hair more than most people.	
I shave, cut or pluck hair more than most people (please specify).	
I use medication to promote hair growth on my head.	
Skin: I clean my skin more than most people.	
I wear more make-up than most people to hide my feature(s).	
I use cover-up stick for spots or blemishes.	
I use facial peel, scrubs or saunas for my skin.	
I bleach my skin.	
I use a sun-bed to darken my skin.	
I pick my skin or squeeze spots more than most people.	
Shape or weight: I exercise to alter my shape or weight.	
I body-build with weights.	

Behavior	Frequency
I use steroids.	
I weigh myself more than necessary.	
I restrict my food to improve my shape or reduce my weight.	
I sit with my toes on the floor to avoid my thighs spreading.	
I eat more food to increase my weight.	
I use diet pills, laxatives or diuretics (please specify).	
Others (please specify):	

The impact of your symptoms on your life

The next step is to rate the impact of your problems on your everyday life. We have provided a standard questionnaire that serves this purpose. It can be repeated at regular intervals (for example fortnightly) to monitor your progress.

QUESTIONNAIRE 5.6: RATING THE IMPACT ON YOUR LIFE

1. If you have a long-term partner, please answer a. If you do not have a partner, please answer b.

a. To what extent does your preoccupation with your feature(s) affect your relationship with an existing partner (e.g. affectionate feelings, number of arguments, enjoying activities together)?

```
   0    1    2    3    4    5    6    7    8
   |____|____|____|____|____|____|____|____|
 Not at all  Slightly  Moderately  Markedly  Extremely
```

b. If you do not have a long-term partner, to what extent does your preoccupation with your feature(s) currently affect you and your potential partner when you are dating or developing a relationship?

```
   0    1    2    3    4    5    6    7    8
   |____|____|____|____|____|____|____|____|
 Not at all  Slightly  Moderately  Markedly  Extremely
```

2. To what extent does your preoccupation with your feature(s) currently have an effect on a sexual relationship (e.g. enjoyment of sex, frequency of sexual activity)?

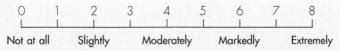

```
   0    1    2    3    4    5    6    7    8
   |____|____|____|____|____|____|____|____|
 Not at all  Slightly  Moderately  Markedly  Extremely
```

Tick, if you have no sexual relationship for reasons other than avoiding sex because of your preoccupation with your feature(s). _

3. To what extent does your preoccupation with your feature(s) currently interfere with your ability to work or study, or your role as a homemaker? (Please rate this even if you are not working or studying: we are interested in your ability to work or study.)

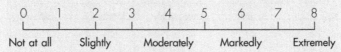

How many working days have you lost in the past year because of your preoccupation with your feature(s)?

4. To what extent does your preoccupation with feature(s) currently interfere with your social life with other people (e.g. parties, pubs, clubs, outings, visits, home entertainment)?

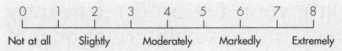

5. To what extent does your preoccupation with your feature(s) currently interfere with your private leisure activities done alone, (e.g. reading; gardening; collecting; walking alone, etc.)?

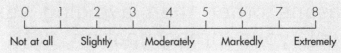

6. To what extent does your preoccupation with your feature(s) currently interfere with your home management (e.g. cleaning, tidying, shopping, cooking, looking after your home or children, paying bills, etc)?

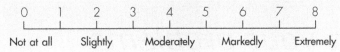

7. To what extent does your preoccupation with your feature also cause you difficulty in its functioning? (For example, if you dislike the shape of your jaw, it might cause difficulty with a poor bite with your teeth; or if your nose is crooked, it might cause difficulty breathing.)

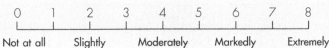

Rating the severity of your depression and anxiety

Rating the severity of your depressive symptoms at the start and at regular intervals will help you to monitor your progress and assess whether what you are doing is effective or not. Even if you decide not to use any self-help techniques or decide to take medication, it is still important to monitor your progress so you should still do these exercises. You can then report back to the doctor and decide whether to try an alternative approach. You can also use the Hospital and Anxiety Depression Scale in Appendix 2 to monitor depression and anxiety.

Listing your problems

Building a list of your problems helps in a number of ways. First it helps you to break down your body image problem into specific areas to tackle. It also gives you a chance to rate these problems overall now, so that you can re-rate them to help measure your progress. This is Catherine's list of problems.

SAMPLE PROBLEM LIST

Severity rating: 0–10 (10 being most severe)
1. Feeling very preoccupied and ashamed about my skin, leading me to worry about it most of the day, and to spend approximately 4 hours applying make-up if I have to leave the house.
Rating: 10
2. Feeling depressed, leading me to spend as much time as I can at home and not

keeping on top of my bills and domestic chores.
Rating: 8
3. Frequently checking in mirror and comparing my skin to people in the media, leading me to feel envious towards people with far better skin than me.
Rating: 7

Now make your own list of problems and rate the severity of each one.

EXERCISE 5.1: PROBLEM LIST

Severity rating: 0–10 (10 being most severe)

1. _____
                                              Rating: _____
2. _____
                                              Rating: _____
3. _____
                                              Rating: _____
4. _____
                                              Rating: _____

Describing your goals

Next, you need to write a description of your goals relating to the problems that you have described and the values you have identified. Start with short-term goals, which are easier to tackle, and set yourself a realistic timetable by which you intend to move onto the next set of goals. Here is Catherine's list of goals.

SAMPLE GOAL LIST

Progress rating: 0–10 (10 being most severe)

Goal:	Progress rating
Short term	
1. To cut down the number of foundations I use to one	0
2. To invite a friend round for a coffee	0
3. To stop comparing my skin with others	0
4. To stop picking my skin and let it heal by itself	0
Medium term	
1. To resume my social life by meeting up with friends outside my home	0
2. To go swimming again regularly	0
3. To be able to go out to shopping centres	0
Long term	
1. To make progress towards returning to work	0
2. To develop an intimate relationship	0

Try to make your own goals as specific, observable and realistic as possible.

Some individuals with body image problems have forgotten what is normal or healthy. To help generate ideas for healthy alternative behaviors, consider the following questions:

• What did you do before you had a body image problem?

• If you had a twin, who was the same as you in every respect but without a body image problem, what would they do?

• What would a healthy role model of yours do?

You will need to ask yourself these questions for goals in the short, medium and long term. You can then monitor your progress towards your goals on a scale of zero to 10, where zero is no progress at all towards the goal and 10 means the goal has been achieved and sustained. Your goals should relate to your valued directions in life and tackle what you have been avoiding. The next section will help you identity your valued directions.

EXERCISE 5.2: GOAL LIST

Progress rating: 0–10 (10 being most severe)
Short term
1. _____
2. _____
3. _____
Medium term
1. _____
2. _____
3. _____
Long term
1. _____
2. _____
3. _____

Focusing more on what's important to you, and less on appearance

Many body image problems are the result of becoming overly focused on your own appearance; other people's appearance; appearance in the media; or the role of appearance in our culture. The aim of the next exercise is to gain an understanding of your values or what you want your life to stand for. This will enable you to engage in a life that has a better balance and is less dominated by appearance. Once you know what your valued directions are, you can start acting towards them.

We have adapted the 'Valued Living Questionnaire' from *Acceptance and Commitment Therapy* (Guilford Publications, 2004) by Steven Hayes, Kirk Strosahl and Kelly Wilson. There are various prompts for each area to help you write down a brief statement. You don't have to fill in every area; just leave an area blank if you think it is inappropriate for you. After writing down your statements, you may want to clarify them with a friend or therapist. Be careful not to write down values that you think you should have just because others will approve of them. Only write down what you know to be true for yourself. It is probably a valued direction if you acted on it consistently before you experienced your body image problem. If you have had a body image problem for many years, you may struggle with this exercise, but you should persevere because it is very important.

Note that values are not goals – they are more like compass points, and they need to be lived out by committed action. Goals are part of this process. With values, you never reach your destination because there is always something more you can do to work towards them. If your valued direction in life is to be a good parent, then your first goal might be to spend a few hours just hanging out with your son or daughter and playing with him or her. Other goals might be to get your son or daughter through school or college. It might take some time to discover all of your values, so here are some prompts to help you:

• Imagine what aspects of life you would be engaging in if you were not feeling shamed or preoccupied with your appearance at this moment. We understand that you might feel upset at the things you seem to have lost but this exercise will help you chart your course on the journey you wish to take.

• Brainstorm all the activities/interests you can think of, and consider which might be close to your valued directions.

• Remind yourself of what you used to value or aspire to when you were younger. Have any of these values simply been 'squashed' by your body image problem?

• Consider whether a fear of what other people will think, or a fear of failing, might be holding you back from pursuing your valued directions.

- Consider a role model or hero and the values he or she holds.
- Have a chat with a trusted friend (or therapist) who knows you well and see what he or she would guess your values to be.
- Be prepared to experiment and 'try on for size' living consistently with a given valued direction to see how it 'fits'.

SAMPLE VALUED DIRECTIONS FORM

Area	Valued direction
1. Intimacy (What is important to you in how you act in an intimate relationship? What sort of partner do you want to be? If you are not involved in a relationship at present, how would you like to act in a relationship?	I want to develop a relationship and be a good partner and spend time doing things together.
2. Family relationships (What is important to you in how you want to act as a brother/sister; son/daughter; father/mother or parent-in-law? If you are not in contact with some of your family members, would you like to be and how would you act in such a relationship?)	I'd like to be a good daughter and less dependent on my parents for support and to help them more in the future. I'd like to spend more time with my brother, getting to know him better.
3. Social relationships (What is important to you in the way you act in the friendships you have? How would you like your friends to remember you? If you have no friends, would you like to have some and what role would you like in a friendship?)	I'd like to be a good friend, more open and available to my friends.

Area	Valued direction
4. Work (What is important to you in your work? What sort of employee do you want to be? How important to you is what you achieve in your career? What sort of business do you want to run?)	I'd like to return to work and be more approachable and help to make it a more successful company.
5. Education and training (What is important to you in your education or training? What sort of student do you want to be? If you are not in education, would you like to be?)	To improve my future prospects of securing a better job in the future, I'd like to do more management and IT training.
6. Recreation (What is important to you in what you do to follow any interests, sports or hobbies? If you are not following any interests, what would you ideally like to be pursuing?)	I'd like to get back to playing tennis and swimming. I might like to learn to play a musical instrument.
7. Spirituality What is important to you in the way you want to follow a spiritual path? If you are not spiritual, would you like to be and how?	I'd like to learn more about Buddhism.
8. Voluntary work (What would you like to do for the community – e.g. voluntary or charity work or political activity?)	I'd like to do more to help others in a charity for body dysmorphic disorder and raise money for them.
9. Health/physical well-being (What is important to you in how you act for your physical health?)	Not relevant.
10. Mental health (What is important to you generally in how you look after your mental health?)	I'd like to be better at managing my stress at the end of the working day.

Now try to define your own valued directions in life.

EXERCISE 5.3: UNDERSTANDING YOUR VALUES

Area	Valued direction
1. Intimacy (What is important to you in how you act in an intimate relationship? What sort of partner do you want to be? If you are not involved in a relationship at present, how would you like to act in a relationship?)	
2. Family relationships (What is important to you in how you want to act as a brother/sister; son/daughter; father/mother or parent-in-law? If you are not in contact with some of your family members, would you like to be and how would you act in such a relationship?)	
3. Social relationships (What is important to you in the way you act in the friendships you have? How would you like your friends to remember you? If you have no friends, would you like to have some and what role would you like in a friendship?)	
4. Work (What is important to you in your work? What sort of employee do you want to be? How important to you is what you achieve in your career? What sort of business do you want to run?)	
5. Education and training (What is important to you in your education or training? What sort of student do you want to be? If you are not in education, would you like to be?)	
6. Recreation (What is important to you in what you do to follow any interests, sports or hobbies? If you are not following any interests, what would you ideally like to be pursuing?)	

Area	Valued direction
7. Spirituality (If you are spiritual, what is important to you in the way you want to follow a spiritual path? If you are not, would you like to be and what do you ideally want?)	
8. Voluntary work (What would you like to do for the larger community? For example, voluntary or charity work or political activity?)	
9. Health/physical well-being (What is important to you in how you act for your physical health?)	
10. Mental health (What is important to you generally in how you look after your mental health?)	
11. Any other values that are not listed above	

6

Thinking about thinking

As we mentioned in Chapter 4, body image problems often occur when your thoughts and images become fused with facts. Thus, if you feel ugly then your ugliness is taken as a given fact and you assume that others will get the same impression as you. Being fused with your thoughts and images thus makes your reality very unpleasant. Many people naturally respond by trying either to escape from the thoughts and images or to control them, but this means that you miss out on rewarding life experiences. This chapter is about developing a different relationship with your thoughts and images so you can treat them as 'just thoughts' or 'just a picture in my mind'. Your life will be more rewarding when you truly accept your thoughts and images about your appearance because trying to suppress (or 'control') them only makes the preoccupation worse and amplifies your discomfort into pain. This chapter also contains a number of practical exercises to help you examine your relationship with your thoughts and refocus your attention away from your mind.

Label your thinking style

You may have forgotten how to observe the process of thinking because you have become bound up with the content of your thoughts. The first step is to thank your mind for its contribution to your mental health. Try to distance yourself from its endless chatter and commentary and rating of yourself. This is a difficult skill, which will take time and practice to master, using a number of different exercises (described below).

Just as having an infection might give you a fever, emotional problems will affect your thinking. In common with other emotional problems, body shame will drive your thinking in a more negative and extreme direction. This unhelpful way of thinking will in turn make you feel worse, and influence what you focus upon and what you do. It thus plays a key role in the maintenance of your problem.

Two of the founding fathers of cognitive behavior therapy, Albert Ellis and Aaron Beck, both identified particular patterns of thinking linked with emotional problems. The great advantage of knowing the ways in which your thinking might be affected by your body image problem is that you can more readily spot a negative thought and learn to take these thoughts (and images) with a huge pinch of salt. Think of it as body shame propaganda, aiming to keep you preoccupied, distressed, and restricted. Just as people during the Second World War had to learn to ignore the negative Nazi propaganda (aimed at lowering their morale) that invaded their radios, you can learn to notice unhelpful thoughts without believing them to be true.

BODY SHAME THINKING STYLES

Here are some of the more common types of thinking styles that arise in body shame.

Catastrophizing

Jumping to the worst possible conclusion, e.g. 'someone will notice my nose and make a really upsetting comment.'

All or nothing (black and white) thinking

Thinking in extreme, all-or-nothing terms, e.g. 'I am either very attractive or very ugly.'

Over-generalizing

Drawing generalized conclusions (involving the words 'always' or 'never') from a specific event, e.g. 'because that person rejected me I know I'll never find a partner.'

Fortune-telling

Making negative and pessimistic predictions about the future, e.g. 'I know I'll never get over this.' 'I will be unhappy unless my appearance changes.' 'If someone saw me without my makeup they'd be really surprised at how bad I look.'

Mind-reading

Jumping to conclusions about what other people are thinking about you, e.g. 'that person is looking at me, I can tell they are noticing my bad skin and thinking I'm disgusting.'

Mental filtering

Focusing on the negative and overlooking the positive, e.g. paying far more attention in your mind to the one person who was not friendly to you and overlooking the fact that the others were very warm towards you; or tending to overlook the positive aspects of yourself and what you have going for you.

Disqualifying the positive

Discounting positive information or twisting a positive into a negative, e.g. thinking 'That person was only nice to me because they thought I was repulsive and felt sorry for me. They'll probably have a good laugh about me with their friends later.'

Labelling

Globally putting yourself down, in an extreme and self-attacking way, e.g. 'I'm a worthless, hideous freak.'

Emotional reasoning

Listening too much to your negative gut feeling instead of looking at the objective facts, e.g. 'I know I'm hideous and will end up alone because I feel it deep inside.'

Personalizing

Taking an event or someone's behavior too personally or blaming yourself, e.g. thinking 'That person pushed in front of me when I was trying to get on the train because they think my appearance makes me inferior.' Recognizing this tendency to misinterpret events in the world around you because of your preoccupation with your appearance can help you reduce the extent to which your body image problem causes you distress.

Demands

Rigid 'should', 'must', 'ought', or 'have to' rules about yourself, the world, or other people. Demands for certainty can be a particular issue for any kind of anxiety problem, e.g. 'I must know just how I look so that I can do whatever I can about it. I should always try to look as good as possible.'

Low frustration tolerance

Telling yourself that something is 'too difficult', or 'unbearable', or that 'I can't stand it', when it's actually hard to bear, but bearable. It is in your interests to tolerate these things, e.g. experiencing some degree of discomfort as you face your fears.

EXERCISE 6.1: IDENTIFYING YOUR COMMON THINKING STYLES

Write down examples of your five most common thinking styles

1. Thinking style

[Space left intentionally blank in the original book]

example

[Space left intentionally blank in the original book]

2. Thinking style

[Space left intentionally blank in the original book]

example

[Space left intentionally blank in the original book]

3. Thinking style

[Space left intentionally blank in the original book]

example

[Space left intentionally blank in the original book]

4. Thinking style

[Space left intentionally blank in the original book]

example

[Space left intentionally blank in the original book]

5. Thinking style

[Space left intentionally blank in the original book]

example

[Space left intentionally blank in the original book]

Labelling your thoughts and feelings

Another strategy for intrusive thoughts is to label the thought or feeling by saying it out aloud and writing it down. For example:

'I am **having a thought** that I am fat.'
'I am **having a memory** of being bullied as a child.'
'I'm **having the feeling** of being anxious.'
'I'm **making a rating** of myself that I am ugly.'

As an alternative, some people find it more helpful to distance themselves from such thoughts by labelling them as products of their mind, e.g. 'My mind is telling me I am ugly.'

EXERCISE 6.2: LABELLING YOUR HABITUAL THOUGHTS

Now try to complete the following for your own habitual pattern of thoughts and feelings:

I am having a thought that (describe)

[Space left intentionally blank in the original book]

I am having a thought that (describe)

[Space left intentionally blank in the original book]

I am having a feeling of (describe)

[Space left intentionally blank in the original book]

I am having memories about (describe)

[Space left intentionally blank in the original book]

I am making a rating about (describe)

[Space left intentionally blank in the original book]

Labelling your thoughts may feel awkward at first, but with practice it will help you to accept your thoughts or feelings without buying into them. Some people find it helpful to speak their thoughts out loud in a funny voice or the voice of a cartoon character. Again, this can help you to distance yourself from your thoughts and defuse them from your 'self'.

The aim of all these exercises is to acknowledge the existence of such thoughts and label them for what they are. It's usually best not to challenge their content, as they are strongly bound up with past memories and in body image problems that are often rigidly held. As you progress, you'll discover that you can experience unpleasant thoughts and feelings and still do what's important for your life, despite their presence. If you keep doing this, they will slowly fade.

Keeping a record of your thoughts

Try making a list of all your recurrent body image thoughts and feelings, label them for what they are, and put a tick in the relevant box each time they occur. Such thoughts are more likely to appear in difficult situations. It can be helpful to monitor them just to see which ones turn up in particular situations and try to bully you. We don't want you to do this repeatedly – just to see what happens over a few days. You will soon start to develop different ways of looking at your thoughts and not buying into them, brooding, comparing, or paying attention to what your mind is telling you. Here is David's chart as an example.

DAVID'S THOUGHT MONITORING CHART

I have thoughts that:	Mon	Tues	Wed	Thurs	Fri	Sat	Sun
1. I will be alone all my life	✓✓ ✓✓ ✓	✓✓ ✓✓ ✓✓ ✓✓ ✓✓	✓✓ ✓✓ ✓✓ ✓	✓✓ ✓✓ ✓✓ ✓✓ ✓✓ ✓			
2. I am ugly	✓✓ ✓✓ ✓✓ ✓	✓✓ ✓✓ ✓✓	✓✓ ✓✓ ✓✓	✓✓ ✓✓ ✓✓			

I have images of:	Mon	Tues	Wed	Thurs	Fri	Sat	Sun
1. Myself looking like an alien	✓✓ ✓✓ ✓✓ ✓✓	✓✓ ✓✓ ✓✓	✓✓ ✓✓ ✓✓	✓✓ ✓✓ ✓✓ ✓			

A blank thought monitoring chart which you can photocopy can be found in Appendix 2. Note that the purpose of monitoring your thoughts is not to challenge their content, or to control or reduce their frequency – just to acknowledge them and to thank your mind for its contribution. If your thoughts are very frequent (and in some people it may be a thousand or more times a day), you might find it easier to use a tally counter and transfer the total at the end of each day to your chart. (You can purchase a tally counter by post. You will easily find a supplier if you type 'buy tally counter' into an Internet search engine.) You can also note the situations in which the thoughts most commonly occur in order to see if there is a pattern. It would be useful to know if there is such a pattern so that you can predict what thoughts will turn up and ensure that you are better prepared for them.

Watching your thoughts pass by

You have gathered by now that what we want you to develop is a sense of distance from your thoughts and feelings. This means not buying into them but being aware of them as a passive observer.

This is best illustrated by closing your eyes and bringing to mind, say, a bowl of fruit, then watching it without influencing it in any way. It's okay if your attention strays away from the orange or if the image changes (for example, the orange falls off the top of the bowl). You should merely be aware of the changing content of your attention without influencing the content in any way. This may not be easy at first, but it's worth persevering. The technique of distancing your thoughts can also be used just to notice your intrusive thoughts and not to engage with them.

Another analogy for watching your thoughts is to imagine them as cars passing on a road. When you are depressed, you might focus on particular 'cars' that tell you that you are a failure and life is hopeless. You cope either by trying to stop the cars or by pushing them to one side (if you're not in danger of being run over, that is!). Alternatively, you may try to flag the car down, get into the driving seat and try to park it (that is, analyse the idea and sort it out until you feel 'right'). Of course, there is often no room to park the car and as soon as you have parked one car another one comes along.

Distancing yourself from your thoughts means being on the pavement, acknowledging the cars and the traffic but just noticing them and then walking along the pavement and focusing your attention on other parts of the environment (such as talking to the person beside you and noticing other people passing you and the sights and smells of the flowers on the verge). You can still play in the park and do what is important for you despite the thoughts. In other words, such thoughts have no more meaning than passing traffic – they are 'just' thoughts and are part of the rich tapestry of human existence. You can't get rid of them. It's just the same as when you are in a city and there is always some slight traffic noise in the background and you learn to live with it. Notice these thoughts and feelings and acknowledge their presence, then get on with your life.

An exercise in distancing

In this exercise, you will need to get into a relaxed position and just observe the flow of your thoughts, one after another, without trying to figure out their meaning or their relationship to one another. You are practising an attitude of acceptance of your experience.

Imagine for the moment sitting next to a stream. As you gaze at the stream, you notice a number of leaves on the surface of the water. Keep looking at the leaves and watch them drift slowly downstream. When thoughts come, put each one on a leaf, and notice each leaf as it comes closer to you. Then watch it slowly moving away from you, eventually drifting out of sight. Return to looking at the stream, waiting for the next leaf to float by with a new thought. If one comes along, again, watch it come closer to you and then let it drift out of sight. Allow yourself to have thoughts and imagine them floating by like leaves down a stream. Notice now that you are the stream. You hold all the water, all the fish and debris and leaves. You need not interfere with anything in the stream—just let them all flow. Then, when you are ready, gradually widen your attention to take in the sounds around. Slowly open your eyes and get back to life.

Attentional biases in body image

In Chapter 4, we described how various attentional biases influence your awareness of your feature. Our attention seeks out the subjects that interest us: it is biased towards those subjects and we become more aware of them. What is on our minds will influence what we notice; it's just part of how the human brain works.

However, in body image problems, this attention bias towards monitoring how you look is one of the factors that keeps the condition going. Being self-focused means being on the outside, looking in at yourself, with an observer's perspective and being very aware of your thoughts and feelings. Being externally focused means being on the inside, looking out at the world around you and at what you see or hear or smell. People with body image problems are frequently self-focused and constantly monitoring their felt impression or picture in their mind. You might want to know exactly how you look and therefore how likely you are to be humiliated (although whether this is accurate or not is a different matter). Or you could be trying to avoid the gaze of someone who you think is being critical.

Another situation where self-focused attention occurs is in front of a mirror. We know from research that people with body image problems are more likely to focus on their felt impression and on certain features that are viewed as defective compared with people *without* a body image problem. Furthermore, when individuals without a body image problem look at themselves in a mirror then they tend to focus more on features that they consider attractive.

Re-focusing your attention onto the outside world gives your brain a rest and allows you to take in what the world has to offer.

Overcoming a body image problem will mean broadening your attention to take everything in, not just focusing on your features and refocusing your attention away from your inner world.

It is important to recognize that biased perception is very likely to lead to biased conclusions. For example, if you constantly live in your head and monitor your impression of how you look, you will feel uglier. Excessive self-focus will also mean that your appearance is much more likely to be on your mind and this will increase the number of hours a day you spend being preoccupied. If you know that you tend to overassume that your features are ugly or likely to lead to humiliation, you can correct your thinking by deliberately acting as if you look OK and are safe from attack.

As we also saw earlier, trying not to notice something, as a way of attempting to correct this bias, is always doomed to failure. (The more you try not to think of the pink elephant, the more you end up thinking about it!) However, you can improve the extent to which you focus on other things. The key question is whether focusing your attention inwards helps you to achieve the goals and valued directions you want.

In summary, most people find that being self-focused causes them to dwell more on the 'ghosts from their past' and to feel more preoccupied, which in turn makes them feel worse and therefore likely to do less, and become more self-focused. The alternative is to be less 'on the outside looking in' at yourself, and more 'on the inside looking out' at the world, and doing what is important to you, despite what your mind is telling you.

Monitoring your self-focused attention

In any given situation, especially when you are feeling more anxious or withdrawn, you can estimate the percentage of your attention that is being focused on:

(a) yourself (e.g. monitoring how you appear to others or how you feel)
(b) your tasks (e.g. listening or talking to someone or writing)
(c) your environment (e.g. the hum of traffic in the background).

MONITORING SELF-FOCUSED ATTENTION CHART

Date	Situation	% attention on self	% attention on task	% attention on environment	Total (100%)	Distress (0–100%)

EXERCISE 6.3: RATING YOUR ATTENTION PERCENTAGES

How self-focused are you? Over the next few days, make a note of different situations (e.g. being in front of a mirror, talking to someone of the opposite sex of the same age, reading, etc.) and then rate the percentage of your attention that is on:

a. yourself (0–100 per cent)

b. your task (0–100 per cent)

c. your environment (0–100 per cent)

d. total percentage (remember the three above must add up to 100 per cent)

e. degree of distress (0–100 per cent)

Try to compare the same situation with a different percentage of attention on yourself. For example, compare talking to someone you know well:

a. being very self-focused (for example 80 per cent of attention on self or your felt impression) with

b. concentrating on what you are saying and really listening to your friend (for example, 80 per cent attention on the task).

How does your degree of distress compare in (a) and (b)?

What effect does your change in attention focus have on your friend? Does he or she find you warmer and friendlier?

The three must add up to 100 per cent, and the ratio is likely to vary in different contexts. When you are very self-focused, about 80 per cent of your attention might be on yourself, about 10 per cent on the task you are involved in, and 10 per cent on your environment. Someone *without* a body image problem might normally focus about 10 per cent on him- or herself, 80 per cent on the task, and 10 per cent on the environment. This is an important observation because it means you can train yourself to be more focused on tasks and the environment and less on yourself.

Adjusting your attention

We hope we have convinced you that it would be helpful to reduce your self-focused attention. When this is difficult, you can use specific exercises that have been proven to help people focus their attention better on the outside world. Think of these exercises as helping you to build the psychological muscle that places your attention on the world around you, rather than on yourself.

Task-concentration training

The first technique is called 'task-concentration training' (TCT), and it was devised by the psychologist Sandra Bogels in the Netherlands. This technique requires practice within progressively more challenging situations.

The technique is that every time you notice that your mind is self-focused (say, above 50 per cent) then you should immediately refocus your attention on to the task or the environment.

Practise being absorbed in a particular task (e.g. having a conversation) and, when you notice your attention is drawn towards yourself, deliberately refocus your attention away from yourself onto something else around you. Similarly, if you tend to focus all the time on how you feel, refocus attention outside yourself on some practical task in hand or on the environment around you. Every time you notice your mind's endless chatter and focus on how you feel, refocus your attention back on to the task or your environment. As a guide, try to aim for self-focused attention in most contexts to be reduced to 30 per cent or less.

If you are alone and have no specific task to do, you will need to refocus on your environment and make yourself more aware of:

- the various objects, colours, people, patterns and shapes that you can see around you (e.g. fabrics, decor, cars on the street, trees, litter)
- the sounds that you can hear (e.g. the hum of a heater, the sound off traffic, a clock ticking)
- what you can smell (e.g. scent of flowers, traffic fumes, fresh air, fabric softener)
- what you can taste (in the case of food or drink)
- the physical sensations you can feel from the environment (e.g. whether it is hot or cold, whether there is a breeze, the hardness of the ground beneath your feet)

This training is done in a graded manner for specific situations. For example, if you experience marked anxiety in social situations, you can practise the exercise starting with easier situations (e.g. listening to someone telling you about his or her holiday) and moving on to the most difficult situations (e.g. being at a party with strangers). This exercise is normally combined with the exercise in exposure and dropping safety behaviors from Chapter 7. You should also keep a record of each exercise on the self-focused attention chart from this chapter (see Chapter 7).

FIRST LISTENING EXERCISE

You and another person (e.g. a relative or friend or a therapist) sit with your backs against each other (so that there is no eye contact). Then other the person tells you a two-minute story (e.g. about his or her holiday). You must concentrate on the story (task) and summarize it afterwards. You should estimate the percentage of your attention that was directed towards your self, towards the task, and towards the environment. Then both of you should estimate the percentage of the story you were able to summarize. The exercise is repeated until the concentration directed towards the task is at least 51 per cent (more than half the total).

SECOND LISTENING EXERCISE

You and the other person now turn your chairs, so that you make eye contact. The other person tells you another two-minute story. As in the first listening exercise, you have to concentrate on the story and summarize it afterwards. You should then estimate the percentage of attention directed towards your self, the task, and the environment. Then both of you should estimate the percentage of the story you were able to summarize. Typically, you may become more self-focused because of the eye contact with another person, and, as a result, memorize less of the story than in the first exercise. Think about how this relates to everyday life. The exercise is repeated as before until the concentration directed towards the task is at least 51 per cent.

THIRD LISTENING EXERCISE

The other person tells you another two-minute story. Try to distract yourself while listening by looking at your appearance in a mirror (and then try to concentrate again on the story). As in the first listening exercise, estimate the percentage of attention directed towards your self, the task, and the environment. Then both of you should estimate the percentage of the story you were able to summarize. Typically, you may become more self-focused while thinking about your feature, and, as a result, have gaps in the summary of the story at the moments where you thought about the problem. Think about how this relates to problems in your everyday life. Repeat the exercise as before, until the percentage of concentration directed towards the task is at least 51 per cent.

FOURTH LISTENING EXERCISE

The other person tells you another two-minute story, which involves worries about being rated (e.g. meeting somebody who has a large nose, if this is the main feature that concerns you).

All four exercises need to be repeated until at least 51 per cent of your attention is focused on the task. The effect of the more complex elements in the later exercise means that most people will become more self-focused as a result, but are able to re-focus on the task after some practice.

SPEAKING EXERCISES

The speaking exercises are practised in the same way as the listening exercises. This time you tell a two-minute story to the other person, while concentrating on the task (speaking and observing whether the other person listens and understands what he or she is being told). The other person listens. The speaking exercises are repeated in the same way as in the second, third and fourth listening exercises (above) until your attention on the task is greater than 51 per cent.

NON-THREATENING SITUATIONS

Practise focusing your attention in non-threatening, everyday situations. An example is walking through a quiet park. You should pay attention to all aspects of the park (what you see, what you hear, what you smell) as well as to each one of your own bodily sensations while walking.

Another example is to listen to music, first to each instrument separately, then to all the instruments at the same time. Focus your attention first on one instrument, and then on all aspects of the music together.

THREATENING SITUATIONS

Draw up a list containing approximately ten social situations in which you are anxious. Arrange these situations in a hierarchy, with the first item being the least fear-inducing. This exercise can be combined with the exposure exercise in Chapter 7, and repeated until the attention you place on the task is greater than 50 per cent.

Your goal is to employ task concentration in each situation and quickly re-focus attention to the task after being distracted by fear of being rated. The exercises are built up hierarchically, since in very fear-inducing situations the feelings will absorb most of your attention. As a result, directing your attention to the task is more difficult. It takes practice to train your brain to stay focused on the world around you and away from thoughts and feelings related to your appearance.

Re-training your attention

The second technique is called 'attentional training' and it was devised by the psychologist Adrian Wells from Manchester University. It will help you reduce self-focused attention in the long term and increase your flexibility at switching attention.

This technique has been shown to be of some benefit in depression and some anxiety disorders for reducing self-focused attention in the long term. It is a form of mental training, like going to a psychological gym and getting your attention muscles in shape. It is also something you can practise at home, rather like practising a musical instrument at home in readiness for playing with an orchestra.

The following exercise should be practised when you are alone and not distracted. In other words, this is not a technique you should use to distract yourself when you feel upset or are brooding. In the long term the training can help you to interrupt the cycle of being self-focused so that you eventually become more naturally aware of your external environment. The technique may seem difficult at first but it is worth persevering and doing it in small steps.

MONITORING HOW SELF-FOCUSED YOU ARE

You can monitor how self-focused you are at any given moment on a scale of between −3 and +3, where −3 represents being entirely focused on your own thoughts and feelings or the impression you have of yourself, and +3 means being entirely externally focused on a task (e.g. listening to someone) or the environment (e.g. what you can see or hear). A zero would indicate that your attention is divided equally between being self-focused and externally focused. Being excessively self-focused is a rating of −2 or −3.

LABELLING SOUNDS

The exercise involves collecting together about nine sounds that you can hear simultaneously. Examples could be: the hum of a computer, the noise of a water filter in an aquarium, a tap dripping, a radio at a low volume, a hi-fi, a vacuum cleaner in a room outside and the noise of traffic. Label each sound – for example, sound number one, the hum of the computer. Try to ensure that one or two sounds do not drown out the others. Sit down in a comfortable chair, relax and focus your gaze on a spot on the wall. You should keep your eyes open throughout. You may experience distracting thoughts, feelings or images that just pop into your mind during the exercise. This doesn't matter – the aim is to practise focusing your attention in a particular way. Also, don't blank any thoughts out or try to suppress them while you are doing the exercise.

FIRST PHASE

The exercise consists of three phases. In the first phase, focus your attention on each of the sounds in the sequence in a sustained manner. Pay close attention to sound number one, for no other sound matters. Ignore all the other sounds around you. Now focus on the sound number two. Focus only on that sound, for again no other sound matters. If your attention begins to stray or is captured by any other sound, refocus all your attention on sound number two. Give all your attention to that sound. Focus on that sound and monitor it closely and filter out all the competing sounds, for they are not significant. Go through all the sounds in sequence until you have reached sound number nine.

SECOND PHASE

Now move on to the second phase. You have identified and focused on all the sounds. In this next stage we want you to rapidly shift attention from one sound to another in a random order. For example, you could pass from sound number six to number four to three to nine to one, and so on. As before, focus all your attention on one sound before switching your attention to a different sound.

THIRD PHASE

Then move on to the third phase. Expand all your attention, make it as broad and deep as possible and try to absorb all the sounds simultaneously. Mentally count all the sounds you can hear at the same time.

PRACTISING THE EXERCISE

The exercise needs to be practised twice a day (or a minimum of once a day) for 12–15 minutes. If possible, try to introduce new sounds on each occasion so you don't get used to them. We appreciate that this is difficult. Keep a record of your attention training on the form below. Like physical training, the exercise needs to be practised repeatedly or your attention muscles won't get bigger.

Motivation for being self-focused

If you are excessively self-focused, and you are having difficulty in switching your attention externally, it can be helpful to explore (a) the contexts in which you tend to be self-focused; (b) the pay-off you think you get from being self-focused; and (c) the motivation for being self-focused. For example, some people might use the picture of themselves as a portable 'internal mirror' that can be easily carried around with them. Thus, you might want to check your appearance internally so you can know exactly what you look like at all times (and especially when there is no external mirror available). After you have completed the exercises on the following pages it will be helpful to discuss what you have written with a trusted friend or therapist.

Brooding, self-attacking thoughts

We described earlier in this chapter how people often have thoughts or images about the way they look that just pop into their minds. Brooding is different and describes a reaction to an intrusive thought or image. It may also be described as 'ruminating'. This is a word derived from the term used for the way cows or sheep naturally bring up food from their stomachs and chew the cud over and over again. It describes perfectly the way a person thinks for long periods of time, going over something in their mind time and time again. Sometimes thinking can be productive and creative in terms of trying to solve a specific problem. However, it is not productive when it involves thinking excessively about past events or questions that cannot be resolved.

RECORD OF ATTENTION TRAINING

Rating scale

−3: entirely focused on your own thoughts and feelings or the impression you have of yourself

0: attention divided equally between being self-focused and externally focused

+3: entirely externally focused on a task (e.g. listening to someone) or the environment (e.g. what you can see or hear)

Date	How self-focused I have been generally today (−3 to +3)	How long the training lasted	Number of sounds I used	Any other comments

EXERCISE 6.4: THE A, B, C, D, E OF SELF-FOCUSED ATTENTION

A ctivating Event

Describe a recent typical situation in which you were excessively self-focused:

[Space left intentionally blank in the original book]

B ehavior

Describe what you were doing. For example, were you checking the picture in your mind to see how you looked?

[Space left intentionally blank in the original book]

Immediate *C* onsequences

Was there any pay-off from being self-focused? Did it give you a sense that you were taking action to prevent something bad from happening?

[Space left intentionally blank in the original book]

Unintended *C* onsequences

What effect did being self-focused have? Did it make you more distressed or preoccupied with your appearance?

[Space left intentionally blank in the original book]

What effect did being self-focused have on the people around you? Did you appear to be less friendly or warm?

[Space left intentionally blank in the original book]

Alternative *D* irections

Could you be more externally focused on an activity that is consistent with your goals and valued directions?

[Space left intentionally blank in the original book]

E ffect of Alternative Directions

What effect did following your alternative direction have?

[Space left intentionally blank in the original book]

Identifying a pattern

Can you see a pattern to the way you cope? What are the typical situations in which you are self-focused? Is there a pattern to these situations that you could change? Can you do anything to prevent such situations?

[Space left intentionally blank in the original book]

EXERCISE 6.5: QUESTIONING YOUR MOTIVATION FOR BEING SELF-FOCUSED

What is your motivation for being self-focused? Do you sometimes think that being self-focused could help you? Do you feel as if it might prepare you for being humiliated or something bad happening? Try to write down your motivation in the form of an assumption. (For example, 'If I am self-focused I can prevent others from humiliating me.')

[Space left intentionally blank in the original book]

The types of questions to ask yourself are:

• Does this assumption or rule about being self-focused help you in your goals and valued directions in life?

• Would you recommend to others checking in an internal mirror or being self-focused? If not, why not?

• Is it possible that the picture in your mind is different from how others might see you?

• What doubts do you have about being externally focused and concentrating on what you see, hear and smell?

• Can this assumption be made more flexible?

• Is the cost of being self-focused too high?

Now decide whether holding such assumptions about being self-focused is really helpful and whether you could try an alternative – being externally focused. Write down what you plan to focus on in your external environment.

There may also be a relentless stream of thoughts comparing yourself to others. These are self-critical, *self-attacking thoughts.* Your mind can be made up of different parts, which may be in conflict (e.g. one part may want to eat some chocolate and another part tells you that would be stupid when you want to lose weight). When you attack yourself, one part of your mind may tell you, for example, 'You are so ugly compared with him', or 'You deserve to look like an alien'. Such thoughts tend to make you fall into submission and you can end up feeling very small.

Other examples of self-attacking thoughts are:

You're disgusting	You're a failure	You're stupid
You're inferior	You're useless	You're worthless
You're inadequate	You're not good enough	You're bad
You're unlovable	You're worthless	You're defective
You're repulsive	You're nothing	You're a freak

People with body image problems tend to put themselves down about:

- their appearance
- having an emotional problem and not being able to 'pull themselves together'
- having done something that may have worsened their appearance
- the consequences of having a body image problem, such as not having a partner.

Here are some examples of what we mean:

- George, who was preoccupied with the idea that his eyes were too big, attacked himself for being 'a freak'.
- Harry viewed himself as a 'total idiot' because he believed that pushing certain areas of his face, initially in an attempt to improve his appearance, had made his looks worse.
- Sarah thought she must be unlovable because she didn't have a boyfriend, although it was really her BDD that meant she tended to stay at home and made it very difficult for her to meet men.

Brooding or self-attacking can lead to a number of unintended consequences, such as:

- feeling more distressed about your appearance
- feeling more depressed
- thinking more about bad events from the past
- believing thoughts in which you put yourself down
- being more pessimistic about the future
- being less able to generate effective solutions to problems and less confident in the ones you do generate
- becoming more withdrawn and doing less of what is important to you
- becoming more likely to be ignored and criticized by others.

When most people brood, it makes them feel worse and they are more likely to avoid getting involved in life. Any counselling that encourages you to search endlessly for reasons why you have a problem can also encourage you to brood.

By contrast, excessive worry is thinking about all the possible things that could go wrong in the future (also called 'catastrophizing) which will make you more anxious. Many people with body image problems therefore use a mixture of brooding and worrying, depending on their mood. When you are more depressed brooding tends to focus on the past, with 'Why?' types of question, for example: 'Why did I have that surgery?', or 'Why was I born this way?' There are variations on this theme, including fantasy thinking, which starts with 'If only', for example: 'If only I could look better'; 'If only I could win the lottery and get the surgery done'. By contrast, worries tend to start with 'What if' type of questions, for example, 'What if my make-up doesn't hide my spots today?'

Spot when, where and how often you brood

The first step is to monitor yourself to see in what times of day, places, and situations you brood and how often you do it. You can do this with a tally counter or a simple tick chart for whenever you ruminate (use the same chart below). This awareness will help you to change your behavior.

BROODING AND WORRYING SELF-MONITORING CHART

WEEK BEGINNING
Write in your most common brooding and worrying thoughts, and tick the relevant

column each time you have that thought, or add the total from your tally counter.

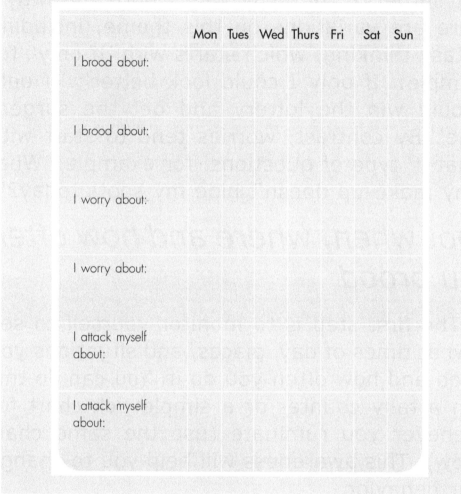

	Mon	Tues	Wed	Thurs	Fri	Sat	Sun
I brood about:							
I brood about:							
I worry about:							
I worry about:							
I attack myself about:							
I attack myself about:							

Understand your brooding, self-attacking thoughts

Now you have understood how difficult brooding is to stop and how powerful these thoughts can be when they are pulled by emotions. However, they can also be very harmful and we are now going to show you ways in which you can begin to escape the power of brooding.

The first step in understanding brooding, self-attacking thoughts and worries is to do a functional analysis on the process. Work out the unintended consequences of your brooding or worrying or self-attacking below.

Your goal will be to stop engaging in the content of your brooding or worries and not respond to the incessant demands. As soon as you have noticed yourself brooding or worrying, refocus attention outwardly on the real world. Choose to do something that you value and which is consistent with the goals that take you closer to long-term reduction in preoccupation with your appearance. Then monitor the effect of this change. This means having a realistic plan or timetable for the activities you are avoiding and what is important in your life rather than doing what you feel. Eventually you will be able to stand back and observe your thoughts, not buy into them and act in a valued direction in your life.

EXERCISE 6.6: THE A, B, C, D, E OF BROODING, WORRYING OR SELF-ATTACKING

Activating Event

Describe a recent typical situation in which you were brooding, worrying or attacking yourself. Did it start with an intrusive thought, image or memory? What were you doing at the time?

[Space left intentionally blank in the original book]

Behavior

What did you tell yourself? Was it a 'Why' or 'If only' question? Were you trying to find a reason? Can you label it as an example of brooding, worrying or self-attacking, or some combination of the above?

[Space left intentionally blank in the original book]

Immediate Consequences

Was there any pay-off from brooding or worrying? Did you avoid anything that was uncomfortable as a result of brooding or worrying?

[Space left intentionally blank in the original book]

Unintended Consequences

What effect did the brooding, worrying or self-attacking have on the way you felt?

[Space left intentionally blank in the original book]

What effect did it have on how self-focused you became on a scale between −3, which is totally focused on what you were thinking, to +3, which is totally focused on environment or tasks?

[Space left intentionally blank in the original book]

What effect did brooding, worrying or self-attacking have on the time you could devote to what is important in your life?

[Space left intentionally blank in the original book]

What effect did the brooding, worrying or self-attacking have on your environment or the people around you?

[Space left intentionally blank in the original book]

Did you do anything in excess as a consequence (e.g. drink more, use drugs, binge-eat, purge?)

[Space left intentionally blank in the original book]

Overall, how helpful was it to buy into your brooding, worrying or self-attacking?

[Space left intentionally blank in the original book]

Alternative *Directions*

What alternative direction could you find that are consistent with your goals and valued directions instead of brooding or worrying?

[Space left intentionally blank in the original book]

***E*ffect of Alternative Directions**

What effect did following your alternative direction have?

[Space left intentionally blank in the original book]

Is there a pattern to the situations that are typically linked to brooding, worrying or self-attacking that you could change? For example, can you do anything to prevent such situations?

[Space left intentionally blank in the original book]

Be sceptical about 'searching for reasons'

As we mentioned earlier, a common preoccupation in body image problems is to try to find reasons for why you look the way you do or what you should have done in the past. The problem is that this type of enquiry takes your mental focus straight back into your mind (trying to solve it as an appearance problem) again, whereas your aim should be to focus on the 'here-and-now' problems in the outside world – like being a good partner, a good parent, employee and member of the community.

Assumptions about ruminating and worrying

Sometimes people brood because they feel they have a good reason to do so. If you are struggling to stop brooding or worrying, it may be helpful to understand your motivations about brooding (or your *thoughts about your thoughts*). Here are some examples of the motivations that people with body image problems give:

- 'I can prepare myself for the worst.'
- 'I can figure out where I went wrong and I won't make the same mistake again.'
- 'If I don't it will let people who have hurt me off the hook.'
- 'It means I don't have to think about the bad things that are happening now.'

People can hold positive motivations about worrying (e.g. 'I must worry in order to think through all the things that could possibly go wrong') as well as recognizing the negative consequences, ('If I worry, then I will go crazy and I won't be able to think straight'). Not surprisingly, this brings on more anxiety and depression. Feeling anxious and de-pressed will pull you back into brooding and being self-focused. Learning to distance yourself and break free from your emotions is tough and requires a lot of practice.

What is your motivation for brooding or worrying?

Do you sometimes think that brooding or worrying could help you? Do you feel as if you need to prepare yourself for being humil-iated or something bad happening? Try to write down your assumptions about the bene-fits of brooding or worrying, e.g. 'If I brood, then I can prepare myself for the worst.'

1. _____
2. _____
3. _____

Now ask yourself:

• Does this assumption about brooding help me in my goals?

• Can this rule about brooding or worrying be made more flexible?

• Does my assumption help me to follow the directions in life that I want to follow?

• Is the cost of brooding or worrying too high?

• While I hold this assumption about my brooding or worrying, do I become more preoccupied and act in ways that are unhelpful?

• For how long am I going to carry on with my solution?

Now decide whether holding such assumptions about your brooding is really helpful. Then write down some alternatives you can try.

1. _____
2. _____
3. _____
4. _____

Assumptions about self-attacking thoughts

People who are critical of themselves (feeling, for example, that they are ugly, weak, or pathetic) might also have reasons for allowing themselves to be bullied by their minds. It is often helpful to ask yourself: What is my greatest fear if I give up criticizing and bullying myself? Criticism can also act as a warning ('If I don't tell you how fat you are and you don't lose weight, then nobody will love you'). Sometimes self-criticism can be triggered by a memory or be linked to your identity. Examples of assumptions behind self-criticism in depression are:

- If I don't put myself down, then I'll be arrogant.
- If I don't get in first with criticism, someone else will.
- I attack myself so I can improve myself.
- I attack myself so I get the humiliation I deserve.
- If I don't criticize myself, I'll get fat.

This sort of reasoning is probably an important factor in maintaining long-standing depression and low self-esteem. You might like to consider the costs and benefits of keeping up such a strategy.

BENEFITS OF SELF-ATTACKING THOUGHTS

What do you think is your motivation or the assumptions behind your self-attacking thoughts?

1. _____
2. _____
3. _____
4. _____

COSTS OF SELF-ATTACKING

• Does self-attacking make your preoccupation and mood worse?

• Does it help you achieve the goals you have set yourself?

• Does it help you stick to your valued directions in life?

• Is self-attacking something you would teach a friend or relative in a similar position? If not, why not?

Having identified what you believe to be the costs and benefits of self-attacking, you could talk these ideas through with a friend or health professional to see whether self-attacking helps or whether there is an alternative to your strategy. You might want to consider whether an alternative compassionate approach might help you to achieve the goals you want in life. Compassion is putting yourself in another person's shoes and being able to understand their emotional experience and be moved by it. It means being non-judgmental and sensitive to the distress and needs of your mind. Thus it is very understandable for your mind to want to try and protect you and prevent you, for example, from being arrogant or being rejected. However, there are other ways of achieving the same goal. It may be helpful to talk to someone about an alternative that does not lead you to feel more distressed and to miss out on life.

Trying to solve the wrong problem

Another activity that takes up a lot of mental time in body image problems is trying to solve the wrong problems. Problem-solving is a good skill to have if the problem is current and exists in the real world, but not if it doesn't. For example, if your car has broken down and you have to get to a job interview, you could brood on 'Why does this always happen to me?' (and just make yourself more frustrated and depressed). Alternatively, you could worry about 'What if I don't get the job?' (and make yourself more anxious). You can problem-solve only if you can turn brooding into a 'How?' question. For example, you could ask yourself: 'How am I going to get to the centre of town on time? I could ring for a taxi, but that will be a bit expensive. I could get a train, but I might now miss the one that would get me there in time. Getting this job is important, so I'll take a taxi.' The most important point is to solve only existing problems or ones that you can do something about. You can also practise for an event, though there aren't that many situations where this applies. For example, if you have an interview coming up, then you might ask a friend to do a role-play and practise being interviewed.

People with body image problems might spend a lot of time trying to solve the wrong problem in their heads. They will spend hours making mental plans about how a 'defect' can be fixed or camouflaged (e.g. 'If I can get my nose fixed, then I can do things I want to do in life' or 'If I can get the right skin product, then it may fix my skin'). Mental planning might appear to instil hope but it usually leads to an endless search for solutions that never help (or make it worse) or do not reduce the preoccupation or distress. If you try to solve it as an appearance problem, rather than an emotional problem, then it will increase your preoccupation and distress about your appearance. If you treat it as an emotional problem, it has a completely different solution. Instead you start to focus on what you are avoiding in life and what you want your life to stand for. You can then begin to test out alternatives to see whether the bad things you are predicting actually happen, or whether there are better ways of coping with the bad things that might happen (for example if you are rejected).

EXERCISE 6.7: THE A, B, C, D, E OF MENTAL PLANNING AND TRYING TO SOLVE THE WRONG PROBLEM

Activating Event

Describe a recent typical situation in which you were mentally planning or investigating a solution for what you believed to be an appearance problem.

[Space left intentionally blank in the original book]

Behavior

What mental plans were you making or what did you do?

[Space left intentionally blank in the original book]

Immediate *Consequences*

Was there any pay-off from mental planning and investigating? Did it give you a sense of hope that you were doing something to solve your 'defect'? Did you avoid anything in life that you find difficult?

[Space left intentionally blank in the original book]

Unintended *Consequences*

What effect did the mental planning have? Did it eventually make you more frustrated or angry?

[Space left intentionally blank in the original book]

What effect did your mental planning have on how self-focused you became on a scale between −3, which is totally focused on what you were thinking, to +3, which is totally focused on your environment or tasks?

[Space left intentionally blank in the original book]

What effect did the mental planning have on the time you could devote to your valued directions and what is important in your life?

[Space left intentionally blank in the original book]

What effect did your mental planning have on the people around you?

[Space left intentionally blank in the original book]

Did you do anything in excess as a consequence (e.g. drink more, use drugs, binge-eat, purge)?

[Space left intentionally blank in the original book]

Overall, how helpful is it to do your mental planning?

[Space left intentionally blank in the original book]

Alternative *Directions*

What alternative direction could you find that is consistent with your goals and valued directions instead of mental planning?

[Space left intentionally blank in the original book]

*E*ffect of Alternative Directions

What effect did following your alternative direction have?

[Space left intentionally blank in the original book]

Is there a pattern to the situations that are typically linked to mental planning, worrying or self-attacking that you could change? For example, can you do anything to prevent such situations from occurring? Can you plan the day using an activity schedule that follows your valued directions? What can you do to stop yourself from being alone at certain times?

[Space left intentionally blank in the original book]

Comparing

Another repetitive thinking pattern in body image problems is to compare your feature with someone else's and then judge yourself against that feature. Comparing is fairly common in people without body image problems (especially in women) but it occurs more frequently in people with body image problems. People typically compare the feature they don't like with the same feature in someone else of the same age and sex. They may compare themselves with air-brushed models in the media or people they meet in everyday life. There is nearly always an upward comparison with people who have the same feature that is considered more attractive. Alternatively, you may compare your feature with the way the same feature looked in the past.

Spot when, where and how often you compare

COMPARING SELF-MONITORING CHART

WEEK BEGINNING _____

Write in your most common comparing thoughts and tick the relevant column each time you have that thought, or add the total from your tally counter.

	Mon	Tues	Wed	Thurs	Fri	Sat	Sun
I compared my:							
I compared my:							
I compared my:							

The first step is to monitor yourself to see in what contexts (times of day, activities and situations) you compare and how often you do it. Being more aware of when you are comparing will help you change your behavior. Self-monitoring, using a tally counter, can increase your awareness of your comparing tendency, as it may be occurring many hundreds of times a day.

Identify the motivation for comparing

The motivation for comparing is usually to know where you stand in relation to someone else as a form of threat monitoring (e.g. 'I have to know where I stand in case I am humiliated'). This usually leads to safety-seeking behaviors such as keeping your head down and trying to camouflage your 'defect'. This makes sense if you are an animal – for example, a puppy will roll over in front of a larger dog and be submissive. This strategy is highly effective at avoiding a conflict and preventing the puppy being harmed. However, when *you* 'roll over' this is another example of treating the body image issue as an appearance problem and has a number of unintended consequences.

Try to understand the function of your comparing using the table below. Instead of comparing, we would encourage to you broaden your attention to all the sights, sounds and smell and textures around you or focus on the whole of a person's appearance rather than just a part – and to fully listen to what another person is saying.

EXERCISE 6.8: THE A, B, C, D, E OF COMPARING

Activating Event
Describe a recent typical situation in which you compared your feature? What were you doing at the time?

[Space left intentionally blank in the original book]

Behavior
Who or what did you compare yourself with?

[Space left intentionally blank in the original book]

Immediate Consequences
Was there any pay-off from comparing? Did you think it prevented something bad from happening?

[Space left intentionally blank in the original book]

Unintended Consequences

What effect did the comparing have on the way you felt?

[Space left intentionally blank in the original book]

What effect did it have on how self-focused you became on a scale between −3, which is totally focused on what you were thinking, to +3, which is totally focused on environment or tasks?

[Space left intentionally blank in the original book]

What effect did the comparing have on your valued directions and the time you can devote to what is important in your life?

[Space left intentionally blank in the original book]

What effect did the comparing have on the people around you?

[Space left intentionally blank in the original book]

Did you do anything in excess as a consequence (e.g. drink more, use drugs, binge-eat, purge)?

[Space left intentionally blank in the original book]

Overall, how helpful was it to compare?

[Space left intentionally blank in the original book]

Alternative *Directions*

What alternative direction could you find that is consistent with your goals and valued directions? What could you do instead of comparing?

[Space left intentionally blank in the original book]

*E*ffect of Alternative Directions

What effect did following your alternative direction have?

[Space left intentionally blank in the original book]

Is there a pattern to the situations that are typically linked to comparing that you could change? For example, can you do anything to prevent such situations occurring? Do you need to buy that celebrity magazine? Can you put old photographs back in the album, etc?

[Space left intentionally blank in the original book]

7

Taking action

This chapter will help you do things in life that are important to you. It will also enable you to enter situations that you have been avoiding because of your anxiety that something bad might happen. This might include public and social situations that you have been anxious about. Some people may be completely housebound. Others may avoid going to family or social gatherings; going to school or university; going to work; going to a doctor to be examined; dating or being intimate; being outdoors or being in bright lighting; having a haircut; shopping for clothes; using a public changing room or going swimming. Sometimes avoidance can include trying to suppress distressing pictures in your mind. Other people might avoid looking at a bodily feature in mirrors (as this might trigger unpleasant thoughts or memories) or because it takes too long to finish a ritual such as checking in the mirror.

We strongly recommend that you work through Chapter 4 (What keeps a body image problem going?) and Chapter 5 (Setting yourself on the right course) before working through this chapter. The earlier chapters will help you to identify the behaviors that are maintaining your anxiety, shame and preoccupation. You can then use those behaviors as targets for change, applying the principles outlined in this chapter.

Behavioral experiments and graded exposure

Behavioral experiments involve making predictions to see whether something is true or not. For instance, you might be predicting that, if you enter a social situation and look into people's eyes and smile, then they will humiliate and tease you.

Such experiments can be incorporated into the principle of graded exposure. With a body image problem, 'exposure' means facing the situations and activities you fear and have been avoiding. This is best done gradually and step by step ('graded').

Exposure also needs to be done without using any safety-seeking behaviors. In body image problems these include many different ways of escaping and trying to cope – for example, keeping your head down, using excessive make-up, wearing bulky clothes, keeping your hand up to your face, checking in a mirror or brooding in your head. However, safety behaviors can have a number of unintended consequences. They may prevent you from finding out that what you are predicting is not true. They also tend to make you more self-conscious, more preoccupied with your appearance and more distressed, as you also have to monitor whether your safety behavior is working. Lastly, they may make you appear cold and unfriendly in social situations.

Sometimes people fear that too much anxiety can be harmful. It's true that exposure is best done in a graded manner, with a series of steps (called a 'hierarchy'), so that you face your less intimidating fears first and confront the most difficult last. But grading your exposure is just a means to an end, and the sooner you can reach the top of your exposure hierarchy the better. Remember that anxiety, though uncomfortable, will not damage you. In dealing with a body image problem, you have to turn your thinking 'upside down': the more you try to avoid anxiety in the short term, the more of it you're likely to get in the long term.

With any exposure program, it really is important to stick with the session until your anxiety has reduced, otherwise you may end up reinforcing the idea that anxiety is harmful. On average, exposure might take up to an hour, but sometimes it doesn't take that long. If the anxiety is persisting for longer than this, then you may be performing a subtle safety behavior or not fully engaging in the exposure. Think really carefully about whether you are doing anything to temporarily reduce or control your fear within the situation. If you think that something you are doing might just be a way of staving off your fear, try your exposure without it. If you still find that your anxiety does not subside even when you've 'stuck with it' for at least a couple of hours then it might be best to seek professional help to make progress.

When you experience fear *without* a safety behavior, the anxiety gradually fades and the urge to use your safety behavior will also fade. When you repeat the exposure (preferably as soon after the first exposure as possible), the anxiety will decrease further, and so on each time you do the exposure. Exposure is best done in a way that allows you to test out your predictions – for example, you might want to test a prediction that your anxiety will go on for ever and ever. This is called a behavioral experiment to see whether your predictions come true, and we will discuss this in more detail in section entitled "More on behavioral experiments".

One way of remembering what exposure and response prevention means is the 'FEAR' acronym:

Face
Everything
And
Recover.

The ten golden rules for exposure and behavioral experiments

1. WRITE DOWN A HIERARCHY OF FEARS

A 'hierarchy' is a ranked list of your triggers – the things you tend to fear or avoid because they activate your worries. These may be activities, situations, people, words or ideas – the range will depend on your particular worry. A checklist of situations or activities that you might be avoiding can be found in Chapter 5. You can use this list as a basis for developing a hierarchy. We have included a table for you to complete, see EXERCISE 7.1: HIERARCHY OF EXPOSURE TO FEARED TRIGGERS.

The nature of an exposure task will depend upon your problem and whether you are someone who is avoiding lots of situations or activities (where it's easier to come up with suitable exposure) or if you are a person who has lots of safety-seeking behaviors (such as checking) where you may need to be a little more creative. We discuss this below. Always plan your exposure in a series of steps, within a particular timeframe, that lead up to your final goals. You then attempt to carry out the steps in sequence, like a set of instructions.

You can measure the amount of distress caused by each trigger using a rating scale of 'SUDs'. SUDs stands for Standard Units of Distress, in which 0 is no distress at all and 100 is overwhelming distress. In the second column of the table, you can give each trigger a rating according to how much distress you would expect to feel if you experienced that trigger and didn't perform a safety-seeking behavior. For example, you may rate being intimate as causing 90 SUDs out of 100. Another individual might rate going swimming as 99 SUDs out of 100, and so on.

Here is a sample hierarchy table.

CHRISTINA'S HIERARCHY OF EXPOSURE TO FEARED TRIGGERS

Trigger (object, place, person, situation):	Estimated distress (0–100)
Going out to the local pub without any make-up on	100
Allowing my friends to see me at home without make-up	80
Allowing my parents to see me at home without make-up	80
Going out to the local pub with only foundation	80
Allowing my friends to see me at home with only foundation	80
Going for a whole day without re-touching my make-up	80

Trigger (object, place, person, situation):	Estimated distress (0–100)
Leaving the house without my make-up	80
Walking to the local shop without mascara	80
Wearing an eye-catching top to the shopping centre	70
Standing six feet away from the mirror without checking	70

Try to group the activities you fear under different themes (e.g. intimacy, social situations). Then, within the themes, try to put them in order of how much distress you would feel if you experienced each trigger.

218

EXERCISE 7.1: HIERARCHY OF EXPOSURE TO FEARED TRIGGERS	
Trigger (object, place, person, situation):	Estimated distress (0–100)

2. FACE YOUR FEAR – 'JUST DO IT'

Decide which targets you will take from your hierarchy and deliberately face your fear. Choose targets that are challenging but not overwhelming. Some of the situations will need to be broken down into smaller steps – thus for someone who is housebound, the first step may be to open the curtains or go into the garden. However, don't spend too much time on the easier targets, if they are not sufficiently challenging. You may need to ask a friend to come up with suitable tasks that are more anxiety-provoking. Always ensure that your exposure is challenging and potent enough. Don't spend time on targets that are mild and only increase anxiety slightly.

3. MAKE PREDICTIONS THAT CAN BE TESTED

One of your predictions might be how severe the distress is going to be, or how long it might go on for at the end of exposure. Or it may be helpful to test whether the result of the exposure bests fits 'Theory A' or 'Theory B' (see Chapter 4). Theory A (the one that you are following) is that you have an appearance problem, which will lead to you being alone and rejected. Theory B is that you have a problem with being preoccupied and worried by your appearance. This predicts that by following Theory A you are increasing your preoccupation and distress about your appearance. When you act as if Theory B is right, then your preoccupation and distress about your appearance will decrease. Other predictions for exposure tasks might include that you will be humiliated or that people will recoil in horror, and these are all testable.

Always ensure that the predictions you make are based on objective information – for example, what you think someone will say or how they will behave towards you. Thus it won't be helpful if your prediction is that people will think that you are ugly, as you can't read their minds. It is more helpful to observe people's behavior and go by what they say and do. In this situation, you need to be especially careful not to use any safety-seeking behaviors. For example if you keep your head down, give poor eye contact and say very little, then you are less likely to be aware of how people are acting towards you, and they are more likely to assume that you are not interested in them and to avoid you. You may, in turn, interpret this as evidence that you are ugly. You should therefore try to practise giving appropriate eye contact and smiling. Make a conscious effort to stand upright and look straight ahead. If you smile, strangers are more likely to respond positively. When you have your head down, hurrying past, then you are more likely to be self-focused and get information about your surroundings from what your mind is telling you.

You should also maintain good eye contact. This signals that you have an interest in others and that you are listening, and tells you whose turn it is to speak in a conversation. Trying to avoid the gaze of others will always be viewed negatively. You are signalling that you do not want to engage in any kind of contact with the other person.

Try to engage in conversation whenever you can. It is harder to do so if you are focused on how you look and how people are responding to you, rather than listening and being involved in what people are saying. Anxiety tends to heighten the temptation to 'self-monitor' so it is harder to focus on what is going on around you. Asking people about themselves, what they do for a living, whether their children go to the local school and similar questions are all ways of initiating a conversation. Similarly, topical subjects are things that other people will have a view about. The result of the latest big football match, the latest soap, the price of petrol, or news headlines are all good subjects to start conversations about.

If you are doing exposure in front of a mirror that you have previously avoided, then do not make predictions about how ugly or unattractive you think you are. Rating yourself as 'ugly' or 'unattractive' is an evaluation that others may or not agree with. We know that such ratings are usually based on 'ghosts from the past' and that various emotions will bias your rating. Stick to objective information, like the colour of your eyes and your height and weight. We will discuss this further in the section on mirrors (see section entitled "Checking and mirrors").

Keep a record of your predictions and whether they occurred or not on your record sheet (see below).

4. MAKE EXPOSURE LONG ENOUGH

Face your fear long enough for your anxiety to subside of its own accord, ideally by at least half. For example, when you enter a swimming pool, don't rush into the water so that your body is under the water immediately. Sit beside the pool for a while or stroll up and down the side and smile at others before getting in to the water. Distress will decrease only when you give it a long enough time and learn that bad things won't happen when you face your fears.

5. MAKE EXPOSURE FREQUENT ENOUGH

Repeat the exposure as often as possible – several times a day – until the anxiety has subsided between the sessions. Remember, you can never do too much exposure. Always think about how you can incorporate exposure into your everyday life so that it makes it easier to carry it out on a daily basis.

6. MAKE EXPOSURE CONTINUOUS

Ensure exposure is done with a constant stimulus, rather than escaping or using a safety behavior and then returning to the situation.

7. DO NOT USE ANXIETY-REDUCING STRATEGIES

Do the exposure without using distraction, drugs, alcohol or a safety-seeking behavior such as saying a phrase to yourself or obtaining reassurance. It's important to 'fully engage' with the situation, allow the intrusive thoughts and images to enter your mind, and for your anxiety to increase and fall naturally. Re-read the section on attention and task-concentration training in Chapter 6 and make sure that when you do exposure you are focused on the world around you and fully aware of what you can see, hear and smell.

If you are not sure whether what you are doing is a safety-seeking behavior, ask yourself what the aim is before you carry it out. If the aim is to reduce what you think is potentially harmful to you, or the degree to which you would be able to control the harm, then it is a safety-seeking behavior.

8. IF YOU DO A SAFETY-SEEKING BEHAVIOR, THEN RE-EXPOSE YOURSELF

If you can't resist doing a safety behavior, you must redo the exposure so that you always finish with exposure. For example, if you put your hand up to your face to hide your skin and keep your head down to avoid any eye contact, then you need to re-expose yourself. This means taking your hand down and smiling at the person.

9. DON'T BUY INTO YOUR INTRUSIVE THOUGHTS

Just 'notice' or 'be aware' of any unpleasant images or thoughts that are self-attacking, judging or blaming that might occur during the exposure. This is especially important if your exposure is reactivating an old memory, which has been traumatic for you. The goal is just to accept the intrusive thoughts and feelings. Distance yourself from them and do not buy into their content. Wait for the anxiety to fade by itself. The issue here is acceptance and not trying to control from or escape from the anxiety. We will discuss this in more detail shortly.

10. MONITOR YOUR EXPOSURE TASKS AND PREDICTIONS ON A FORM

Always monitor your exposure so you can learn from it and see your progress. Re-rate your distress at the end of exposure and see whether you over-estimated the degree of distress that would occur or how long it would last for.

This is also essential when you are seeing a therapist so that he or she can monitor whether you are doing the exposure that you negotiated with your therapist in the previous session.

226

1. Task that I planned (e.g. when, where, how, and with whom. Include a description of how I will act without safety behaviors)	2. How distressing I am predicting task will be at the peak (0–100%)	3. How long I am predicting that the distress will take to halve (minutes or hours)	4. What I am predicting will happen (e.g. how others will behave towards me) or whether the result will best fit a particular theory and how strongly I believe it (0–100%)	5. What I actually did during the task (including using any safety behaviors and degree of self-focused attention)	6. How distressing the task was at the peak (0–100%)	7. How long it actually took for the distress to halve (minutes or hours)	8. What actually happened? Does this differ from what I predicted in column 4? Do the results best fit my theory that I have a problem with my appearance or the alternative – that the problem is being excessively preoccupied by my appearance?

Obstacles

A common obstacle is the belief that I can only stop avoiding situations or drop my safety behaviors 'when I feel comfortable or "right"'; or when 'I know for certain that the consequences I fear will not happen'; or when 'I feel confident enough to test out my fears'. This applies to a wide range of avoidance and safety behaviors. There may be a high-level emotional intolerance and a struggle to stop controlling events. Progress will occur if you are willing to accept and embrace uncomfortable thoughts and feelings and willing to take a 'leap of faith'. This means doing tasks uncomfortably, with some uncertainty and lack of confidence in the short term, in order to obtain the long-term gains. Some people may have a good intellectual understanding of the problem but not be ready to change their behavior in order to test out their predictions. In such situations, you may have to think about taking smaller steps and get professional help. Whatever happens, you need to really commit yourself to testing out an alternative, otherwise your suffering is likely to persist.

The problem with 'normal' – treatment first, normal later

You might be concerned at some of the suggestions that a therapist or we might make for exposure at the top of your hierarchy but they are a means towards an end. As soon as you have overcome your body image problem, you can bin them. People sometimes complain that what they are being encouraged to do during exposure is 'abnormal' and therefore unreasonable. Thus, someone who is preoccupied with their spots or the redness of their skin may be encouraged to exaggerate their redness or spots by the use of make-up. Another person who has been encouraged to refrain from washing their hair or applying make-up for two weeks might say something like 'Even someone without a body image problem wouldn't do that!' as if the therapist is being entirely unreasonable. (We're not saying therapists are never unreasonable; it's just that this is more likely to be a problem of misunderstanding!) However, for someone with a body image problem who believes that others would reject her and she would be alone all her life, then it is a powerful way of testing this out.

Thus, the ultimate tasks will not only involve the dropping of safety behaviors but also the highlighting or exaggerating of the 'defect'.

If you think about it, many treatments for human ailments involve doing the unusual. Consider how 'abnormal' it is to swallow toxic chemicals every day; but chemotherapy treatment for cancer involves exactly that. Likewise, it's not exactly normal to wrap a leg in plaster, but if you have a broken leg, it's very helpful! We accept these 'abnormal' activities as part of 'normal' treatment for physical problems. Part of the problem when tackling a psychological problem is that, because of the stigma and shame surrounding psychological and emotional problems, the normal processes of overcoming fears are not so readily discussed and understood.

Would you expect a medication to be effective if you took less than the recommended dose and took it less often than prescribed?

More on behavioral experiments

We have discussed how you can make predictions to see whether something is true or not – this is called a behavioral experiment. If you are not sure whether something you do helps or not, compare the effect of increasing and decreasing the behavior (e.g. checking in a mirror more often than usual compared to not checking at all) for a sufficient period of time to see whether you become more or less preoccupied.

Here is another example of a behavioral experiment. Katja was preoccupied with lines on her skin over her arms. She used a thick moisturizer daily to reduce 'wrinkles'. She was very reluctant to give up using it but agreed to compare the effect of (a) using the moisturizer on one arm; and (b) using no moisturizer on the other arm.

I will use moisturizer as usual only on my left arm. I will not use it on my right arm. I will not make a special effort to conceal my arms.

It will be very distressing (100%) to see my right arm developing wrinkles.

My distress over my wrinkles is likely to increase over several days.

I predict others will notice my wrinkles and say something.

I did leave the cream off my right arm as planned.

My distress was about 70%.

The distress decreased over several days and I began to think less about it.

Others were unable to predict which arm had been moisturized either by looking at it or feeling it with their fingers. The results best fit the theory that I have a problem with being excessively preoccupied with my skin and that it is my solutions that maintain this preoccupation.

Checking and mirrors

For people with body image problems, mirrors (and other reflective surfaces) can present a real problem. Mirrors or reflective surfaces are commonly used as a safety behavior to check on appearance. If this is a problem for you then the first step is to see how often you are checking in a mirror. You can do this using a record sheet like the one overleaf. Some people check in a mirror 30, 50 or hundreds of times a day. If this is the case with you, it's best to use a tally counter and to carry over the total to the chart. This method will tell you exactly how often you are checking and will give you a baseline so that you can tell in future whether or not your checking is decreasing over time.

Keeping a record will also make you more aware of when you are checking so that you can resist it in future. There are of course many different ways of checking. These might include long checks in front of a mirror, doing something like styling or cutting your hair, plucking eyebrows, picking spots, applying make-up and trying to do mental cosmetic surgery. Or it may take the form of brief glances in shop windows or the backs of CDs. Alternatively, you may be doing internal checking of the picture in your mind or your memory of how you last looked. If your feature (e.g. your thighs) can be examined directly, you might not need a mirror to check. Add a tick or a click on your tally counter whenever you do any of these checking activities.

EXERCISE 7.3: FREQUENCY OF CHECKING

Date _____

	Mon	Tues	Wed	Thurs	Fri	Sat	Sun
I check in a mirror for a long period (e.g. applying make-up, grooming, etc.)							
I check briefly in a mirror or reflective surface (e.g. a window)							
I check by looking at a feature directly, without needing a mirror							
I check the 'picture in my mind' or memory of how I last looked							
I check by feeling my skin with my fingers							
I check my feature using a camera or photobooth							
I check by feeling the elasticity or amount of fat by pinching my skin							
I check by measuring my feature							
I try to convince others of how unattractive my feature is							
I ask others to confirm the existence of my defect							
I seek reassurance about whether my feature has got worse							
I seek reassurance about whether my feature is camouflaged (e.g. by make-up)							

The next step is to try to understand more about your motivation for checking and the pay-off you obtain in the short term as well as the unintended consequences in the long term.

EXERCISE 7.4: THE A, B, C, D, E OF UNDERSTANDING YOUR CHECKING

Activating Event

Describe a recent typical situation in which you were checking the feature (e.g. looking in the mirror or a reflective surface or pinching your skin). Did you experience a picture in your mind or memory before the checking started?

[Space left intentionally blank in the original book]

Behavior

What did you actually do? What was your mind telling you as you checked? How long did it last?

[Space left intentionally blank in the original book]

Immediate Consequences

Was there any pay-off from checking? For example, did you avoid anything that was uncomfortable? Did you briefly feel more certain about how you do look? Did you feel you were doing something to improve your appearance?

[Space left intentionally blank in the original book]

Unintended Consequences

What effect did the checking have on the way you felt?

[Space left intentionally blank in the original book]

What effect did the checking have on how you acted? What effect did it have on the time you were able to devote to what is important in your life?

[Space left intentionally blank in the original book]

What effect does checking have on the people around you?

[Space left intentionally blank in the original book]

Did you do anything in excess as a consequence of checking (e.g. drink more, use drugs, binge-eat, purge?)

[Space left intentionally blank in the original book]

Overall, how helpful was it to give into your urge to check?

[Space left intentionally blank in the original book]

Alternative *Directions*

What alternatives could you find that are consistent with your goals and valued directions instead of checking?

[Space left intentionally blank in the original book]

Effect of Alternative Directions

What effect did following your alternative direction have?

[Space left intentionally blank in the original book]

Is there a pattern to the situations that are typically linked to checking? For example, can you do anything do to prevent such situations arising?

[Space left intentionally blank in the original book]

Reasons for checking

Examples of the reasons that people with body image problems give for checking are:

- I hope that I don't look as bad as I think I look

How long does the hope last for? What happens after that?

- I have to know what I look like before I do anything.

Might there a better way of knowing how you feel?

- I have to know for certain how I appear in public.

For how long do you feel certain that you know what you look like? Then what happens?

- I believe that if I stare long enough, I might see a different image.

Does staring make you more objective?

- If I resist looking in the mirror then I will feel worse.

Does this really fit in with your experience?

- I need to see what I don't like about myself.

Does this teach you anything new?

- If I don't look then I might forget how ugly I am.

What is the cost of having this on your mind? Will you really forget?

Some of these assumptions can be tested in an experiment, using two different time-frames. Compare checking once a day with checking 20 times a day and ask yourself whether increasing the checking leads you to be more or less certain about how you look. You should also ask yourself whether increasing the checking makes you more preoccupied and distressed.

Goals for mirror use

We hope you agree that mirror checking is unhelpful and needs to be used only for functional reasons. We would encourage you to work towards the following goals:

(a). To use mirrors at a slight distance or ones that are large enough to incorporate most of your body.

(b). To deliberately focus your attention on your reflection in a mirror, rather than on an internal impression of how you feel.

(c). To only use a mirror for an agreed function (e.g. shaving, putting on make-up) for a limited period of time.

(d). To use a variety of different mirrors and lights, rather than sticking to one which you 'trust'.

(e). To scan your body and focus your attention on the whole of your face or body, rather than on a specific 'defect' or detail. (People without body image problems tend to focus their attention on features that are considered to be more attractive. This is an alternative strategy.)

(f). To avoid making any judgements about your appearance. Just be aware of any intrusive thoughts and images about being ugly without buying into them. Take the position of an observer of passing traffic, rather than trying to control the traffic and believing that what enters your mind must be true.

(g). Not to use mirrors that magnify your reflection.

(h). Not to carry small hand mirrors around with you to make checking 'easier'.

(i). Not to use ambiguous reflections (e.g. windows, the backs of CDs or cutlery or mirrors that are dusty or cracked).

(j). Not to use a mirror when you have the urge to check but to try and delay the response and do other activities until the urge has diminished.

(k). Not to 'swing' from excessive mirror checking to avoiding mirrors all together. It's important to learn to resist the urge to check or scrutinize whilst in the presence of your own reflection.

For some people, it is more important to monitor how long the mirror gazing lasts. For example, a single use of the mirror can sometimes last several hours. Here, the criteria used to finish a check may be problematic. Thus, someone may finish mirror gazing when they feel 'comfortable' or 'just right'. Deciding whether you are going to stop checking or applying make-up based on how you 'feel' will inevitably cause problems. When finishing a ritual, do not go by how you 'feel'. Instead, refocus your attention and concentrate on the environment around you and what you see. This means finishing using the mirror when you still feel anxious, acting against the way you feel. This goes against the grain when you believe you have to be guided by your feelings or 'sixth sense'. The problem is that you are receiving a false signal of danger and you have now got used to it. The goal is to finish using a mirror or grooming or combing your hair when you can *see* that it looks 'good enough'. As an experiment, you might want to alternate between using a 'just right' feeling and 'just doing it' without using internal criteria.

If you can reduce the amount of make-up or grooming, then this will reduce significantly the amount of time you spend in front of a mirror. It is also worth remembering that when women reduce excessive camouflage on their faces, they may well receive comments from others that they look different. This is not the same as being 'ugly'!

Mirror avoidance

Some people may avoid 'unsafe' mirrors. Avoiding mirrors altogether is an unrealistic goal and will cause problems in the long term.

Mirror feedback is sometimes necessary in people who are avoiding all or certain mirrors. It can be done as graded exposure with varying degrees of light or the amount of body exposed. If the problem is with the whole body then a swimming costume can be worn if someone else is present. When you look in the mirror, it is important to describe your appearance objectively, e.g. the colour of your eyes, your complexion, height, build, etc. Observe and describe but do not 'rate' or value these features. Scan the whole of your body and do not focus attention on a specific 'defect' or go into any detail. Look at the person in the mirror as if they were a stranger.

Photographs

Like mirrors, photographs can present a real difficulty for people with body image problems. Many people will avoid having their photograph taken, or tear photographs up. Alternatively, they might repeatedly have their photograph taken in a photo booth to 'check' whether their appearance has changed. Photographs can also fuel the brooding tendency, when you look at a photograph taken at a time when you thought you looked acceptable and repeatedly go over the thought 'if only I looked like that now'. As with mirrors, try to integrate photographs as part of your normal everyday life and allow your mind to become used to them again. This may form part of the 'exposure' program described above. Alternatively, if you are using photos to check your appearance, then monitor how often you are checking, using the Exercise 7.3 form above, and carry out the same analysis as you did for mirror checking.

Photo or video feedback

Photo or video feedback can sometimes be helpful if you can make a specific prediction beforehand of how you look and you are not using a camera for frequent checking. For example, the degree of redness can be calibrated against a colour chart showing varying degrees of redness. Other predictions can be made by drawing what you imagine, and it may be possible to superimpose an outline of a drawing onto an actual photo of the feature using photo editor software. Thus, a person who feels he has a disproportionately large forehead or chin, which he has drawn in profile, may have it superimposed onto a photo of his actual face to examine the difference between the two.

In general, these approaches probably need the guidance of a therapist. For example, they may not be helpful for people with a disfigurement. Good-quality lighting and equipment is also important to avoid adding unhelpful shadows or distortions.

When watching a video or looking at a photo, make sure that you are not self-focused but look at it as if you are watching a stranger. Only make observations on what you see (not what you feel and not making a rating of how ugly you look). Remember that a video camera may also have the effect of making you look heavier.

Now ask yourself:

• Were the things that you were afraid of as noticeable as you felt they would be?

• What does the photo/video tell you about using the picture in your mind to judge how you come across?

8

Building a new attitude towards yourself

This chapter is aimed at helping you to develop a new perspective on yourself. First, we'll introduce an approach to combating low self-esteem called self-acceptance. Second, we'll encourage you to look at your past, and to re-consider events that may have contributed to your negative self-image.

Accepting yourself

As we've already seen, many body image problems stem from a tendency to over-identify appearance with your 'self'. That is, to measure, rate and value yourself according to appearance or physical attractiveness alone. In simplistic terms this can be presented as the following formula:

> GOOD LOOKS = WORTH AS A PERSON
> LESS GOOD LOOKS = LESS WORTH AS A PERSON

The danger is that such a philosophy has great potential to make a person feel unhappy if they either a) are visibly different from others in their appearance; or b) have a thought or image in their mind that their appearance is very different from and not as good as other people's. It can also lead a person to become excessively critical of their appearance, leading them to scrutinize their appearance for any possible flaws.

Condemning yourself, overall, as repulsive, and unlovable is a form of over-generalizing called 'labelling'(see Chapter 6 for more on this) or 'self-attacking'. It is this particular thinking error that people are usually referring to when they talk about 'low self-esteem'. Labelling yourself will make you feel worse and is very likely to lead to counter-productive action such as avoidance, rituals or other safety behaviors.

You have worth because you are human

Would you teach a child to value themselves according to the way they look, their popularity or their success? Or would you want them to develop an unconditional sense of self-worth? Yes, our society seems to hold beauty in high esteem (and people with body image problems tend to over-focus on this), but do you really agree with this value? Do you choose your friends solely on the basis of what they look like? Self-acceptance is part of being warm and decent to yourself and will put you in the best possible frame of mind to engage fully with life.

Accepting yourself has two important implications for overcoming body shame and body dysmorphic disorder. First, it means you are equal in worth to other human beings just as you are, and this will help to improve your self-esteem and reduce shame. Second, it means that, because you're not distracted by attacking yourself, you'll be better able to concentrate on facing your fears, reducing your safety behaviors, and re-focusing on the world around you and what will make life more rewarding.

You are too complex to measure or rate globally

Self-acceptance involves the following assertions:

1. As a human being, you are a unique, multi-faceted individual.

2. As a human being, you are ever-changing and developing.

3. You may, to some degree, be able to measure specific aspects of yourself (e.g. how tall you are), but other things are harder to place a value on (e.g. how kind you are).

4. It is in the very nature of being human to be fallible and imperfect.

5. Because you are a complex, unique, ever-changing individual, you cannot legitimately be rated or measured as a whole person.

To overcome disturbing feelings such as shame and anxiety about your appearance, it helps to regard your feature(s) as only one aspect of you, rather than defining you. (For example, you are more than your nose!) Naturally, it's foolish to deny that some people and indeed some aspects of 'society' place an overly large importance on appearance, but you don't automatically have to go along with them. Concentrate on the effect of putting yourself down based on your feature. Is it helping? If not, you can certainly develop greater levels of self-acceptance. This means accepting yourself (including your flaws), and recognizing that you are a unique, fallible, human being like everyone else, without globally condemning yourself.

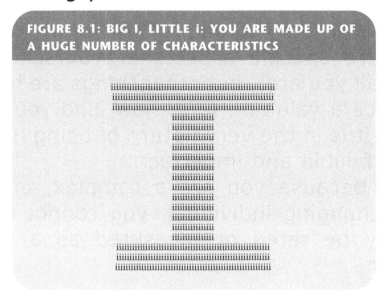

FIGURE 8.1: BIG I, LITTLE i: YOU ARE MADE UP OF A HUGE NUMBER OF CHARACTERISTICS

Consider the 'Big I, little i' illustration above. This is one way of showing that each and every one of us is made up of a huge number of parts, and that appearance is only a part (or even a few parts) of who we are.

PRACTICAL EXERCISE

Take a pack of sticky notes and a large wall or a door (or another person if they're prepared to help out). Write down on a note a characteristic that you, as a whole person, possess and stick it on the wall, door, or a volunteer. Keep doing this, trying to think of all aspects of yourself, until you run out of characteristics (or notes!). This can be a very memorable illustration of how multi-faceted you are.

SALLY AND GEORGE

Sally decided to practise the idea that her nose made her imperfect, but that she could accept herself as a person with many other good points.

George concluded that even if his eyes were bigger than he would ideally like, he was a fallible human being, not a freak.

The way to develop self-acceptance is to think more self-acceptingly and to act in a way that reflects self-acceptance.

Self-acceptance and humiliation

Another important factor in body image problems is of course worries about other people's reactions. As social animals, we human beings naturally place some importance on what other people think of us. However, like other parts of us, this can become a problem if it gets over-developed. Our patients often tell us about their fear of dropping a safety behavior (such as camouflage) and this resulting in someone responding in a way that they feel humiliated by. Their fears include:

- Someone laughing at me.
- Someone making a negative comment about a flaw in my appearance.
- Someone making a negative comment to another person about my appearance.
- Someone thinking something negative about me but not saying anything.

Psychologist Windy Dryden has provided a useful analogy to help people cope better with the idea of other people putting us down, which he calls the 'Dryden invitation technique'. The invitation technique involves considering negative evaluation by other people as an invitation for you to evaluate yourself negatively. Think of it like an invitation to a party; at the bottom it usually says 'RSVP', the message being 'let us know whether you accept or decline'. The great thing about invitations is that you can decline them, so when someone evaluates you negatively, even if they are harshly critical, you don't have to accept their invitation to criticize yourself.

INVITATION
Dear _____
YOU ARE INVITED TO:

CONSIDER YOURSELF UNATTRACTIVE AND UNLOVABLE
For having an imperfect appearance Please RSVP as to whether you accept or decline.

Remember, whatever triggers your own negative and self-critical thoughts, you can choose to recognize those thoughts as simply thoughts, not the truth. Again, we say more about this in Chapter 6.

Accepting and normalizing imperfections

Imagine a bowl of really good-quality fresh fruit. Now imagine that one of the apples in the fruit bowl has a bruise on it. Would you consider the whole bowl of fruit to be ruined and inedible? Of course not! It's a delicious, nutritious bowl of fruit, with an apple that has a bruise.

Celebrities and models

Many people with body shame and body dysmorphic disorder compare themselves with highly polished celebrities or models. This puts further distance between your self-image and your ideal, making you feel more dissatisfied.

You may also be focusing on the better aspects of other people's appearances and overlooking their flaws, whilst doing the reverse to yourself. Think about the way you look at other people when you meet them for the first time. Do you tend to focus on the part of their appearance that worries you about yourself? You're trying to reassure yourself that you are no different from others – but this bias tends to have the reverse effect because you tend to focus on and remember those who you think look better than you. Try to focus on the whole person: they may have some very nice features but none of us is perfect. Like you, they will be a mixture.

Ghosts from the past

For some readers, this will be one of the most important parts of this book. Here, we are going to encourage you to identify early experiences in your life that relate to your shame, anxiety or preoccupation about your appearance. We'll introduce some 'pen-and-paper' strategies that will help you to challenge the unhelpful meanings you have in your mind related to early experiences. We will also teach you some techniques that focus more on your imagination. Remember: if you have memories of a highly painful or traumatic nature you should probably not use these techniques involving imagination without the support of an appropriately trained therapist.

QUESTIONNAIRE 8.1: IDENTIFYING EARLY EXPERIENCES THAT MAY BE RELEVANT TO THE DEVELOPMENT OF YOUR BODY IMAGE PROBLEM

1. Are there any early experiences that you can remember that may have contributed to your developing unhelpful patterns of thinking and acting about your appearance? These might be experiences of teasing, bullying, humiliation, sexual abuse, or what you learnt from your parents or peers. These links may not necessarily be about your appearance but something that you learnt about yourself that made you think you were different or abnormal. To begin with, simply list any memories that come to mind.

[Space left intentionally blank in the original book]

2. The second way to identify relevant memories is to use your experience of the picture in your mind or the felt impression you have of yourself. Try to think of a recent time when you felt upset about your appear-

ance. What was the situation? Where were you?

[Space left intentionally blank in the original book]

3. What was happening at the time?

[Space left intentionally blank in the original book]

4. How did you feel emotionally?

[Space left intentionally blank in the original book]

5. What was the picture or felt impression in your mind? Can you draw yourself or describe the impression you had of yourself?

[Space left intentionally blank in the original book]

6. Did you have any bodily sensations? Where in your body did you feel them (e.g. tightness in your skin)?

[Space left intentionally blank in the original book]

7. How old were you when you first experienced that picture or felt impression of your feature? Please describe your experience in the first person, present tense (e.g. 'I am about six years old and playing in a school playground. A boy who is quite popular with other girls just comes up to me and tells me I look ugly').

[Space left intentionally blank in the original book]

8. What was the most upsetting meaning that this experience had for you? The meaning might influence your views about yourself (e.g. 'I am ugly and I'll be alone all my life') or how you think others will behave towards you (e.g. 'People will always humiliate me').

[Space left intentionally blank in the original book]

9. Can you remember the first time you had this meaning in your mind?

[Space left intentionally blank in the original book]

There may be several painful experiences that have all contributed to the views you have of yourself and others. Try to repeat this questionnaire for the most important experiences.

Changing the meaning of past events, part 1: the 'triple column' method

This is a 'pen-and-paper' strategy for taking another look at distressing or unhelpful experiences. The aim is to describe the meaning you attached to an experience when it happened, and then to look at the experience as an older, wiser person and generate an alternative way of understanding the situation. To help yourself do this, use the table in Chapter 8 and consider the following:

• What would be the effect of a kinder, more compassionate way of looking at the situation?
• How would you help a child, close friend, or loved one look at the situation?
• What is a more balanced and non-extreme point of view?
• How would someone you respect look at the experience?

Changing the meaning of past events, part 2: Re-scripting memories in your imagination

This is a technique for tackling one specific memory at a time and is usually best done with a therapist with experience in this approach. The memories might be of being abused, teased, humiliated – anything you think that might have contributed to your body image problems. The principle is that you, in your imagination, go back in time to talk to your younger self and deliver a more helpful way of understanding a difficult experience.

STEP 1

Select a memory from those you have identified earlier in this chapter. Re-live the upsetting memory in detail, as if it were happening now, imagining that you are the age you were when the event happened. It is important to keep your eyes closed and describe it in the first person present tense so that it feels as if you are re-experiencing it.

STEP 2

Re-live the memory again but this time imagining that you enter the scene as an adult and intervene. You might simply observe and offer your younger self comfort, or you might actively change the course of events and help your younger self escape. The important thing is to find out what your younger self wants and help your younger self in whatever way you can. Sometimes the younger self may need you to bring with you an authority figure to stop the bad things happening.

STEP 3

Imagine again that you are your younger self (as in Step 1) and describe out aloud what it feels like to see your older brother or sister arriving on the scene. Consider whether your younger self would need anything else to happen to help it feel better. If necessary repeat Step 2 depending on whether the younger self needs more to happen.

Early experience	Meaning	Alternative meaning

STEP 4

Now 'ground' yourself back into the 'here and now'. Look around you and remind yourself of where you are, the time, and the date.

JIM

A male client, Jim, who suffered from BDD recalled the first time he felt really ashamed about his appearance. This was when he was being hit by a bully at school. One of the bully's friends made a comment during this upsetting experience that he remembered very well: 'Stop hitting him, it won't make him any better-looking.' At the time Jim thought 'I'm being hit because I look disgusting', and later concluded 'I must always look good to avoid people hurting me'. This rule drove a considerable degree of his preoccupation with his appearance. If he focused on the memory, Jim would get an image of a bully standing over him, hitting him, with a crowd of people standing around him, watching. He reported that he had the distinct impression that the onlookers were enjoying the spectacle, a bit like a Victorian freak show.

Jim considered alternative meanings using the triple column method first, and then went on to imagine himself as an older person going into the memory to intervene. He imagined himself grabbing hold of the bully and throwing him to the side. Drawing from his work on the triple column method, he then imagined himself explaining to his younger self that he was being bullied simply because he was shy and had moved from another school. He explained that the comment from the bully's friend was the only comment of its type he'd ever been on the receiving end of in his life. As such, it was a rare, unusual event, not the norm for his life and therefore not something from which to draw general conclusions.

Strengthening your helpful beliefs

A fundamental process that maintains the way you feel about your body is 'thought–event fusion'. Thus if you feel ugly or have the thought that you will be alone all your life, then that becomes very real to you. Rating yourself as ugly and the future as being hopeless is treated as a fact in the same way as 'the sky is blue'. Sometimes other people reinforce this tendency (for example, friends or relatives who say 'I'd be depressed too if I went through what you did').

While you focus on your negativity, you don't notice the process by which your thoughts and reality are becoming fused. Instead, you totally buy into the content of your thoughts as facts. These thoughts are really just mental chatter, rather than objective evidence that everyone can agree with. When the way you feel about your body is very rigid, we understand you won't believe the alternative meanings. However, it may be more helpful to consider your relationship with your thoughts and how you react to them. If you have fused your thoughts with reality and believe them to be true, it's not surprising that you want to escape from them or from the feeling of being ugly. Thus, in order to escape unpleasant thoughts and feelings, you might start to put in place things which seem to be protective, but which actually make your life much harder. For example, you might want to:

- avoid activities and people that you normally enjoy and become more focused on yourself
- withdraw from friends or family
- make excuses to yourself (e.g. 'I am not in the mood' to see other people)
- use alcohol or drugs to numb your feelings
- brood about the past and try to work out reasons for the way you feel
- avoid calling friends because you think you may be humiliated or rejected

- spend a lot of time watching TV or DVDs or spend excessive amounts of time on the Internet
- ignore the doorbell or telephone.

One of the best ways of truly viewing your thoughts as mental chatter is to act *as if* you already really believe the alternative. The way you act or behave has a big impact on your thinking. So if you deliberately act against your negative beliefs you are simultaneously eroding them and building up your new beliefs. This strategy is extremely helpful, so practise it often. Here is a questionnaire to help you get acting 'as if':

QUESTIONNAIRE 8.2: ACTING 'AS IF'

1. Write down the new belief or attitude that you wish to strengthen (e.g. 'I have a feature that others do not notice or believe to be that abnormal. The problem is that I worry a lot about my feature.')

[Space left intentionally blank in the original book]

2. Now consider, if other people in your life could see positive changes in you, what do you think they might notice? How would

you be behaving differently if you truly believed in your new way of thinking about yourself, others and/or the world? Think of people you know who seem to hold the kind of attitude that you wish to strengthen in yourself. How do they behave in ways that reflect that way of thinking? Write down how you can act 'as if' you believe in your new healthy belief:

[Space left intentionally blank in the original book]

3. Where and when could you act in the ways you have described above?

[Space left intentionally blank in the original book]

9

Principles in action

This chapter offers some examples of people with body image problems and gives brief descriptions of how they overcame them. You will notice that some of the examples are of people who have 'flaws' in their appearance that most people would agree are observable. Other examples are of people who do not have a 'flaw'. In other words, most people would agree that their feature is not observable or 'out of the norm'. However, all the people described in this chapter are distressed about their appearance and this distress is interfering with their lives. Even more importantly, they all managed to reduce their distress and improve their lives by following many of the principles outlined in this book. These examples may not be exactly like your own, so please concentrate on the application of the principles, rather than any slight differences in your own situation. Virtually no one starts a process of recovery from a significant body image problem feeling totally confident that they can recover, so please recognize thoughts like 'I can see how it could work for someone else but it won't for me' as a common by-product of the problem. Just let such thoughts pass through your mind, and give the principles a try.

Eileen: Adjusting to visible scars following burns

Eileen is in her mid-twenties. She lives on her own in London and used to work as a supply teacher. Her family live in Cornwall, but she has many good friends whom she used to see regularly. She recently split up with a boyfriend but this was a mutual decision. She used to describe herself as reasonably attractive, happy-go-lucky and a good friend. A year ago she was a passenger in a car that crashed. Although not badly injured, she has some scars on her forehead that have healed well, but are visible to other people. Eileen is devastated about these scars. She has been unable to return to work and increasingly stays on her own in her flat day after day. She will only go out with a baseball hat pulled down low over her face and looks at the ground to avoid catching anyone's eye. She is frightened that other people will notice her scars and thinks that people have started to back away from her and feel uncertain. Her mood is low and she cannot understand what has happened to the cheerful girl who once confidently stood in front of a class of boisterous children.

First of all, Eileen identified the main problems using the checklist from Exercise 5.1 and rated their importance:

1. Feeling very anxious and ashamed about my scars, comparing myself with the way I used to look. Worrying about this most of the day, and having to wear a baseball hat if I have to leave the house. Rating: 10

2. Feeling depressed and tearful about my face. Worrying about other people's reactions if they see the scars, leading me to spend as much time as I can at home. Rating: 10

3. Worrying about whether I will ever get back to work and have a relationship in the future. Rating: 8

4. Worrying about my treatment and whether it will be possible to remove the scars. Rating: 8

5. Not feeling as if I am 'me' any more. Rating: 8

Eileen then kept a record of her activities for the week. From this, it was clear that she spent all her time alone. She spent long periods reading or watching television or thinking about her face. In the morning she spent an hour looking at her scars in the mirror and trying to cover them with make-up, and she returned to check on whether they were visible every one to two hours. Three times a week, she had to go out to get milk and food, but she bought large enough quantities to last for a few days so that she did not need to go out more often. When she went out, she prepared for at least two hours, pulling a baseball cap as low as she could and hurrying back without talking to anyone. She rated her anxiety before going out as 10/10, and coming home again was associated with a huge feeling of relief and a fall in anxiety to 3/10.

To help motivate herself to overcome her problems, Eileen worked through the 'Exercise 5.3: Understanding your values' worksheet (see Chapter 5) and identified the directions in life that were important to her. Here are some examples of what she wrote:

- *I would like to meet someone and feel that I am the same happy and supportive friend that I used to be, not always talking about my own problems.*
- *I'd like to be a good sister and see more of my family.*
- *I'd like to return to work, which I really used to enjoy.*

The first step towards helping Eileen change some of her behavior was to encourage her to increase her level of activity and to cut down on her avoidance of leaving the house. To do this, we had to explore the reasons why she was fearful, remove any parts of her behavior that were currently unhelpful (safety behaviors) and put in place some positive strategies.

For Eileen, the most frightening part of going out was the feeling that everyone was staring at her and her scars. This is a very common feeling if there is something about your appearance that is visible to others, and it can often be confirmed by people doing a double-take or staring and asking questions. For this reason, Eileen needed a good response. If someone was staring, she decided that she could:

• Act in a positive way by looking firmly at them and smiling. If someone asked about her scarring she could:
• Respond in a positive way by saying e.g. 'I was in a car accident. It was several months ago and I'm much better now.' She could then comment on some aspect of the other person's appearance, e.g. 'I like your scarf – do you mind me asking where you got it?'

By responding in such a way, Eileen would demonstrate that there was nothing odd or strange about her.

Eileen also needed to modify her safety behaviors such as wearing the baseball cap. She was invited to write down the way people seemed to respond to her and to see if there was another way of explaining this.

Eileen is very tall. Because she was wearing a cap, she was also wearing jeans and an anorak, rather than her normal skirt and top. Add to this the fact that she was looking at the floor to avoid eye contact, and trying to get in and out of a shop quickly, and her behavior could appear very suspicious. This had not occurred to Eileen but she could readily see that this was a possibility. This helped Eileen to prepare a simple plan for increasing her activity.

First of all she considered her hat. Taking it off completely seemed very frightening. She therefore looked at home for different hats, and chose one without a large brim. She chose a small beret in a soft colour. Because this seemed more feminine, she decided to wear a skirt.

We then worked out a simple exposure program:

Day	Task	How long I spent	How uncomfortable I felt (0–10)
Monday	Go to local shop, buy milk		

Day	Task	How long I spent	How uncom-fortable I felt (0–10)
Tuesday	Go to local shop, buy milk and other groceries		
Wednesday	Browse shelves, buy recipe ingredients		
Thursday	Go to local shop: ask if they have a particular item		
Friday	Go to next shop along: ask for items		

Although this table is presented in daily format, Eileen was asked to repeat each task without her safety behaviors, and to focus her attention on her surroundings until her anxiety level dropped to 5 or less, before going on to the next task.

To her surprise, Eileen found this much easier than she had thought, once she got going. One thing that helped immediately was that someone asked her where she had got her hat. She therefore had a very good example of a naturally occurring behavioral experiment, which had disproved the idea that people:

   (a) were staring because of her scars (they were looking at her clothes); or

(b) thought she looked freakish or strange (they thought she looked approachable and friendly).

This was the first conversation Eileen had had with anyone for weeks, and it greatly improved her mood and sense of self-esteem. She started to initiate conversations herself, commenting on the weather or the newspaper headlines.

As Eileen began to increase her activity, she found herself worrying less about other people and their response to her. However, she still had lots of worries about her appearance, and felt preoccupied about what she looked like and whether she would ever look as she had before the accident.

We rated Eileen's ideas about the noticeability of her scars and her preoccupation with them on a scale of 1–10.

The target was to get as close to 0 as possible on both counts. However, if we could reduce the level of worry or preoccupation to 0, then Eileen would be able to achieve all the things she had listed on her valued directions scale, whether or not she still felt the scars were noticeable.

Eileen rated the noticeability of her scars as 8/10, and the amount she worried about them as 10/10.

Eileen decided to keep a record of her thoughts about her appearance and to try to identify her thinking styles (see Chapter 6). She then rated the strength of her belief about the noticeability of her scars and tried to find another way of looking at it.

By focusing on unhelpful thoughts, Eileen could see that she was making her mood lower and triggering more unhelpful beliefs. By questioning whether there was an alternative but equally plausible explanation, she could stop her thoughts spiralling downwards. She now felt able to go and see her family for a short holiday. Whilst there, she tried hard to take part in family activities and, although she found this very anxiety-provoking at first, she was gradually able to relax once she was in the situation. She prepared herself to answer questions about her scarring – but was surprised that no one mentioned it. Eventually, at the end of a long evening at the local pub, someone asked her: 'I hope you don't mind me asking, but were you in an accident?'

Date, time	What was going through your mind?	Rating	Thinking biases	How could you challenge this?	Rating
Tuesday 7.30 pm	I saw a program about teaching. I was thinking that I would never get another job looking the way I do.	8	Black and white thinking	Lots of people with visible difference work and have happy, successful lives. It is how good you are at what you do that interests employers. I know I am a good teacher.	3–4
	I will never have the confidence to stand in front of a class of children.	9	Fortune telling	My confidence is growing with each new step. Last week I was not confident enough to leave the house.	2–3
	I will never be able to work again – no one will have any respect for me, I will never have a partner...	8	Catastro-phizing	I have no evidence to support the idea that I will never be able to do this. It is a question of tackling things step by step. I need to act as if this is just a thought even if I don't yet believe it.	2–3

```
 0   1   2   3   4   5   6   7   8   9   10
 L___|___|___|___|___|___|___|___|___|___J
 No distress, calm    Moderate distress    Panic
```

Eileen actually laughed! 'Thank goodness! I am supposed be practising answering and no one has asked!'

This proved to be a landmark event for Eileen. She had relaxed enough to discover her old sense of humour, and she went back home feeling much more positive and ready to tackle the next steps in therapy.

(This sometimes happens – a marked success really builds up confidence. But of course the reverse can also happen. You can have a situation that you feel has gone badly. If this happens, don't jump to negative conclusions. Carefully examine the event, trying not to make value judgements. Look at what happened as feedback. What could you have done differently? What could you have said? How could you have behaved? Decide how you would manage this event if it happened again – make a plan and then move on. Don't brood! In this way every event provides feedback for change. There is no such thing as failure so long as you keep on learning!)

Eileen re-rated her scores on noticeability and worry. Not only had her level of worry dropped to 3/10, but her sense of how noticeable her scars were to other people had also fallen.

Eileen kept up her progress with an activity schedule which included going out every day, even if it was just for some shopping, seeing friends and building up her confidence step by step. She kept regular records so that she could talk about her progress during her therapy and to encourage her on days when her mood was lower. Occasionally she had a 'bad day', but she focused on the good days, and noticed that things got back to normal much more quickly if she did not brood.

She now began to think about returning to work. This meant planning, reading adverts and completing an application form. Eileen organized this by setting herself manageable goals in a sensible timeframe. Once she had been invited to an interview (this took a number of weeks), she role-played certain interview skills – such as keeping good eye contact, smiling and focusing on other people rather than monitoring her own behavior and responses (see Chapter 6).

At her interview, Eileen took the initiative with regard to her scarring. Rather than having people wonder why she had had so much time off work, she explained about her accident and the scarring. Taking the initiative like this is very helpful in building confidence.

Eileen is now back at work. Of course she wishes the accident had not happened. She still has some visible scarring and people occasionally ask her about it. However, she recognizes that people are curious, that the way she responds means that they very quickly see past the scars, and that her appearance is not the thing that defines her. Her preoccupation and worry has fallen to 1–2. She feels like 'herself', recognizes herself when she looks in the mirror, and has plans to start doing some voluntary work for children with special needs.

Fugen's preoccupation with the shape of her nose

Fugen was preoccupied with the shape of her nose. She believed that it was misshapen, too big, and did not suit her face. Overall she felt that her nose was very noticeable and abnormal but others could not observe anything that noticeable or abnormal. When she highlighted her nose to a friend who viewed it very closely, the friend could only see a small bump where Fugen thought it was misshapen. However, her friend was viewing her as a whole and did not regard her nose as her identity.

Fugen had had a number of cosmetic procedures earlier in her life, most notably work on her chin, which she said she was happy with, but that it made her nose look worse by contrast. She had approached a number of cosmetic surgeons who did not consider her a good candidate for further surgery. She was spending at least six hours per day preoccupied with her appearance, felt down much of the time, and frequently anxious about her appearance. She worked a few hours from home, having withdrawn from her office, and rarely socialized. She experienced a felt impression of her nose in her mind, which she looked at as an observer. Sometimes this led to doubts as to how exactly she did look and to frequent checking of her nose in mirrors which had to have the right lighting. This often led to further doubts. She avoided bright lights, which cast a shadow. She compared herself to old photographs of how she used to look, and compared her nose to the noses of other women of the same age. Her relationship had broken down, as her partner as was unable to cope with her behavior.

There were two alternative theories to be tested out in therapy:

Theory A (which she had been following for several years) was that the problem was her nose and that this had to be fixed before she could do anything else in life, or she would be humiliated and be alone all her life.

Theory B (which was to be tested during therapy) was that she had an emotional and thinking problem about her nose and that her solutions (by treating it as Theory A) was making her preoccupation and distress with her nose worse.

Fugen identified some of her ways of coping with their unintended consequences for her preoccupation and distress, using the vicious flower diagram below.

Her commitment for change was to treat her problem 'as if' she had an emotional and thinking problem, rather than a problem with the appearance of her nose (even though she didn't believe it). After all, if treating it as Theory B for several months didn't work, then she could always go back to her previous way of treating it as Theory A. She also recognized that there could have been ghosts from the past (such as when she was bullied as a child) that influenced the way she felt about her appearance. Furthermore, she recognized that some of her ways of coping were making her preoccupation worse and that she was on an endless treadmill of further checking. She was very fearful of being humiliated and left alone in the world. However, she also knew that many of her solutions were now the problem. They were causing much of her unhappiness and isolation.

The first step was for Fugen to keep a record of how often she checked her nose both with her fingers and in the mirror, using a 'tally counter' she bought via the Internet. This helped her to monitor her checking, made her more aware of just how much checking she was doing, and helped her to steadily reduce and stop the checking.

FUGEN'S HIERARCHY OF SITUATIONS

Trigger (object, place, person, situation):	Estimated distress (0–100)
Asking an attractive man out on a date, without my hat, and without checking beforehand	100
Going to an interview	90
Sitting and having a meal in a brightly lit fast-food restaurant	80
Asking for directions in the street on a bright, sunny day	70
Going for a walk around the local park on a busy day without my hat	70
Going for a walk around the park on a quiet day without my hat	65
Sitting and having a meal in a dimly-lit restaurant	60
Standing, profile on, in a long queue in a shop	60
Having a friend over to my house for coffee and deliberately allowing them to see me from the side	50

She learnt how to use mirrors in healthy way and to refocus her attention more on what she saw without making any judgement. At the same time, Fugen developed a hierarchy of situations she was anxious about or was avoiding.

Fugen found using a hierarchy helpful in three main ways:

Re-focuses my
attention and
stops me from
tolerating doubt

Comparing nose
in my mind
to how I would
ideally want it to look

Checking the size
of my nose with my fingers

I feel dissatisfied
and I can seem
distracted to
other people

Fuels my belief that my nose
is very noticeable to others.
May appear odd to other
people and make them feel
less warm towards me

Preoccupation
and shame
about my
appearance

Checking the size
and shape of my
nose in the mirror

Wearing a baseball
hat to make
nose look
less long by contrast

Makes it seem
more important.
Makes me late
which annoys people

Makes me feel
self-conscious
and distracted

Adjusting my posture
to stop people seeing
my nose in profile

Fugen's vicious flower

1. It helped her see more clearly that recovery could be a series of gradual steps, rather than taking her usual 'all or nothing' view of 'stop being so silly' or 'of course I'm devastated; so would anyone else be'.

2. She used her hierarchy as a guide for areas in which to conduct 'behavioral experiments' (see example below).

3. She used her hierarchy as a guide to help her practise approaching situations without her safety behaviors. She could then re-direct her attention into the surroundings, away from her felt impression of how she was coming across. This

was particularly difficult and the main strategy to re-focus her attention was 'task concentration training' (see Chapter 6). She rediscovered her love of nature, and found it especially helpful in the early stages to practise re-focusing her attention onto trees and plants as she walked. This helped to 'anchor' her attention in the outside world and then she found she could more readily move it around to other aspects of her task or environment.

Fugen eventually learnt to stop brooding about her nose. This was a great relief, as the brooding just made her feel worse and more preoccupied. Her mind constantly generated more questions, to which there were no solutions.

After she had made some progress with changing her behavior, Fugen learnt to develop a different relationship with her intrusive thoughts and images about her appearance. She viewed her thoughts and images about her appearance as her internal 'BDD TV'. She considered that her thoughts could be like a 'history channel' (for when she brooded about the past), the 'BDD propaganda newsflash' (for when an upsetting image or thoughts would suddenly enter her head), or 'adverts' for when her mind was telling her that she 'needed to know how exactly she looked' or how she could fix it and had a strong urge to check her appearance. Over time, these 'BDD TV broadcasts' became less frequent and distressing. She was able to return to work in her office. She contacted some of her old friends and about six months later developed a new relationship.

Roz's preoccupation with her weight and shape

Roz, aged 32, was preoccupied with her weight and shape. She was especially concerned with her stomach and the upper part of her thighs. She frequently stood in front of the mirror, changing the angle she looked at herself from, attacking herself in her mind for being 'fat and disgusting'. She would poke, squeeze, or even hit areas of fat on her body. She did not have a diagnosed eating disorder but would spend a lot of time researching different diets and slimming products on the Internet, and was usually 'on a diet'. She avoided foods that she considered extremely 'unsafe' such as white bread. And she would usually avoid eating in public. If she deviated from her diet plan she would feel guilty about having 'let herself down' and become very angry. She would then very often try and starve herself the next day or try

FUGEN'S BEHAVIORAL EXPERIMENT SHEET

1. Task that I planned (e.g. when, where, how, and with whom? Include a description of how you will act without safety behaviors).	2. How distressing I am predicting task will be at the peak (0-100%).	3. How long I am predicting that the distress will take to halve (minutes or hours).	4. What I am predicting will happen (e.g. how others will behave towards me) or whether the result will best fit a particular theory and how strongly I believe it (0-100%).	5. What I actually did during the task (including using any safety behaviors and degree of self-focused attention).	6. How distressing the task was at the peak (0-100).	7. How long it actually took for the distress to halve (minutes or hours).	8. What actually happened? Does this differ from what I predicted in column 4? Do the results best fit my theory that I have a problem with my appearance, or the alternative – that the problem is being excessively preoccupied by my appearance?
Going into brightly lit restaurant without my hat, make-up or checking my in the mirror 100%.	100%	Never	People in the restaurant will notice my nose. The waitress will be awkward and uncomfortable; other people will stare and make comments to each other, trying not to let me hear. I'll have to run into the bathroom to see what everyone else is noticing.	I tried really hard to keep my attention focused on the outside world. I resisted feeling my nose or checking in the bathroom. I remembered that thoughts about people thinking negatively about me were mind-reading and being driven by my own preoccupation.	80%	45 mins	Nobody really paid much attention to me. I have no evidence that anyone said anything to anyone else about me, even though I did feel self conscious, which was more down to my anxiety than anything anyone else did or said. The waitress was nice enough but was really too busy to pay me much attention. This does confirm the theory that I tend to worry far too much about how people will respond to my appearance. I need to practise this more until I feel much more comfortable.

and burn off more calories at the gym. She would tend to either weigh herself excessively, or avoid weighing herself for fear of finding out that she had gained weight. She would frequently compare herself with other people, especially focusing on people who were her ideal size and shape. One way of comparing herself with her ideal size and shape, which often provoked a significant drop in her mood, was to put on clothes that she had worn when she was in her early twenties.

She recognized that her solutions – monitoring her weight and shape and constantly comparing herself with others – were making her very unhappy and had become self-perpetuating. However, change was going to involve real commitment to experiencing some unpleasant thoughts and feelings. A number of her problems had developed after two of her relationships had broken up. Throughout her life, her family had always commented on how pretty she was, and how it was very important to look after herself and to have a happy marriage.

As part of getting to grips with her body image problem, Roz built her own vicious flower, overleaf.

As part of her recovery, Roz resolved to stop buying fashion magazines for herself, and to replace them with novels and magazines on music. She practised using a mirror in a healthier way, as described in Chapter 7. A crucial step in recovery for Roz was what she called 'positive eating'. This meant that she concentrated on eating regularly, three meals with a mid-morning snack, but with an empha-sis on health rather than weight loss. She therefore took great care to eat plenty of fruit, vegetables, whole grains, nuts, lean meat and fish. She also made exercise part of her weekly routine, focusing more on boosting her fitness and stamina than on burning off calories.

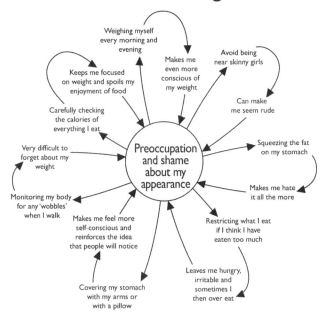

Roz's vicious flower

Roz identified an early memory of her family sitting watching television when she was a child. She recalled that whenever a celebrity appeared on the screen, her parents and older sister would comment on whether that person-ality had gained or lost weight. She realized that this had led her to fear gaining weight and being criticized. She took one of those memo-ries and restructured it in her imagination. She imagined her older self walking into the living room and scolding her family, and them apologizing and admitting that it was a bad habit. This helped her to feel more confident in reducing her own self-attacking.

An important symbolic step for Roz was to throw away her 'twenty-something' clothes, and update her wardrobe to clothes the right size for her now. She also increased her social life, but initially found it very hard to resist comparing herself with others. She shocked herself by keeping a frequency record of her comparing for a few days. Over the next couple of weeks, she deliberately focused on the sounds, smells, and décor of the places where she met friends, to help keep her attention away from comparing.

Roz practised thinking of her critical thoughts about her appearance as 'mental traffic', and considered herself as a pedestrian standing at the side of the road watching the traffic go by. One thought that she found particularly hard to allow to pass was an idea that if she stopped worrying about her weight she would become obese, and feel much worse than she already did. She decided to think of this thought as a particularly unpleasant-looking, dirty and polluting 'lorry' driving down her psychological 'street' – harder to ignore, but not worthy of her attention. She realized that fears of losing control of her weight were entirely natural, in view of the fact that she had given it so much importance over the years. However, she decided that she would see how her healthy living worked out for at least six months before considering any changes.

Happily, six months later, she was far happier and less consumed by anxiety about her weight, and was even more convinced that it was not worth focusing on. Her social life had improved and she was able to be a better friend. Her friends liked the fact that she was no longer preoccupied with her weight and shape and was fun to be around.

Tom: Adjusting to assault and a facial scar

Tom is a student. He enjoys a drink with his mates, particularly when the pub is showing the premier league football games. He describes himself as amiable, friendly and the last person to be aggressive or get into a fight.

Unfortunately, Tom was unlucky. He was in the wrong place at the wrong time when a fight developed. Someone smashed a bottle and caught him across the face. He now has a characteristic glass injury with a scar running from the corner of his mouth across his cheek.

He was referred to the plastic surgeons asking for 'scar removal'. Although the scar will soften and fade over time, it will remain visible.

Tom had a number of problems when he first came for treatment.

He disliked the change in his appearance and was preoccupied with the idea that the injury was 'unfair'. He kept brooding about the injury. ('If only I had not gone that night, if only I had left when I planned etc.')

He felt irritable, his mood was low and he felt jumpy with other people. He also reported that girls looked at him oddly and were inclined to avoid him, whilst other men seemed more aggressive. He started to avoid pubs and stopped spending evenings with his friends.

Like Eileen, Tom was concerned about his appearance. However, his case included some additional problems. The first is related to trauma. Some disfiguring injuries occur as a result of an accident, and this can cause a post-traumatic stress disorder with flashbacks of the incident, avoidance of the scene or reminders of what happened. Mood can be low, with heightened awareness and poor sleep. People may have episodes of 'dissociation' or blanking when their mind seems to switch off. But it's also important to recognize that some of these symptoms are the body's normal response to trauma. In the first few weeks after an accident it is not at all unusual to experience these effects, and they usually get better without treatment. The best thing to do is get back to as normal a life as possible, talk to friends about what happened and try not to avoid people or situations.

But Tom had the additional problem that his injury seemed to bias people's response to him. He now looked 'tough'. He gave this example:

'As I walked into the pub, there was a girl just ahead of me, so I opened the door for her and stood back. She looked at me as if she was going to smile and then she froze and hurried in, just nodded at me.'

Tom thought that this girl had concluded that he was rough and not the sort of person she should be talking to. He found himself 'catastrophizing' and telling himself that he would 'always' have this problem and that girls would 'never' want to go out with him.

Tom found this situation very difficult to manage because it was so different from his actual character. In order to deal with it, he needed to take charge of the situation before anyone else came to inappropriate conclusions. Instead of looking down and avoiding eye contact, or trying to hide his face, he needed to do the opposite. He needed to look directly at people and smile. He had to get in first, before people made judgements about him, and he needed some ice breakers to show that he had a sense of humour and was not aggressive. He settled on the following:

'I know I look tough – but I was just in the wrong place at the wrong time.'

'You should have seen the other chap.'

James Partridge, from the charity Changing Faces (see Appendix 1), has a good way of diffusing the tension when walking into a room, which Tom also found helpful. This is a particularly useful strategy if you are wearing bandages or dressings or have recent scars:

'Good evening everybody – not looking my best tonight I'm afraid!'

The key is not so much what is said as how it is said – and being ready with an immediate response in a way that gets rid of any tension. Tom had to practise this strategy, rating his response.

Situation	How anxious I felt	What I did/said	What happened next?	How anxious I felt
A girl looked at me and then did a double-take.	9	'Never cheer for Arsenal in a Spurs supporters pub.'	She laughed, and I ended up chatting to her.	2
Someone I did not know suddenly asked me about my face.	7–8	'It's a long story – I'll tell you about it another time. Did Arsenal win today?'	We talked about football for a while.	1–2

Situation	How anxious I felt	What I did/said	What happened next?	How anxious I felt
A girl I really fancied asked me about my face.	9	'I was just trying to help a damsel in distress.'	Not a brilliant response – it opened up a lot more questions, but she was really sympathetic so in the end it turned out to be a good reply.	3
This bloke who had been drinking starting baiting me about being hard.	9–10	Finished my drink – left the pub.	I was irritated, but I decided that he was not in a rational state – the positive thing was to walk way.	8 – but then 3–4 when I thought about it afterwards. It was a good move.

As you can see, sometimes the best thing to do was walk away. It is important to recognize, especially when other people have been drinking or are showing off in front of friends, that taking control of the situation can mean removing yourself, even if briefly, before other aggressive behavior develops. This is not a negative avoiding response, but a controlled judgement and a positive way of coping with a potentially dangerous situation.

Tom built up a number of different ways of answering questions and behaving in a way that put other people at their ease. As he increased his social activities and time spent with friends, so the flashbacks and 're-experiencing' of the attack faded, he started to sleep better, and, although he remembered what happened, he no longer felt as though he was constantly reliving it. Like Eileen, he would far rather he did not have the scar. But he no longer searches for a surgical solution, nor does he let it get in the way of doing what he wants to do.

Nicola's birthmark

Nicola is six. She was born with a port wine stain or birthmark on her face. The red colour makes the birthmark very visible to other people, and the texture is slightly less even than the other side.

Nicola's parents were very protective. They did not want her to play rough games with other children at playgroup because they feared 'another injury'. They also worried about her being bullied by other children and spent a lot of time on the Internet trying to find new forms of laser treatment that might help her. Nicola's father worried that she might be promiscuous when she was older because this would be 'the only way she could get a boyfriend'. Her mother thought that it was good that she had an older sister because 'she would be able to stand up for Nicola and stop other children teasing her'. (It is important not to anticipate problems. It is equally possible that Nicola will be the confident child and stand up for her sister!)

As we discussed in earlier chapters, younger children are very accepting of visible difference. As she goes through school, however, she may encounter more problems, as appearance becomes more important for her social group.

We made the following changes with Nicola: First of all, her parents contacted her school and ensured that everyone there knew what a port wine stain was, how it is treated and that there was no reason to exclude her from any activities. They quickly agreed that they wanted her to be treated just like the other children.

Next we all 'brainstormed' what Nicola could call her port wine stain. We wanted something easy to remember that everyone would understand and which she could use to answer questions. We called it her 'birthmark'.

The idea that one's appearance is *special* rather than *abnormal* is important here. No feature is ever ugly or horrible or nasty, but rather pink, bumpy or different.

Nicola's parents practised this when other people asked them about her. In doing this, they were illustrating or 'modelling' a positive coping response for Nicola, instead of avoiding situations where other people might ask them about her. Her sister, grandparents and teachers all learnt to refer to this as her 'birthmark'. As she grows older, Nicola will copy them and use the same kind of response when she is on her own.

Many children's' stories make a link between 'beauty and goodness'. This is not a helpful link for a child. There are lots of books that celebrate difference or simply avoid this kind of comparison. The charity Changing Faces (see Appendix 1) has a list, but they are not difficult to find if you browse in a bookshop or on the website of an online book retailer.

Some parents like to meet others who manage similar issues for their children. Again, Changing Faces offers this kind of peer support and contact, which can help parents exchange good ideas. Nicola's parents met others through the charity and felt supported by being part of a group working towards better acceptance of variation in appearance.

Nicola is still growing up. As she does so, there will be more challenges for her, but because she has the support of a strong family and social network she is likely to cope with them well. Like others with the same condition, she will choose what she wants to do in life and with whom. Her 'birthmark' will not limit her opportunities or force her to compromise in relationships or in her career.

Sabine's preoccupation with her skin

Sabine was a 24-year-old single woman who lived with her parents. Her main problem, of several years' duration, was a preoccupation with her skin. She felt that her cheeks had become saggy and there was fullness of the lower face, causing lines and ageing, and that she had acne scarring. She was preoccupied to a lesser extent with wrinkling and sun-damaged skin. She wanted intense light therapy or cream for ageing and wrinkling skin, and a skin peel. It was on her mind for at least 10 hours a day, and she was checking in mirrors or reflective surfaces about 20 times a day. She avoided having a photo or videos taken, though she would take a photo of herself on her camera-phone, which she used to compare with photos of when she was much younger.

She was constantly comparing her features with others in the media or to people she met, and with old pictures of herself. She tried to hide her face with her hair. She had been significantly depressed for some time and did nothing at home apart from watching TV, and trying to change her appearance in her mind. She felt constantly tired, and often slept during the day and woke early. Her appetite was variable and she had lost a bit of weight. She often believed the future to be hopeless. She was extremely self-conscious and fearful of others quietly laughing at her and humiliating her and avoided social, public situations.

She had no enjoyment of anything and did not plan anything. If she did go out, then her mind was elsewhere, comparing herself with others. She might try to convince her mother about how unattractive she was. She might push her cheeks up to where they used to be, as she used to look. She tended to brood on the past and why she was born this way and how she could change her skin. Overall, she felt that her face was extremely noticeable (e.g. to a stranger passing at a distance in the street), but others could not observe anything abnormal. She had some acne problems when she was about eight to ten years younger, when she was teased about having a 'pizza face'.

There were two alternative theories to be tested out in therapy.

Theory A (which she had been following for several years) was that the problem was her skin and that this had to be fixed before she could do anything else in life.

Theory B (which was to be tested during therapy) was that she had an emotional problem about her skin and that her solution (by treating it as Theory A) was making her preoccupation and distress with her skin worse.

The first step was to understand that the 'solutions' were the problem, and while she continued to treat her skin as the problem, her preoccupation and distress would persist and her life would continue to be severely limited.

She was desperate to change and agreed to test out Theory B (that the real problem was her preoccupation with her appearance and being excessively self-focused). She focused on a felt impression of herself, which had become fused with reality. What she saw in the mirror was therefore what she felt. She then believed what her mind was telling her about being ugly as a witch.

She spent some time developing a good understanding of what was keeping the problem going and identified a number of ways of coping that maintained her preoccupation. She put all this in her vicious flower diagram opposite.

She recognized that, in order to test the theory that the problem was her solutions, each of these petals would have to be pulled off. Logically, she thought, if her situation improved by treating her problem 'as if' it were a preoccupation problem, she would learn more about what the true nature of her problem was. However, one strategy she found particularly difficult was checking her appearance using either the mirror or her mobile phone. She decided to conduct an experiment to help make the link between checking and her preoccupation clearer. She recorded the number of hours she was preoccupied with her appearance, and how much distress it caused her on a 'normal' checking day. Then the next day she increased her checking by at least 50 per cent. She had thought that she might need to repeat this again to really help herself 'get the message' but in fact the middle of the afternoon on day two she was so anxious and disturbed about her appearance that she resolved to try as hard as she could to resist checking for the next few days to see how that affected her. Happily this was a very significant step on her road to recovery.

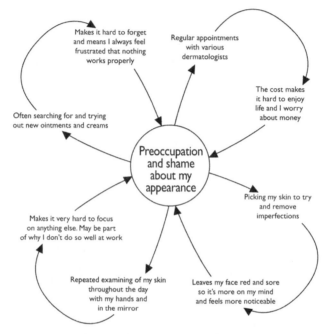

Makes it hard to forget and means I always feel frustrated that nothing works properly

Regular appointments with various dermatologists

The cost makes it hard to enjoy life and I worry about money

Often searching for and trying out new ointments and creams

Preoccupation and shame about my appearance

Picking my skin to try and remove imperfections

Makes it very hard to focus on anything else. May be part of why I don't do so well at work

Repeated examining of my skin throughout the day with my hands and in the mirror

Leaves my face red and sore so it's more on my mind and feels more noticeable

Sabine's vicious flower

Sabine defined her problems as follows:

1. *Feeling anxious and ashamed about the condition of the skin on my face.*

Rating: 10

2. *Feeling down and as if my life is over.*

Rating: 7

Sabine also completed the Exercise 5.3 'Understanding your values' worksheet and became clearer in her mind that she no longer wanted her appearance to stand for her life. She was particularly inspired to follow her valued directions in the area of contributing to her community through working with children, and in the area of socializing with friends.

Having realized just how much of her attention had become trained onto her appearance, Sabine consistently practised switching her attention away from what her mind was telling her towards the outside world, using 'task concentration training' (described in Chapter 6). To make her attention more flexible, she practised 'attention training' in the dining room most days (also described in Chapter 6).

To help lift her low mood, Sabine drew up an 'activity schedule' to restore some routine to her life, and become more productive. She also started to spot when she was engaging in brooding and thinking about the past, and practised bringing her attention back into the outside world in the 'here-and-now'. She viewed much of her activity scheduling as taking care of her life and herself, and ignoring the negative messages her depressed brain was sending her.

Sabine developed a hierarchy of situations she was anxious about and/or avoiding, and conducted a number of behavioral experiments and exposure to such situations whilst gradually dropping her safety behaviors. One of her experiments is shown below:

SABINE'S BEHAVIORAL EXPERIMENT SHEET

1. Task that I planned (e.g. when, where, how, and with whom? Include a description of how you will act without safety behaviors).	2. How distressing I am predicting task will be at the peak (0–100%).	3. How long I am predicting that the distress will take to halve (minutes or hours).	4. What I am predicting will happen (e.g. how others will behave towards me) or whether the result will best fit a particular theory and how strongly I believe it (0–100%).	5. What I actually did during the task (including using any safety behaviors and degree of self-focused attention).	6. How distressing the task was at the peak (0–100)?	7. How long it actually took for the distress to halve (minutes or hours).	8) What actually happened? Does this differ from what I predicted in column 4? Do the results best fit my theory that I have a problem with my appearance or the alternative – that the problem is being excessively preoccupied by my appearance?
Going to my local shopping centre to look around the shops, without checking my appearance and excessively applying face cream and make-up.	90%	2 hours	I'll feel much worse and it will show me that I can't cope. Shop assistants won't want someone as ugly as me in their shop as I'll put off the other customers.	I used my task concentration skills to keep me focused on the décor of the shopping centre and what was on sale in the shops. At times I lapsed into staring too hard at my face in reflective surfaces.	75%	1 ½ hours	I coped better than I thought I would, although I noticed I struggled in brightly lit shops with lots of mirrors. I need to practise not getting drawn into scrutinizing my face in the mirror.

As part of her desire to keep her body image problem at bay in the long term, Sabine used imagery re-scripting on experiences of when she had been teased and bullied (see

Chapter 8 for more on this). She was moved to tears when she imagined her younger self being bullied, and became far more sympathetic towards herself about her worries. She re-framed her body image problem as being like a bully itself, and resolved not to let it push her around into self-focus, avoidance, camouflage or checking. She decided that her negative, threatening, and critical thoughts about her appearance were like a bully's threats, and she became determined to do what she wanted to do, in spite of the threats. Gradually, she introduced more of what was important in her life. She started to do some voluntary work and new skills so that eventually she could return to work. She caught up with old friends and developed a new relationship after about six months.

10

Helping someone with a body image problem

This chapter is primarily written for family members or friends of people with body dysmorphic disorder (BDD), although much of it is also relevant to people with other body image problems.

One of the practical things a friend or relative can do is become an ally for the individual in overcoming their BDD, if he or she wishes you to. If a child has BDD, parents must be involved in therapy, but teenagers should be given a choice as to whether or not their parent is involved.

In cognitive behavioral therapy (CBT), the person who acts as an ally in this way is called a 'co-therapist'. Such allies can be of enormous value and can help in numerous ways. If you decide to be an ally or co-therapist for a relative with BDD, it will make sense for both of you to work through this book, and review it together as you progress. However, be aware that your relative may come to feel that you are over-involved with monitoring their homework or progress. If this happens, you will need to negotiate your degree of involvement.

If your relative is in therapy and you think they are not being honest with the therapist, it is usually possible to inform the therapist of your observations without the therapist breaching confidentiality. Ultimately, though, it's up to the person with BDD to do their homework and to be honest with their therapist about their difficulties. As their ally, you can gently remind them that having setbacks is part of overcoming BDD.

General guidelines for relatives

Know your enemy!

If you are a relative or a friend – or, especially, partner – of someone with BDD, get to know as much as you can about the condition (for example, by reading books like this), the common behaviors and the treatment. It's worth emphasizing three key points:

• However odd the behaviors may seem, they are just part of BDD. BDD is not a sign of madness – it's simply a disorder, of the kind that can affect many people at some stage in their life. BDD is not 'bad' behavior done to annoy you.

• If you have a relative or partner with BDD, it's still important to set consistent boundaries with behaviors that are unrelated to BDD, and to problem-solve BDD behavior where it impinges on your family life (e.g. the length of time the person spends in the bathroom when everyone is getting ready in the morning).

• BDD is not something that can be easily stopped. It will take time, commitment, and the right guidance to improve everyone's quality of life. Each person needs to overcome his or her problems at his or her own pace, and this may be a lengthy process. Avoid comparing your relative or friend with other individuals with (or, indeed, without) a mental health problem.

Avoid the blame game

No one should be blamed for BDD – it's not the fault of the person who has it, and nor is it your fault as a relative. Hence there is no need to feel guilty for 'causing' BDD, even if there is a possible genetic link. If you start blaming your genes then you can go all the way back to Adam and Eve!

Encourage your relative to seek help

Encourage your relative with BDD to try out the principles explained in this book, and to seek professional help with therapy or medication if they need it. Support them in either or both routes, and do everything you can to help them change. This means:

• helping them to understand and define their problems clearly
• if they want you to, being an ally as described above
• encouraging them to persist with their treatment, and
• praising improvement, however small.

Don't participate in BDD

Families should not try to adapt their ways of doing things to accommodate a relative's worries. Don't put family life on hold. Accept that BDD may complicate family life, but get on with it anyway, and encourage your relative to maintain as normal a lifestyle as possible:

• Don't take on their responsibilities (unless of course you are a parent of a child).

• Don't make excuses for them (e.g. about their being late for work or for an appointment).

• Don't collaborate in trying to find 'magic solutions', such as cutting details about cosmetic surgery out of the paper or offering to pay for surgery or provide a loan.

• If necessary, compromise in the short term in the way we have described, but draw the line when new avoidance behaviors and safety behaviors start.

If you have been participating in your relative's BDD up to now, start to find ways of changing this:

• If the person is in therapy, ask your relative if you can see the therapist with him or her and discuss a program of reducing your involvement in your relative's BDD.

• If the person is not in therapy, try to negotiate a program of gradual withdrawal from the person's safety and avoidance behavior before you implement it.

- Make sure that you communicate that you are changing your involvement in order to help rather than punish.
- Practise saying 'No' or 'No, thank you' to requests for reassurance or checking.
- Help your relative to see the downside of your participating in avoidance and safety behaviors and the effect on your relationship. Highlight how long the effect of the reassurance lasts for and what the effect is on their doubts.

Anticipate how you will deal with your relative becoming stressed or irritated by your new way of responding and have a plan that you can both agree upon if he or she becomes aggressive or angry. Where aggression is a problem, always ensure your own safety, if necessary by calling the police. You may have to be very persistent until requests for reassurance or rituals stop happening, because if you respond just once, it immediately becomes more likely that they will involve you again.

Remember:

• Individuals with BDD will not come to any harm as a result of anxiety, though they may be distressed in the short term.

• Accommodating rituals and avoidance means that you are helping to fuel BDD in the long term – and you are not taking care of yourself. It may feel as if you're protecting yourself from stress and helping someone with BDD, but the effect is the opposite.

What is good for the family is good for the person with BDD, and this can only occur when no one else engages in the BDD. A family that is all pulling together can provide better support for your relative with BDD. Its members can also better support each other and solve problems more efficiently.

Be a coach and cheerleader

You and your relative both need to see BDD, and not the individual experiencing it, as your shared enemy. Approach the problem as a team, working together. As your relative improves, see yourself as a coach shouting encouragement from the sidelines, or cheerleading, as you become less involved. Enthusiasm, understanding and general support are the best help you can provide.

Look after your own needs

Maintain your own interests and have your own sources of support. At times you may need time out (or respite care). When this happens, tell your relative that you need a break but have not given up on them, and try to get others to help.

- Feelings such as guilt, sadness or anger are normal in those caring for a relative with any long-term disability.
- Try not to engage in self-pitying thoughts such as 'Why me?' or 'Poor me, I don't deserve to have BDD in the family.' These will only make you feel worse and feed another vicious circle.
- Try to detach yourself emotionally from your relative's BDD and take it less personally.
- If you're not coping emotionally or it is affecting other areas of your life, seek help. There might be a local caregivers' group or, even better, a group for caregivers of individuals with BDD. Alternatively, see your family doctor for a referral or go directly to a therapist. You might also find it helpful to read our book *Manage Your Mood,* published by Robinson.

De-catastrophize anxiety and discomfort

We've met many family members who seem to believe that anxiety and discomfort should be avoided, and have even been critical of CBT because it requires the tolerance of discomfort. In some cases this is entirely understandable, given the profound distress that the individual with BDD, whom they care about, experiences as they wrestle with a doubt or intrusive thought.

Some families share 'rules' about emotions that can be *unhelpful* in overcoming BDD. For example:

- Emotions are a sign of weakness and should be controlled.
- If something upsets you, don't think about it.
- Being upset is terrible, and it's important to do something to make yourself feel better as soon as possible.
- If something bothers you, do something to take your mind off it.
- Be careful about showing that you feel upset to other people, or they might use it against you.

- If you get too upset it could make you ill, so it's best to avoid intense emotions.

These rules are unhelpful as they interfere in someone's ability to recover from BDD. They are sometimes explicitly taught; at other times they are taught by the way a family or person within that family behaves.

If you think you or your family share any rules like these, which might make experiencing emotions even harder, try to communicate to the person with BDD the message that you are confident that feeling short-term distress is a sensible and helpful thing to do when overcoming BDD.

Be prepared for setbacks

It's likely that on some days your relative will be better able to deal with symptoms than on others. It will be harder for both of you at certain times – for example, when either of you is feeling tired or stressed by other problems. Setbacks are to be expected, and to a certain extent can be planned for. Taking time out can be helpful at these points.

Each person with BDD will need to overcome their problems at their own pace, even though this may be a lengthy process. It's entirely normal to experience setbacks along the road to recovery. Don't lose heart. You can help by staying optimistic and encouraging them to keep trying. You probably won't see the hundred times that BDD doesn't get in the way, but you are bound to notice the time that it does!

Keep a sense of humour

People with BDD are often aware of the humorous aspects of their worries. BDD support groups are frequently filled with laughter, and many people are relieved at not having to take things too seriously. Such mirth can be used to help people with BDD distance themselves from the condition and their catastrophic thoughts. However, it is very important that friends and relatives resist any temptation to mock the person with BDD for their symptoms, as this may cause additional stress, shame and embarrassment.

Keep communicating

Make sure that you communicate, both with your relative who has BDD and with everyone else in your family.

• Remember that you may need help and support yourself.

• Make sure that you continue to do things you enjoy and have people to talk to about your own feelings and concerns.

• Eventually, you may decide that, for the sake of your own mental health, you can't carry on caring for your relative with BDD. In that case you'll need to communicate as a family and get help from the local services.

What if your relative has BDD but doesn't appear to want help from a mental health professional? This can be a very trying situation, as the following case study makes clear.

SARAH

One of us had a telephone call from Sarah. She told us that she and her husband were desperate for help for their daughter, who was now aged 23 and still living with them. She was quite attractive but had suffered from BDD since the age of about 12 but it had become worse when she was at college. She had dropped out of her degree course and now rarely went out. She had refused any help from her family doctor or local mental health services. She spent several hours a day in various checking rituals in the bathroom and skin-picking. She avoided going out unless it was late at night. She tended to neglect herself. Her sleep/wake cycle was reversed so that she would spend much of the night awake watching TV or using the Internet/computer. Their daughter did not accept that she had BDD and did not believe that she had a mental health problem that needed help; she would get a job and get on with her life when she felt she looked right.

Sarah and her husband understandably felt helpless and desperate in the face of their daughter's plight. They found some benefit in attending a support group for people with BDD, which gave them a welcome opportunity to get some support and stop blaming themselves. They began to realize that they couldn't take responsibility for their daughter's behavior. They also came to realize that their daughter's BDD was dominating their household and that they were talking about little else. They continued to encourage her to seek help and reduce her avoidance and rituals, but also began to try harder to talk to Sarah about things that weren't related to her BDD.

There is a significant minority of individuals with severe and chronic BDD who are hidden in the community. Many are cared for by ageing parents who become increasingly concerned at the effect BDD is having on their son or daughter. As professionals, we find this is one of the most difficult situations in which to help. We recognize the limited influence we have on someone with BDD. No one can make someone with BDD change.

We would normally recommend that Sarah tries to engage her daughter in therapy by asking for a home visit by a psychiatrist and subsequent visits by a qualified CBT therapist, who would focus on what Sarah's daughter really wants to do in life and her real values, which are being obscured by the BDD. If this were not possible, the therapist could try to engage her over the telephone. An exceptional mental health team with therapists familiar with BDD may provide this service. However, the success of any treatment will still depend on the cooperation of the person with BDD, and ultimately on their willingness to see a therapist and do the homework.

When you have an adult with chronic BDD in your home, it can be difficult to get them to accept help. The road ahead may be a long and hard one, and you'll need to look after yourself as well as your child. We offered some suggestions on how to do this in the 'General guidelines for relatives' earlier in this chapter.

What if a relative plays down the problem?

If your relative insists that BDD is having hardly any effect on their life, there are various things you can do to encourage them to face up to the problem and seek help.

Try to find out:

> • what their real feelings are about having such a problem (shame, for example, can make people very reluctant to acknowledge it; see Chapter 4 in this book)
> • what they fear and/or
> • what doubts they have about therapy or change.

Ensure that as a family, or if possible as a wider group, including friends, you take a consistent approach, and that nobody is accommodating the BDD. Agree upon your message, and if necessary talk to the individual both within the family (or wider) group and with a mental health professional.

One person in the group might draw up, along with the relative with BDD, a list of costs (or disadvantages) and benefits (advantages) of:

    1. staying the way they are, or
    2. engaging in a program of therapy.

A blank copy of the cost–benefit analysis form is included in Appendix 2. Each of the costs and benefits may be divided into those for the 'self' and those for 'others'. Even if your relative sees few disadvantages in staying the same, you can emphasize the costs of BDD to others in the family and the benefits to him or her self in the long term. Do go on emphasizing that you will still provide support and help during therapy. If your relative finally agrees to seek help, discuss the timeframe within which this can be done, and the process it will involve.

What if a relative refuses to seek help?

If your relative continues to refuse help and you decide that you cannot go on any longer with things the way they are, you will need to explore your own options, such as finding your relative independent living arrangements by getting help from your local mental health services.

Local mental health services do not always respond positively to requests for help for a relative with BDD who does not want help. The main priority for a psychiatrist in public health services is patients with 'severe mental illness', especially those who may be suicidal or a danger to the community. UK and US mental health law allows a patient to be detained in hospital against their will in certain circumstances; but in the absence of a risk to themselves or self-neglect, patients with BDD are unlikely to be admitted to a hospital and would, in any case, be unlikely to benefit much from admission to the average acute psychiatric ward. Short-term in-patient care in a national specialist unit where the staff are used to dealing with BDD patients and regular CBT is available, is more likely to be helpful. In others a trial of medication can be given against a person's will and this might be helpful to some people.

It must be emphasized, though, that CBT is powerless without the cooperation of a person with BDD. It is both unethical and counter-productive to forcibly expose someone to feared situations or activities. Therapists will encourage and challenge a patient, but would never force exposure or spring something on their patient unannounced. Nor should you ever do this to a relative with BDD. A program of CBT has to be followed voluntarily, and the motivation has to come from the patient, if it is to be ethical and effective.

Is anyone with BDD untreatable?

Many people who successfully overcome their BDD have made previous unsuccessful attempts, and some have even been diagnosed as 'untreatable'. This book is not the place to discuss the practical and ethical aspects of deciding under what circumstances a person should be considered unable to recover from BDD. What is clear, however, is that many people with BDD (and some less well-informed healthcare practitioners) arrive at the 'untreatable' conclusion much too quickly. On the whole, the best advice you can give to your relative with BDD is to keep fighting to change the BDD, rather than fighting to change one's appearance and to hide from the world.

A very few individuals with BDD are beyond the skills of mental health professionals and the provisions of mental health law, and cannot be engaged in treatment. Such individuals often have values that have become idealized and central to the person's identity. Such values are more likely to be seen in those who cannot bear anxiety and strenuously avoid situations that may provoke any distress.

They feel that they must have a high degree of control so that everything has to be done their way and at a time and speed that suits them. In this case, as a relative, we would advise you to seek help for yourself from your family doctor. It's perfectly acceptable for your mental health, if you decide you can't carry on caring for your relative, to ask local services to find suitable independent living arrangements for them.

Remember: recovery from BDD is a process

When your relative is recovering, you might expect everything to go back to how it used to be. However, this may not be how it happens at all, and the family might need to go through various stages of adjustment. This is normal. Each person will adjust and recover at a different rate. You might want to see BDD as something that is 'over' or 'finished', but remember that setbacks are part of the process.

In summary, BDD can have a profound effect on the person with BDD and on the person or people who looks after them. However, though the situation may sometimes be difficult, it is never hopeless, and there is a lot that you can do as a team to help each other.

11

Overcoming compulsive skin-picking

Compulsive skin-picking refers to excessive scratching, picking, gouging, lancing, digging, rubbing or squeezing of normal skin or skin with minor surface irregularities. It's known by a variety of different names, such as 'pathological skin-picking' or 'psychogenic excoriation'. It can cause significant distress and disability and may lead to visible disfigurement and chronic infections.

Compulsive skin-picking (CSP) is a fairly common feature of body dysmorphic disorder (BDD). It is sometimes a symptom of obsessive compulsive disorder (OCD) – for example when there is a desire to get rid of contamination under the skin. It is also a feature of borderline personality disorder when it is a form of self-harm.

People who pick their skin usually have healthy skin or minimal acne. They target pimples, scabs, mosquito bites, 'large' pores, 'bumps', 'small black dots', 'white dots', 'ugly things', 'cysts' or apparent imperfections or dirt, pus or 'impurities' from under their skin. More often than not, individuals with CSP have healthy skin, or at least they had healthy skin until they picked. If you have CSP then you might be using your fingernails to pick, pinch or squeeze your skin. You might use utensils such as tweezers, needles, pins, razor blades, staple removers, or knives to pick. The damage caused by skin-picking ranges from red patches, swelling, blisters, denuded areas and crusts to cuts and scars.

Sites chosen for picking are those that you can reach with your hands. The face is the most frequent site for picking. Other popular areas include the back, neck, scalp, ears, chest, cuticles, hands, arms and legs. It may lead to marked scarring, infections and visible disfigurement on the skin. You are likely to avoid activities that involve letting others see damaged skin such as intimacy, sexual activity or sports. You might be trying to camouflage yourself with cosmetics, clothing or bandages to cover the damage on your skin. We understand that most people are extremely ashamed of their picking and don't want to do it. Some people become housebound or suicidal because of their picking.

Skin-picking tends to occur in the evenings and, for women, either pre-menstrually or during menstruation. The most common trigger is standing in front of a mirror or touching your skin when you are alone at home. Other triggers include a feeling of itchiness under your skin, or a sensation of something underneath the surface of the skin.

Physical complications of skin-picking can include bleeding, infections, ulcers, permanent discolouration, and scarring that is disfiguring. This in turn leads to further scabs or imperfections, which become a further target for skin-picking, creating a vicious circle. The complications can require dermatological treatment for which you should seek advice. If inflammation is a problem then dermatological treatment can help (e.g. hydrocortisone) or Eurax cream (hydrocortisone and crotamiton) and decrease the sensation of itching. Dry skin should be moisturized regularly (e.g. using Eucerin). Don't be ashamed to reveal you have a problem with picking – doctors are used to seeing such problems. If, for some reason, they do not seem to understand, you should think about seeing a different doctor.

In addition to skin-picking, people often have other repetitive behaviors such as nail-biting, hair-pulling (trichotillomania), lip-biting, knuckle-cracking, cheek-chewing or body-rocking. These are all habit disorders which can be treated in a similar way to skin-picking. Research into skin-picking is limited but the recommended treatment consists of a type of behavior therapy called self-monitoring and habit reversal, which we describe below.

QUESTIONNAIRE 11.1: UNDERSTANDING THE PROBLEM OF SKIN-PICKING

The first step in overcoming skin-picking is to have a good understanding of the problem.

1. How old I was when I first started skin-picking?

[Space left intentionally blank in the original book]

2. How old I was when skin-picking first became a problem?

[Space left intentionally blank in the original book]

3. What was happening at the time my skin-picking started (e.g. acne or a stressful event)?

[Space left intentionally blank in the original book]

4. Which areas of my body do I tend to pick?

[Space left intentionally blank in the original book]

5. What do I target for picking (e.g. pimples, scabs, mosquito bites, scars, healthy skin)? Has this varied over time?

[Space left intentionally blank in the original book]

6. What methods have I used to pick (e.g. fingers or fingernails, scratching, squeezing, razors, picking, digging or lancing with pins, tweezers)?

[Space left intentionally blank in the original book]

7. What are the typical times of day when I pick and how long does each episode last for?

[Space left intentionally blank in the original book]

8. Why do I want to stop picking now? Am I ready to stop?

[Space left intentionally blank in the original book]

If you are ambivalent about stopping, you might find it helpful to do a cost–benefit analysis? What are the costs and benefits of stopping? What are the costs and benefits of continuing to pick?

COST–BENEFIT ANALYSIS OF PICKING	
Costs – for you and other people. Consider short- and long-term costs.	**Benefits** – for you and other people. Consider short- and long-term benefits.

A blank version of this form can be found in Appendix 2, for further cost-benefit analyses.

The shame of skin-picking

Like many other sufferers, you might feel ashamed of your excessive skin-picking, thinking that you are odd or a freak, which is likely to make you quite secretive about it. Perhaps you even have a parent, friend, or partner who has already been quite critical of your skin-picking and this further increases your desire not to get caught. This can lead to a destructive cycle in which more of your attention gets focused upon hiding your skin-picking than on overcoming it. To help combat your shame, you need to begin by taking a self-accepting and compassionate attitude towards yourself for having the problem. No matter how alarmed someone else might be about your picking, remember that you are in good company and that it is a recognized problem. With calm determination, you can overcome skin-picking, especially if you can detach from unkind and critical thinking about having the problem.

Analysing your skin-picking problem

1. Triggers (or 'Antecedents')

This section asks you to describe in as much detail as possible the chain or sequence of events that lead up to picking. There are two types of triggers – the events immediately before you start picking and events that make the picking easier or harder to do.

a. Triggers before the pick

Two types of triggers usually occur before picking – those that are external (i.e. generated outside of you) or those that are internal (i.e. generated inside you). Examples of external triggers include different:

- Settings (e.g. being alone in front of your bathroom mirror, putting on make-up, driving, planning to go out socially and coming out of the shower, being up late at night on a computer).
- Implements (e.g. the presence of a mirror or a pair of tweezers).
- Visual triggers (e.g. 'looking in a mirror and seeing a scab').

Examples of internal triggers include:

- Emotional states. Any emotional state can be a trigger for picking or pulling but the most common are being bored, lonely, empty, hurt, or anxious.
- Tactile sensations (e.g. 'feeling a bump on your skin with your fingers' or 'feeling a tingling sensation on your skin').

- Physical sensations at the site (e.g. an itch, irritation, burning under your skin, or feeling greasy).
- Thoughts. A specific intrusive thought or rumination or image (e.g. 'my skin is dirty and disgusting and has pus under it, I have to get it out. Maybe the pus has been pushed inwards, or maybe it is just swelling up in preparation for a spot appearing but hasn't formed yet.')

We want you to describe in as much detail as possible the *chain or sequence of events* that lead up to your pick, e.g. 'I come home feeling tired, I start to think about my skin, I then feel for bumps with my fingers, I go to the bathroom and look for imperfections in the mirror. I see a mark' or 'I start doing my homework in my bedroom, I'm feeling bit bored, and I get a tingling sensation on my skin, I have a thought – that sensation means there is something that shouldn't be there and my hand goes up to my face'.

Describe in as much detail as possible your particular chain of events. There may be several different scenarios you need to describe. If so, continue on another sheet.

_____

_____

_____

_____

_____

_____

_____

How aware are you of the triggers before you start picking or during your actual picking? Is the picking done 'on auto-pilot' (where you have little awareness of what you are doing)? Or is it planned? Or is it a mixture of the two?

_____

_____

_____

_____

b. Triggers that make it easier or harder to pick

The next step is to identify the things that make it easier or harder for you to pick. Examples of external triggers are being with someone or not having a pair of tweezers.

Both of these make it harder to pick. However, having a drink might make it easier it to pick. Examples of internal triggers that make it easier include certain postures such as 'holding my hand near my face'. Thoughts that make picking easier include 'I deserve this pick'.

What makes your picking easier to do?
[Space left intentionally blank in the original book]
What makes your picking harder to do?
[Space left intentionally blank in the original book]

2. Picking behavior

Next, write down a detailed description of your actual picking in sequence. There are usually three different stages:

• In the preparatory stage, you might go to a specific place, find your implements, choose a site on the body, inspect or clean the skin excessively.
• In the second stage, you might pick the skin, squeeze it, gouge it, remove and examine it.

• The final stage usually involves getting rid of the skin and perhaps camouflaging it with cover-up sticks or using make-up.

Describe the sequence of what you do in as much as detail as possible.

_____
_____
_____
_____
_____
_____

3. Consequences – the effects of picking

What are the immediate consequences of your picking that provide a pay-off? For example, you might get a positive feeling of satisfaction from removing a scab; or it might be escape from bad feelings such as feeling lonely or bored or a physical sensation.

_____
_____
_____

What are the unintended consequences of your picking? Examples might include the physical damage, such as ulcers or scarring, or a deep sense of shame or criticism from others.

4. What leads you to finish picking?

Examples might include feeling ashamed (which could also act as a trigger for further picking) or because you become aware of the damage you are causing or you are feeling pain. Alternatively, you might finish because a relative interrupts or you have to leave for an appointment.

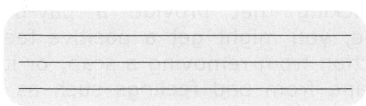

Taking steps to overcome your picking

Having done your analysis, you will now be able to choose the most appropriate steps to take and when to use them. We'll assume that you are 'ready' to change and you want to stop (or at least reduce how often you pick), rather than just wanting to stop feeling ashamed about your picking.

If you are not ready to change, then it won't work and you may need to talk through some of the benefits and costs of picking with a therapist first.

You may also need to test out your motivation to pick. For example, if you believe 'I must have smooth skin or I will be rejected', you can test this belief by seeing whether others do indeed respond to you differently on a day when you feel worse about your skin. You may find that they don't react to you any differently, or that you can cope with this belief differently.

Step 1: Self-monitoring

The first step towards overcoming compulsive skin-picking is self-monitoring. The rationale for self-monitoring is that:

SKIN-PICKING MONITORING FORM

DATE:

Date/Time	Duration: How long did you pick for?	Location: Where were you?	Activity: What were you doing before picking?	Strength of urge to pick on a scale of 0 to 10, where 0 is no urge	Degree of awareness of picking on a scale of 0 to 10, where 0 is no awareness	Notable feelings before you picked	Notable thoughts or images before you picked	Notable sensations before you picked (e.g. itching or burning)
1.								
2.								

• You increase your awareness of your picking so you are better able to resist the urge.

• You can build on the analysis you have already done and identify different chains of events so it is possible to predict when and where future episodes of picking will occur. Being more aware of the chain of events allows you to anticipate high-risk situations, and therefore to resist the urge to pick.

• You can monitor whether what you do to help yourself works or not by a change in how often you pick.

Try to complete the self-monitoring form overleaf while you are picking or immediately after the picking so it will be as accurate as possible. Do this for at least one or two weeks and keep a record of the number of times you picked each day. When it is frequent you might find it easier to count how often you pick by using a tally counter, which you can order from a website.

Step 2: Using habit reversal

You can train your mind to stop picking by using a method called habit reversal. First, you need to identify a 'competing response' that is incompatible with picking (for example, clenching your fist, squeezing a ball or sitting on your hand).

Whatever you choose:

- it should be incompatible with the habit
- it should be possible to maintain for a minute or more
- if you are with others you should be able to do it without behaving oddly
- it should not interfere with normal activities
- and lastly it should heighten your awareness that the picking is not occurring.

Practise the competing response at times of the day when you are not picking so that it becomes a habit. It should be held for at least a minute until an urge to pick has subsided. You should also practise the competing response in your imagination and several times a day when there is no urge to pick. In this way it will eventually become automatic and a part of your routine. It is often helpful to practise relaxing and breathing with your diaphragm when the picking urge occurs, before applying the competing response.

Now introduce the competing response as soon as you are aware of your urge to pick. If you start to pick, use the competing response to interrupt the picking or use it as soon as you have finished picking. If the urge persists, then the competing response should be repeated. When you get the urge, just notice the urge and any intrusive thoughts and feelings, without buying into them. Thank your mind for its contribution and quietly ignore it whilst you relax and use the competing response. When you successfully use the competing response instead of picking, give yourself a reward or treat. Make sure you give it to yourself immediately after successfully resisting an urge to pick.

Keep a record of your practice (see overleaf) and the number of times that you use the competing response on the habit reversal form below. Note whether you used the competing response before, during or after an episode of picking. You can also use the form to keep a record of the number of times you practised the competing response when there was no urge to pick.

You should have identified a typical chain of events in your analysis. Although the goal is to use the competing response before the chain begins, you may have to start by introducing the competing response near the end of the chain. With practice, you will be able to add the competing response earlier and earlier in the chain so that it eventually replaces the picking.

It is worth emphasizing that the success of the technique cannot at first be measured in terms of reducing how often you pick but whether you are using the competing response at all (even if you use it after you pick). This is important, as many people will otherwise give up too early.

Step 3: Making it less likely that you will pick

There are various things you can do to help you relax in the high-risk situations that you identified in your monitoring chart. You could use meditation or exercise, take a warm bath, or use muscle relaxation or diaphragmatic breathing. Have an action plan ready with a list of the activities you can do when you get the urge – for example, do some exercise, make a phone call, bake a cake. Try to distract yourself when the urge occurs (e.g. have a bath or shower (possibly a cold shower); apply an ice pack, especially if you have an itching or burning sensation on your skin; or put on a facial mask).

Some people have found that it is easier to resist the urge to pick by wearing gloves; using artificial (acrylic) nails over their real nails; or cutting their fingernails short. These strategies may also enhance awareness training as they alter the sensations on the skin. Try posting 'High risk area' signs at the door of the bathroom and other areas associated with picking.

HABIT REVERSAL FORM						
Site: Where did you pick?	What effect did picking have on your feelings?	What effect did picking have on your thoughts?	What effect did picking have on your sensations?	How strong was your effort to resist picking on a scale of 0 to 10, where 0 is no effort at all	What did you do to try to resist picking?	
1.						
2.						

There are various strategies that can help block the habit by decreasing the opportunity to pick, for example agreeing not to touch your skin unless it is for an agreed activity; wearing bandages on the fingers used for picking; wearing white cotton dermatological gloves in bed or other high-risk areas; keeping your nails trimmed and smooth. Some people have enlarged a photo of the area of picking, taken at its worst, and kept it by the most common locations for picking.

Others have used a reminder of all the un-intended consequences of picking, which you can easily read in locations where you are likely to pick.

Step 4: Disrupt your triggers to pick

Try to disrupt the chain of events in your daily routines that lead to picking. This might mean altering the settings in which you pick to disrupt your opportunity to pick and reducing the time spent in high-risk areas. For example, you could:

- remove or temporarily cover mirrors (especially magnifying mirrors) or bright lights
- wear dark or tinted glasses when around mirrors
- remove any glasses or contact lenses before looking in a mirror

• give the equipment you use for picking to a significant other or throw it away

• switch grooming and applying make-up to times of the day when they are less risky

• stay out of certain high-risk area rooms or find an alternative

• tell a significant other(s) about your picking and allow them to point it out when you pick

• reduce time spent alone and use a different routine

• use plasters and petroleum jelly or antibiotic ointment on scabs and skin to aid healing

Step 5: Stimulate or distract yourself

It may also be necessary to replace or increase stimulation in your fingers in high-risk situations. This can include activities such as knitting, crocheting, embroidery, sewing; playing a musical instrument (or taking lessons); stroking or massaging a pet; playing with Silly Putty or squeezy balls; popping the bubbles on bubble-wrap; playing with worry beads; playing a video game that requires the use of both hands on a controller; nibbling food (e.g.

sunflower seeds); or taking a facial steam bath (to provide a feeling that impurities are being removed from your face).

Step 6: Penalties

You might be able to decrease the likelihood of picking by the use of a penalty. This should be used as a last resort but, if you do, use it immediately after picking. You could, for instance, donate a set amount of money each time you pick to your most hated organization. This is an under-researched strategy so we would be interested to hear of your outcome.

Step 7: Exposure to triggers

When you are ready, and have managed to stop picking for a few months, try re-exposing yourself to those situations that are associated with picking. You should begin with low-risk situations for short periods of time (e.g. up to 5 minutes). You can then gradually increase the time and location, eventually reaching high-risk situations. Continue to resist the urge to pick, and try to visualize your desired outcome instead of picking.

SHARON

Sharon is 29 years old. She usually picks her skin in the bathroom mirror at night when her boyfriend is asleep and she has privacy, or when she has just come home and checks her skin when she feels feel dirty and tired. This is more likely to occur if she feels anxious, bored, brooding, hurt or frustrated. When she sees or a feels a spot or blemish, immediately she will squeeze it and it will lead her to check and squeeze the rest of her face. Sometimes she will feel a scab in the morning in bed and mindlessly pick it, even if it has not healed. Touching and looking at scabs often will lead her to pick it off before it is healed (which then leaves a scar and a further bout of squeezing and scabs). Physical sensations such as feeling greasy or throbbing will also make her more likely to pick. Her picking might also start while feeling her face for small imperfections which is done automatically with no intention of picking. The problem becomes more voluntary if she happens to find a blemish. She then becomes like a shark smelling blood, something else takes over and she feels she cannot stop.

She will not squeeze in front of others (apart from very superficial squeezing in front of a family member). The absence of tweezers will probably help for the rare occasions that she might use them. The absence of mirrors or hand compact and bright lighting helps her not to pick. If it is hot and humid and she feels sweaty, then she feels her skin gets spottier and so her urge to squeeze it increases. She then thinks her skin is greasy and pus is gathering under the skin and her skin is getting out of control. If she aimlessly puts her fingers over her skin, that encourages picking. If she has scars forming, then she tells herself that she will allow herself to just pick at one spot, as if to appease her craving. Unfortunately this always triggers further picking. Very occasionally if she has resisted the urge to pick then she thinks she can reward herself and release the tension and allow herself to squeeze. Initially it feels like a relief, but it is short lived as this prompts further picking and she then feels deflated and angry with herself.

When she does pick she just squeezes it with her fingernails. Usually she will squeeze it a bit more than necessary to ensure everything is out. If it is deep down, sometimes she will scratch off the first layer of skin with her nails and then squeeze it, so it has a way of being expelled rather than sinking deeper. If the pus will not come out, sometimes she makes it worse when she really scratches at her skin till it bleeds and she presses the flesh together to squeeze it in a very violent way. Sometimes she will use tweezers to pluck the flesh and hairs away. The amount of stuff becomes insignificant and laughable when she see how little it is, but she feels satisfied as it is no longer feels under her skin. If it has been an insignificant picking session that hasn't caused much damage, she will usually just splash her face with cold water and cover up the spots with make-up and go to sleep (so that her boyfriend will not be able to see her spots in the darkness.) But if she has caused a lot of damage to her face, usually she will have to wash her face, and apply make-up for hours, in between holding a tissue or cloth to her wounds to soak up the fluid. She has to stop the fluid flowing so that she can apply the make-up powder in a way that it sticks.

The immediate pay off is a sense of satisfaction if she has squeezed a lot of pus out, especially if it is a 'problem spot' which means one she has been trying to expel the pus from for a while but been unable to. Very occasionally if the squeezing is straightforward and not messy, and hasn't left any significant damage or red marks, she feel extremely proud of herself that she has managed to clean up her face without losing control and hurting herself.

However, the long-term consequence is shame and anger against herself. This just triggers her to pick more. Ultimately what usually stops her is when she is feeling out of control in her picking and there is nothing more to squeeze, making her face an absolute mess. In these cases it is not shame or realization of damage that stops her. It is simply impossible to squeeze anything else out.

Sharon found the functional analysis helpful in making sense of her compulsive skin-picking. The act of self-monitoring started to make her more aware of her picking and times of vulnerability and how her picking became a self-perpetuating cycle. She found it particularly helpful to identify frequent chains of events that inevitably resulted in skin-picking. Having identified the chain of events, she found it important to talk to her boyfriend and get his support in encouraging her to go to bed earlier. She would also talk a friend on the telephone or have a cold shower in order to disrupt the chain of events when she came home and felt vulnerable. She found it helpful to have a Turkish bath at a gym so she felt that impurities were being re-

moved. Of course it was not all plain sailing and there were frequent setbacks. However, she practised habit reversal as soon as she was aware that the chain had begun. At first she practised clenching her fist after she had picked and in situations which did not lead to picking. She then gradually managed to increase awareness of her actions and to implement habit reversal at an earlier stage, so that eventually she was able to use it before she picked. Her skin improved and she had help to reduce her self-consciousness learning not to engage with her intrusive thoughts and images.

12

Special problems of disfigurement

This chapter is written for people with disfigurements. If you have body dysmorphic disorder (BDD) or an eating disorder and are preoccupied by a minor defect in your appearance you may be interested to know how people with severe disfigurements cope with an unusual appearance. This is something that health professionals have found interesting too. You may assume that someone with very severe burns scarring is going to find life more problematic than someone with, say, minor scarring from acne – but in fact this is by no means inevitable, as shown by the following case studies. Someone with BDD might find it helpful to assume, temporarily, that the 'flaw' in their appearance *is* as bad as they think it is, and then follow the advice outlined in this chapter.

GERALDINE AND LOUISE

Geraldine has very severe burn scarring caused by a house fire. The scarring is visible all over her body. One of the practical problems she has is keeping cool in the summer, since she cannot lose heat though her skin by sweating. The easiest thing is to swim. She does so several times a day when it is very hot. She knows that people notice her scarring and sometimes ask about it. She has therefore developed some good answers to questions, which give a minimum of information but satisfy other people's curiosity. 'I know I am unusual, and I understand that people are curious, but I don't intend to tell them my life story'. Geraldine is confident, successful and good fun to be with. She has a partner and her appearance is not a barrier to living a full life.

Louise has very minor scarring on her face following a car accident. She is very aware of it, but it is hardly noticeable to other people. She manages this by wearing a baseball cap pulled down low so that no one can see her face, and she avoids eye contact or speaking to other people. She has stopped working and any kind of social activity and does not go out. Her life has changed dramatically and her mood is low. She is very pessimistic and feels that her chances of a happy life are now over. She is not unusual in feeling devastated by a relatively minor change, and what makes this worse for her is the well-meaning rela-

tives and friends who tell her that she is making a fuss about nothing and that, compared with other people, there is nothing really wrong with her.

Even though Geraldine rates her condition as far more noticeable than Louise, she is less preoccupied by it. The target of treatment for Louise will be to reduce her level of preoccupation and worry; Geraldine, of course, does not need any treatment!

Many people with very obvious disfigurements live totally normal lives – so what is it that makes concerns about appearance such a problem for some people and not for others? Why is Geraldine able to manage, whilst Louise is finding life so hard?

The answer has a lot to do with the value we place on appearance. In the diagram below, a circle has been divided up to represent the importance of different aspects of her life to Geraldine's identity.

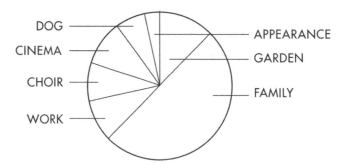

In Geraldine's pie chart (above), appearance occupies quite a small 'slice' of the pie. Most people are concerned about fitting in with their peer group and not standing out in a negative way. For teenagers, this slice might be larger or, for very fashion-conscious girls, part of this slice might be about being slim. But there are lots of other slices too. More important, to Geraldine, are 'my family' and 'my garden'. 'Work' is a slice, 'cinema ' and 'choir' are additional slices, and so on.

For some people, the 'appearance slice' can take over the whole circle. The preoccupation with a particular feature and the search for a means of changing it become more important than anything else in their life. Before treatment, Louise's pie chart looked like this. She felt very self-conscious and unable to cope with the idea that people would notice her face. Her self-esteem had sunk very low. After treatment, her preoccupation with her appearance was much reduced, she was able to go out and her social life started to take up more space in the circle again.

Psychological treatments aim to help people manage their concerns about their appearance and gradually shrink their appearance 'slice' back down to a small or moderate level of importance. Self-esteem and self-confidence depend on far more than what you look like. We all like to feel that other people think about us in a positive way. Although we may believe (and the media encourage us to believe) that appearance has a lot to do with this, our behavior and personality are actually far more important in how we are regarded by other people. One of the most attractive things about other people, and something that makes you feel good about yourself, is being comfortable in social situations and able to demonstrate an interest in other people rather than yourself. People who we know cope well with a visible difference or a disfigurement tend to be those with very good social skills.

In this chapter, we look at the particular challenges faced by someone who has an obvious facial difference, together with some practical ways of meeting these challenges. Even if you do not consider yourself to have a facial difference, it is worth reading this section and using some of these skills and strategies yourself. They will help you to focus 'out' on what is happening in social situations, rather than focusing 'in' and becoming preoccupied with what people are thinking about you. This is the key to becoming more comfortable with other people and gradually building your self-esteem.

Causes of visible difference

Visible difference is more common than we think. Severe burn injuries, accidents and traumas, such as dog bites, account for some changes in the way people look. Skin conditions, cancer and other diseases account for others. Thyroid gland problems can have an impact on the appearance of your eyes, and rheumatic diseases can change the appearance of your joints, particularly in the fingers. Steroid medication can alter the shape of your face and body; chemotherapy can cause hair loss. Surgery to remove cancer can leave scars. There are therefore many people who experience visible changes in their appearance related to accident or illness.

A second group of people are those who are born with a visible difference. This includes conditions such as cleft lip and palate, birthmarks such as port wine stains and other craniofacial syndromes which affect the way in which the bones of the skull are fused together and therefore the appearance of the face. Research has demonstrated many similarities between all these groups in terms of the kinds of challenges they face in day-to-day life. We therefore treat any problems that arise in the same way.

The problems of visible difference

Staring

Staring by others is commonly reported. The human brain is hard-wired to take note of anything that is unusual or outside our experience. You may have noticed babies and children constantly gazing at objects and people, as they build up a picture of the world. This curiosity never leaves us – we can learn some social skills that prevent us from staring at others, but most of us will notice, or do a 'double-take', when we see someone who looks unusual. It is important to note that this is a response stimulated by curiosity. But it can feel like a problem if it is accompanied by comments, questions or a whispered aside to a companion.

However, some people feel they are being stared at, when the problem is more to do with being excessively self-conscious and worrying about what others are thinking. You may only be sure that people are staring, for example, if it is confirmed by someone else who is with you, or the person staring is asking questions or pointing at you.

Questions

Questions are common. Curiosity is often followed by the impulse to ask more. 'I hope you don't mind me asking – but what happened to you?' There are not many people with a visible difference who are not familiar with this response from other people. Choosing how to answer this question is important in determining whether the encounter is going to be a positive one.

Comments

Comments, either directly to you or about you to others, are often infuriating, even if kindly meant. 'I think you are so brave, dear' is designed to be reassuring, but can feel patronizing and unhelpful. 'People like you should stay at home' tells you far more about the ignorance of the person who makes the comment than the person it is made about, but can still be experienced as hurtful and aggressive.

Loss of anonymity

Many of us underestimate the luxury of being able to walk down a crowded street and know that no one is taking any notice of us. The sense that we stand out, that others notice us or pay us special attention, can be uncomfortable. Indeed, people whose faces are well known, who have become celebrities, often complain about this kind of intrusion. Attention does not have to be negative to impact in a negative way – it simply needs to be unsolicited, or outside your control. The fear of standing out, of people looking at us, is extremely common in all kinds of body image disorders and can lead us to make un-helpful choices in how we respond. The easiest thing is avoidance. If you stay at home or avoid crowded places, then this apparently solves the problem – except, as we have seen elsewhere in this book, it is important to confront fears, by learning the skills that allow us to stay in situations we find difficult. By doing so, we become able to do everything that anyone else can, without constantly worrying about whether people are looking at us or what they think.

For many people with body image concerns, it is the fear of standing out, of looking unusual or 'ugly', that preoccupies them and prevents them participating fully in social activities. For someone with a visible disfigurement, the fear that someone will notice is often a reality. People *do* notice, they are curious and they do ask questions. But this is manageable. In treating people with a visible difference, we work on the basis that intrusions will definitely happen so we are going to learn how to manage them – from dealing with staring to answering questions in different ways. Mastering these skills is not difficult – in fact they are useful life skills for anyone to develop. For most people with body image problems, working out how you would deal with the thing you fear most is far better than simply dreading it happening and avoiding other people in case it does. This might mean practising a role-play with a friend so you will know how to cope with questions or comments.

Interpreting the world around you

Before we go on to think about managing an unusual appearance, it is worth considering some key pieces of research that tell us more about how the way in which how you think, your beliefs or expectations, colour the way in which you interpret what happens around you.

In the 1980s, psychologists interested in social research used make-up to mimic different kinds of visible difference including port wine stains (purple marks) on the face and facial scarring. They were interested in measuring the experience that people who had these conditions were reporting. The participants in these experiments were asked to report back on how it felt to stand out in a crowd – and they reported many experiences of discomfort, staring by others and generally feeling conspicuous. This seemed to support what people with a visible difference had been telling us. However, half this experimental group did not in fact appear disfigured at all. Before sending them out to gather data, the researchers had removed the make-up with a solvent, whilst pretending that they were 'fixing it' or setting it so that it would not rub off. These groups reported just the same experience of intrusion, and staring from others as the group who really did look different.

How can we make sense of this? The best explanation is that we tend to see what we expect to see. So if we go into a situation with a preconceived idea of what is going to happen, it is very easy to interpret what happens in line with this. There is another explanation. It could be that when we expect a hostile or intrusive response from others, we change our behavior, and it is this altered behavior that attracts people's attention. For example, we avoid eye contact, walk with our head down, pull a baseball cap low over our head – all patterns of behavior that are very understandable when we feel conspicuous, but which have the opposite effect from that intended; they attract rather than reduce attention. Whilst both of these theories explain what the researchers discovered, they are not mutually exclusive – in other words the finding might be due to a little of both.

The psychologist Professor Nichola Rumsey was very interested in the second explanation – the idea that people change their behavior when they have visible differences. She continued to carry out research into this 'behavioral' explanation for the problem of facial difference. She was intrigued, partly because she had observed 'avoidant' behavior in people who had problems managing facial difference, but also because she believed that social skills training (learning to behave differently in social situations) might be a way of teaching people skills that they could use to cope more positively. By chance, she met James Partridge who had set up a charity helping people with facial disfigurements, following his experience in managing his own burn injury. They discovered that they had come to the same conclusions from their completely different backgrounds in the subject. Good social skills could profoundly alter and improve the experience of facial difference. The charity Changing Faces (see Appendix 1) then developed this social skills idea further, whilst Professor Rumsey evaluated their findings and demonstrated that their ideas really worked.

Managing facial difference using cognitive behavioral therapy (CBT)

As you have seen in this book, CBT is a means of changing the way you think about a problem and how you actually behave. Psychologists working in this field have developed the CBT approach to include social skills training, and have shown that this is the most effective way to help people who do not cope very confidently with a visible difference. The aim is to teach people to manage as effectively as those for whom having a visible difference is not a barrier to achieving all that they want to. Changing Faces has made a huge contribution to the development, evaluation and publicizing of these approaches, and the following section draws on their work.

Identifying and challenging unhelpful beliefs

We have seen that certain kinds of 'thinking styles ' or unhelpful patterns of thinking can become automatic (see Chapters 4 and 6). Many people, particularly if their appearance changes suddenly, can 'write themselves off' and convince themselves that they no longer have the opportunities that the rest of us may have.

'All-or-nothing' thinking often lies behind this.

Examples include:

> 'No one is going to employ someone who looks like this'

> 'I am never going to get a girlfriend looking the way that I do'

> 'None of my friends will want to know me any more'

> 'How can I take the children to school when I look like this?'

These are all real examples of all-or-nothing thinking that can lead to people writing themselves off.

One way of reducing the harm that these negative thoughts can cause is by keeping a record of them on paper. You can then distance yourself from such thoughts and not engage with them (see Chapter 6). You can also examine the evidence for each belief and see if there is an alternative. For example, for the belief 'No one is going to employ someone who looks like this', is it true to say that no one would employ someone with a visible difference? Clearly not. Many people with an unusual appearance have jobs just like anyone else. So an alternative belief might be:

'Most employers are looking for someone with good skills and experience who is prepared to work hard and who is reliable.'

Similarly, the belief 'I am never going to get a girlfriend' is about partnerships. Many people with a visible difference are married or in happy long-term relationships with others. So a more realistic belief might be:

'Happy relationships are based on who you are and not what you look like.'

The belief 'None of my friends will want to know me any more' can be challenged with the alternative belief:

'Good friends enjoy being with me because they have a good time – not because of how I look.'

Finally, children are far less interested in appearances than adults are. Given a good explanation, and provided they see that you are coping well with your altered appearance, they will cope well too.

Note that these alternatives avoid the 'all-or-nothing' patterns that are typical of the unhelpful beliefs. We are not challenging the idea that finding a partner or a job may sometimes be harder – we live in a very appearance-conscious society where some people may make judgements that are overly dependent on appearance. But it is not true that all or even most people think in this way.

Remember the example we gave earlier with the make-up experiments, of how anticipating a problem can become a self-fulfilling prophecy? This is very true when it comes to finding a job or developing a relationship. If you write yourself off before you get there, this will come across in the interview. If you appear confident and self-assured, this will act in your favour. It is very tempting to blame lack of success on appearance. But the reason you do not get a job is equally likely to be because there was a better candidate with more experience. The reason someone does not want to go out with you may equally be because you do not share the same interests or think very differently about important issues.

Another very common example of all-or-nothing thinking is the belief:

'Everybody's staring at me!'

(This is so common in fact, that the charity Changing Faces has produced a booklet with this title.) Again, a cognitive behavior therapist would examine the evidence for holding this belief. One way of doing this is to design a 'behavioral experiment'.

GEORGE

George, who was anxious about being stared at, conducted the following behavioral experiment: he decided to count how many people he passed on the way to his office from the train station. He also kept a note of how many people stared hard in his direction.

How many people I expect to stare	Most of them – 90 per cent
How many people did I pass?	About 100
How many people stared?	1 – i.e.1 per cent

George noted that he had passed about 100 people and only one person had stared at him. So he was easily able to challenge his all-or-nothing thinking. In fact, 99% of people took no notice of him. (There was a nice bonus to this experiment; the person who had been staring hard at him finally came up and asked him directions. So, far from being identified in a negative way, George had been identified in a positive way as someone who looked friendly and helpful).

Other common types of thinking errors that characterize people with appearance-related concerns are described below.

Personalization

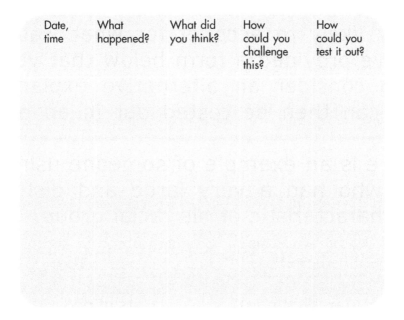

This is the tendency to think that every mention of appearance is somehow stimulated by seeing you. For example, if someone comments that someone else is looking fatter, has let themselves go, should get a haircut – or anything similar, you may think:

'They are really thinking that I should do something about my appearance.'

'*It is really my nose that is making them think about another person's appearance.*'

Again, you can challenge these thoughts by looking for evidence to support them, and then find an alternative explanation that is equally likely to account for what was said. We have provided a form below that you can use to consider an alternative explanation, which can then be tested out in an experiment.

Here is an example of someone using this form, who had a very large and distinctive nose characteristic of his racial group.

Date, time	What happened?	What did you think?	How could you challenge this?	How could you test it out?
Saturday, 8.00pm	I was sitting with friends in the pub and they started talking about a program they had seen on TV about plastic surgery.	It is because they have noticed my nose – it has reminded them...	Lots of people are interested in plastic surgery. They may be thinking about surgery themselves. I could say:	'I thought it was interesting too. Would you ever think about surgery?'

When he asked this question, his friend responded by telling him about his sister who had recently had a breast reduction operation. He was then able to reduce the strength of his belief that it was his appearance that had triggered the conversation

Are you making the most of your appearance?

Before considering behavior and how to change it, it is worth making a particular point about appearance. We have talked about 'write-off thinking' above. However, one common mistake people can make is to think that, because they have a visible difference, it is not worth bothering with other aspects of their appearance. This could not be further from the truth! If you give other people a strong message that you have given up on yourself, why should they be interested in you?

So – you *do* need to have your hair cut or styled regularly. You *do* need to dress in a way that is appropriate for your lifestyle. Wearing appropriate clothes, looking tidy and ensuring that you do not have food spilt all down you is important. Your personal hygiene should be good. Making an effort to fit in with your peer group will help people to see you for who you are and not as an outsider. In this context, it is important to note that sometimes clothes or make-up designed to disguise a feature can have the opposite effect. Baseball hats are particularly unhelpful and we work hard with our patients to get rid of them. In the UK, people associate them with aggressive behavior and you can easily make yourself look threatening, especially if wearing them is combined with poor eye contact. (It usually is – reducing eye contact is why people wear them!) Look back at the example of Eileen in Chapter 9. Similarly, wearing very large jackets in the summer can draw attention, rather than disguise problems, and unskilled use of camouflage creams can make a facial disfigurement more, rather than less, obvious.

Catastrophizing

This is a common pattern that people fall into. So, having noticed someone glance your way, the negative automatic thoughts follow this sort of course:

'Oh no, I hope she doesn't notice my face. She is thinking how awful I look and wondering how she can get away from me. She is just like everyone else. What's the use of coming to places like this, it always ends up the same way. I will never fit in; I will never have any friends or be able to enjoy my life. What's the point of living like this?'

You can see that the first automatic thought has triggered a whole spiral of further negatives so that just the thought of being noticed has led to the feeling that life is not worth living. You may then start you to brood, as described in Chapter 4. This catastrophic outcome has evolved in six steps from the simple question of whether or not someone has looked your way! This is also an example of writing negative scripts for other people based on no evidence. In fact when we do some behavioral experiments, we often find that people have not noticed anything unusual. They may find it hard to describe the person who believes their appearance to be so distinctive. Or, they may express surprise that the person is so worried by it, because it makes no difference to the judgments they make about them. It is therefore really important to stop yourself and challenge the automatic thought at the start, before you allow these unhelpful beliefs to depress your mood and change your behavior.

Developing a positive approach to visible difference

Social skills are a good place to start. We talked about making the most of your appearance earlier. Go through your wardrobe and check anything that needs either washing or mending. You do not have to always wear black. One of the things we encourage people to do as they become more confident is to wear clothes that are more colourful and help to challenge the idea that you are trying to hide. How do you style your hair? It can be tempting to wear a long fringe or to try to drape your hair over your face to cover a facial condition, but keeping this in place means walking with your head down. Like hats, this is less helpful than it might seem. If you have a disfiguring condition elsewhere on your body, then wearing long sleeves and high necks can be automatic, but you can become dependent on them.

VERONICA

Veronica, who had a skin condition called vitiligo, developed patches on her skin that lacked pigment. She always used make-up to camouflage her skin. Veronica was worried that she would get constant questions from other people. As her skin condition progressed, she got fed up with the time it was taking to put on the make-up. She decided to try going out with her face bare. To her surprise, although people glanced her way, they really took very little notice of her. She decided that she would wear her make-up some but not all of the time. Now, if she is going to work, or if she is dressing up to go somewhere special, she wears it. But if she is home with her family or with friends she knows well, she does not bother.

This example illustrates the kind of cognitive errors that we described earlier. The belief that 'everyone will notice and ask me questions' and 'everyone will think the marks on my skin are ugly' were successfully overcome by putting them to the test.

Posture

How you stand is important. If you tend to look down and away from people, your behavior is not open and inviting. (Think how difficult it is to communicate with someone who wears dark glasses.) Try to make a conscious effort to stand upright and look straight ahead.

Smiling

You will be amazed at the difference it makes when you look at other people and smile. This gives a positive message instantly! Sometimes when people have a facial condition making their face move either asymmetrically (more on one side than the other) or, for some people without a facial nerve, not at all, they are unable to smile or try to avoid it. Using other forms of communication – commenting on the situation or using touch – can provide alternative ways of signalling pleasure. For those of us who can smile, responding to others in this way, on the bus, in a queue, in the street, gives a very different message from hurrying past, head down.

Eye contact

Eye contact is the basis of communication. We use it to signal interest, that we are listening, and whose turn it is to speak in a conversation. Trying to avoid other people's gaze will always come across as negative, giving a clear signal that you do not want to engage in any kind of contact with them. It is very easy to misinterpret other people's gaze as intrusive – staring at a feature you dislike – when in fact people are simply trying to talk to you. There are lots of good books and information about improving social skills. For instance, Changing Faces (see Appendix 1) publish information and run workshops where you can practise developing your non-verbal communication skills.

Developing verbal skills – learning to have a conversation

People often describe the fear of going blank in social settings – being unable to think of what to say. This is more likely to happen when you are focused 'in' on your own appearance and how people are responding to you, rather than listening and involved in what people are saying. Anxiety tends to heighten the temptation to 'self-monitor' so it can be doubly hard to relax and really focus on what is going on around you, rather than other people's reactions to you. (See Chapter 6 for some strategies to help you overcome problems with inattention.)

It can also be hard to get going again if you have been avoiding social situations because of concerns about staring or questions. (This is another reason to avoid withdrawing from others. It is much harder to pick up your social life again if you have let it stop completely rather than to keep it going, even if it's at a slower pace).

Developing verbal skills is mainly a matter of practice but there are some simple things that will help. First, it is helpful to listen. What do other people talk about in different settings? The easiest place to start is at work or in a situation where you have lots in common with the other people there, or are with a group of people that you know well. You might have friends in common and can ask how they are. You might have a job in common and can ask about that. Asking people about themselves is a very good way to get a conversation started.

So asking if people live nearby, what they do for a living, whether their children go to the local school and similar questions are all ways of initiating a conversation. Similarly, topical subjects are things that other people will have a view about. The result of the latest big football match, the election, the price of petrol, or news headlines are all good places to start.

It can be a good idea to identify something about the other person that you can use as a question if there is a pause in the conversation. So, you might notice that someone is wearing a particular piece of jewellery or an interesting tie. T-shirts often have slogans or flags or something you can comment about. If someone looks tanned you can ask if they have been on holiday. (Note that, in this context, it is not surprising that people ask about your appearance if it is something that stands out – it is something about you that is unusual and therefore an ideal way of getting you to talk about yourself. Other people are simply using the same tactic as you are using yourself.)

Role-play exercises

Practising with a friend is good way to build your skills and confidence. Try these role-play exercises:

1. You are arriving at a crowded party. You can't see anyone you know. Another chap is standing on his own, looking as if he does not recognize anyone. He is wearing an Arsenal football shirt. Ask your friend to play this role. Now you go over and start a conversation with him.

2. Imagine that you have broken down miles from anywhere. You phone the AA, but the mechanic can't mend your car. He calls for assistance and decides to wait with you. What can you talk to him about? (There is a good chance that he is interested in cars!) Ask your friend to role-play the AA man, and see how long you can sustain the conversation.

Answering questions about your appearance

We have already seen that questions from others are likely, but are related to curiosity and not a negative judgement about you. However, it is important that you do not feel trapped into giving away more information than feels comfortable. You do not have to 'tell 'your story' to other people unless you want to. We would advise you to develop three different ways of answering questions about your appearance.

First, think about answering the question:

Q: *'What happened to your face?'*

A: *'I was in a house fire. It started at 2.00 in the morning and the first thing I remember is waking up and all the heat and the noise. My mother ran into the room...*

This kind of answer is the full, detailed and often lengthy one. It is best reserved for the medical team who have been involved in your care and those very close to you when relevant. However, interestingly, for people who worry about answering questions about their appearance, it is often the only one they ever use – with the result that they feel conspicuous and as if their private life is an open book to anyone who wants to know. Not surprisingly, they dread that opening line 'I hope you don't mind me asking, but...'

The second answer is the complete opposite. It is a simple response which closes down the questioning firmly, whilst giving little or no detail.

Q: *'What happened to your face?'*

A: *'That's a long story. I'll tell you about it sometime.'*

Or

    A: *'It was years ago – you don't want to hear all about that.'*

Together with firm eye contact and a smile, both these answers work superbly at turning off the questioning. They are particularly effective if you then switch the attention to the questioner, for example:

    Q: *'What happened to your face?'*

    A: *'That's a long story. I'll tell you about it sometime. I hear you've just come back from America. How long were you there?'*

The third way of answering the question is to give a more general response – about your condition rather than about you. For example:

    Q: *'What happened to your face?'*

    A: *'I was injured in a fire. Luckily, now that smoke alarms are available, injuries like mine are far less common.'*

It is a really useful exercise to write down some of these alternative answers and personalize them so that they apply to you. Then practise, and see how much more in control of the situation you feel. There are no right or wrong answers, although some answers tend to invite more questioning. For example, look at these answers to the question:

Q: *'Why are you wearing that scarf on your head?'*

A: *'I have my reasons!'*

Or

A: *'I've had a small operation and I am keeping the stitches covered.'*

The first answer invites all kinds of speculation about what is under the scarf. The second answer gives a very simple explanation. Any further questioning can be managed with the 'turn off the questions' approach above.

Answering children's questions is very straightforward. They say exactly what they think, but they are equally happy with a simple explanation.

Q: *'Why have you got a funny arm?'*

A: *It's because I was burned in a fire. So don't play with matches, will you?'*

Sometimes humour can be helpful.

Tom, who is in his early twenties, was recently asked how he had lost a finger. To which he responded: 'it wouldn't fit up my nose so I cut it off!'.

This is a great reply! It made the questioner laugh, gave nothing away and made Tom feel comfortable and in control. You will find as you develop your own answers, that there will be certain favourites that you use again and again, and then some new ideas that you add in. The aim is to have them at the tip of your tongue so you are never caught out. Sometimes you can be ambushed by the question that comes in the middle of a conversation about something else, but, provided you have an answer ready, you won't be caught unawares.

Try using the chart below to plan some good replies. Think about some questions that people have asked you. What did you say? What could you have said instead? Try developing three different ways of answering the question, one with lots of detail, one which closes down the questions and one which distances you from the subject, as above.

Questions I have been asked	What did I say?
What could I say instead?	
To give lots of detail:	
To close down the questioning:	
To distance myself from the conversation:	

Managing staring

Sometimes it is actually easier to answer questions than to be in a setting where you can see someone is staring at you, but does not ask. Often when they get into conversation with you, the curiosity will pass. People may become firm friends with others without ever discussing why one of them has a visible difference, and over time it simply becomes insignificant. However, sometimes the staring can be very intrusive. Sitting on a bus or tube with a pair of eyes that keep drifting back to your face is annoying. A firm stare back is often very effective. Or a question:

> *'Have we met before? You seem to be trying to remember who I am.'*

An aggressive response, though sometimes tempting, is not usually helpful.

Distraction is another very easy way to focus away from the situation. A newspaper or book to read, particularly if you can hold it up and interrupt the staring, is helpful. A 'shoe review' when you estimate who has the most expensive trainers or exotic sandals is a simple distraction. You can also use visualization methods to imagine shrinking down the person into a tiny little figure or putting them into a different context (for example, in their pyjamas). All of these strategies will allow you to feel more in control of the situation and, as you feel able to manage more situations, so going out becomes less of an ordeal.

Changing Faces (see Appendix 1) is a very good source of more ideas about managing staring, comments and questions. In addition to written information, they have a website and video materials and are developing on-line interactive programs that help you to practise different social situations before you start doing them for real.

Putting it into practice

The key to successfully managing a visible difference is to take a positive approach to social situations, work on developing your social skills and then practise them in a graded way. By this, we mean tackling some of the things you find easiest before tackling something harder. Fran's case is a good example.

FRAN

Fran had been bitten by a dog and had a very visible 'V'shaped scar on her cheek. She was a very stylish woman in her thirties who liked clothes and make-up and was devastated by this change in her appearance. She stopped work, stayed at home and became increasingly depressed. Her greatest fear was that, if she went out, someone would notice her face and ask about it.

We started treatment by developing some answers to questions. Fran settled on a very simple answer:

Q: 'What happened to your face?'

A: 'I was bitten by that Alsatian at number 32'.

We then designed a 'hierarchy' of exposure tasks (as in Chapter 7), which is a simple ladder with easier items at the bottom and harder items as you climb each rung. Fran's ladder looked like this:

10	Go back to work
9	Go to the supermarket
8	Go out with the family at the weekend
7	Invite a good friend back to the house for tea
6	Go to the corner shop and browse for groceries
5	Go to the corner shop and ask for a newspaper
4	Go to the corner shop, pick up a paper and offer a £5 note
3	Go the corner shop with exact money for the paper so I don't have to speak
2	Walk to the corner shop but don't go in
1	Fetch the milk bottles in from the front step

Fran then carried out each step and repeated this until she felt comfortable doing it. She very quickly managed number one. She then spent a week going up to the shop and back every day but without going in. Gradually, her anxiety about going into the shop lessened. She then went in and picked up a paper and came home. She repeated this twice more and then went up to number three. Fran successfully completed this treatment and went back to work. There is an interesting aspect to Fran's program. When she got to number 6, she waited patiently in the queue rehearsing her answer to the question she was expecting – and nothing happened. In the end, she got so tired of waiting that she pointed out her dog bite herself. 'What do you think of this then? I was bitten by the dog at number 32!' The shopkeeper had noticed, but had politely refrained from asking. Fran laughed as she told me about this. You do not necessarily have to do the same thing, but it does illustrate how taking control of the situation had so lessened her anxiety that she felt able to introduce the topic of her face to a stranger. This was very different from how she imagined herself behaving at the start of her treatment.

If you find certain situations very daunting, it is worth trying to work out your own hierarchy like Fran did. Take it steadily, with not too big a jump between one step and the next. Then make sure you only progress to the next rung when you are completely happy on the rung below. It does not matter how long this takes you. Regular practice is more helpful. Doing an activity every day means that you will progress much faster than if you do it once a week. Be ready for a bad day but don't let this put you off. You can often have an experience that does not go so well, just before a real breakthrough in behavior change. Go back to the rung below to build your confidence, and then try again.

Ending the search for surgical solutions

All the examples given in this chapter are real examples drawn from our clinical experience. They all have something else in common. All these people went on to successfully change their behavior and live normal lives without surgical removal of their disfigurements. They all had surgery at some point in their lives, and some were able to improve their appearance slightly. But all of them learned to live with a visible difference for which no further surgical treatment was possible.

Plastic surgery achieves an enormous amount for people who have disfiguring conditions. However, the media can sometimes portray surgery as offering 'magic' solutions. All surgery has its limitations. All surgery leaves a scar, but some scars can be concealed better than others, for example, in the natural contours of the skin. It is impossible to completely modify a disfiguring condition so that the person looks exactly as they did before an accident. Even cleft lip and palate repairs, which produce very good results for children born with this craniofacial condition, will leave a fine scar.

At some point, a decision must be made about whether the benefits of further surgery are outweighed by the costs. Going on and on with surgical procedures is no guarantee of being able to restore appearance. The real goal, after all, is to be able to live a normal life. So draw a line under surgery when your surgeon suggests it, or when you yourself feel that the results are 'good enough'. Addressing any challenges that you still face using a psychological approach, like the people in the examples we have given, is a very healthy way forward.

Visible difference and CBT

This chapter has considered the special case of disfiguring conditions, within the context of body image concerns. We have seen that objectively minor conditions can cause considerable distress, whilst other people cope with a very significant difference without any distress.

Positive coping strategies, taking the initiative, good social skills and social support are helpful. Avoiding difficult situations, increased social withdrawal or coping using non-prescription drugs and alcohol are not helpful.

CBT, which helps you challenge unhelpful beliefs, develop social skills and practise positive coping behavior can enable you to manage your condition even when surgery has no more to offer. This is achieved in a gradual way by tackling difficult situations step by step. Staring, comments and questions are intrusive but everyone can learn to manage them.

For people whose concerns are less to do with objective difference, and more to do with an internal dissatisfaction with appearance, these approaches are still very helpful. The preoccupation with appearance, which is typical in BDD, can be a real barrier in social situations. If you believe that other people are distracted, for example, by your nose, as you are, then it becomes very difficult to focus on the situation, rather than on other people's response to you. Anxiety about how to interact in this situation means that it can be hard to concentrate on what is really happening and not to write an agenda based on what you think or fear might be happening. For this reason, the section on social skills will be helpful for you too. It is also useful to note that there are answers to appearance-related anxiety that do not involve surgery, and that people with a very obvious visible difference can live just as happily and successfully as anyone else.

13

Psychological aspects of cosmetic procedures

'If I looked better, then I would feel better.'
Cosmetic surgery is often thought of as 'body image surgery', and most people who request cosmetic procedures agree with the statement above. It seems self-evident that if you dislike your appearance, a procedure which can change that appearance must be a good thing. However, understanding the impact of surgery, whether it works, who will benefit and for whom surgery is a bad idea, is much more complicated. In this chapter, we will attempt to untangle some of these issues and help you to decide whether surgery is really a good option for you.

What is cosmetic surgery?

Plastic surgery can be reconstructive or cosmetic. Reconstructive surgery involves repairing or modifying the body to restore function and appearance after injury or disease. The term cosmetic is usually used to describe surgery that alters appearance in cases where there is no apparent injury or abnormality.

However, many surgical procedures include both reconstructive and cosmetic elements, as in Jessie's case below.

JESSIE

Jessie was on a safari holiday when she was involved in a car accident and was thrown from the vehicle she was travelling in. She received severe facial injuries and needed many procedures to reconstruct her face. Her insurers were happy to pay for the initial surgery, which they regarded as reconstruction, but challenged later procedures to reduce scarring because they described these as 'cosmetic'.

In the example above, Jessie's insurers are defining all surgery that is modifying appearance only (not treating disability or disease) as *cosmetic,* regardless of the cause of the problem or whether there is an objective disfigurement.

PAULINE

Pauline had breast cancer and had a mastectomy (removal of the breast), which successfully treated the disease. She then underwent a breast reconstruction operation in which skin and muscle from her abdomen were used to recreate the breast.

Pauline's operation is classified as a reconstructive procedure because it is addressing a problem caused by disease and its treatment. However, it is also true to say that it is entirely aimed at recreating the appearance rather than the function of the breast, so there is a cosmetic aspect to the procedure.

TANYA

Tanya is a beautician. She places a high value on her own appearance and feels that this is important in her career. She is dissatisfied with the size of her breasts. Although she has well-shaped breasts, she feels that she would prefer more fullness and would like to be two cup sizes bigger.

Tanya has normal breasts for her build and no history of disease. There is no reconstructive element in this surgery; her surgery would be classified as entirely cosmetic.

These examples are relatively straightforward. However, in practice, deciding whether a procedure is cosmetic or not can be very difficult. This is important because there is increasing pressure on the NHS in the UK to provide procedures traditionally defined as cosmetic. Guidelines as to when and for whom these can be provided vary from place to place, and usually depend on whether an individual's need is exceptional and whether there is good evidence that surgery will be effective. For example, a breast reduction operation, which can reduce pain in women with very large, heavy breasts, is available in some parts of the UK as long as the individual case meets the guidelines. In other parts of the UK it is regarded as a cosmetic procedure and is not available on the NHS. As with many other aspects of healthcare, there is a real need for more consistency across the country. In reality, and given the increase in popularity of cosmetic surgery and the competing financial pressures on the NHS, it is increasingly unlikely that any cosmetic procedures will be available in the future, except in the private sector. This is not of course an issue in the USA and most other countries where all cosmetic procedures are done privately.

Cosmetic procedures also include a whole range of non-surgical procedures such as dermabrasion, laser treatment and botox. Even less is known about the psychological effects of such procedures compared with surgery.

Why do people request cosmetic procedures?

The most common reason for requesting cosmetic surgery is because someone feels 'abnormal'. They compare their own feature with their idea of what a 'normal' feature should look like and decide that there is room for improvement. Often, people worry that this will be seen by others as vanity. Sometimes there is a sense of wanting to improve their appearance to be better than others, but there is usually a much stronger desire to fit in. They do not want be different from, or not as good as, others.

There are different reasons why people may feel abnormal or unusual and these are tremendously important. Sometimes these reasons are based on 'ghosts from the past' or incorrect information.

Impact of media images

> *'This isn't about other people. I'm not thinking about surgery because of what other people think of me – I'm doing this for myself.'*

The fact that you may be undergoing cosmetic surgery for yourself, not for someone else, is far from being a safe reason to go ahead with a procedure. You may well have become dissatisfied with your body because you have been comparing yourself with an ideal. This ideal will have come from what you see around you – whether or not you want surgery for yourself, to improve your career prospects or for other reasons

Fifty years ago, it would have been unheard of for magazines, TV shows and other media to blatantly display pictures of semi-clad models and celebrities with 'ideal bodies'. People were generally more reserved in how they dressed and how much of their bodies they displayed. Nowadays, the media bombard us with images of ideal bodies in our everyday lives. This can substantially raise expectations of the image you develop for your 'ideal' self, and may mean that you are more ready to compare your appearance with others.

DEBORAH AND JANE

Deborah was very unhappy about the shape of her breasts. Compared with the pictures that she saw in magazines, she felt that her breasts were excessively lax. She described them as 'droopy'. In fact, when she was examined, her breasts were completely normal. When Deborah produced the pictures that she was using for comparison, it was clear that she had selected pictures of women with artificially high or prominent breasts following breast en-largement procedures. For Deborah, these images seemed normal.

Jane had a similar belief that her breasts were abnormal. But for her, this was based on comparison with her own breasts before she had children. Breast shape changes for most women following pregnancy regardless of whether or not they breast-feed. Breasts also fall under their own weight over time. So although Jane no longer looks as she used to look, her breasts are not abnormal.

These examples show that there may be a difference between having a normal feature and an ideal feature but that this does not necessarily mean you are abnormal.

Not only do different individuals value appearance to a greater or lesser extent, but the amount that body image impacts on their lives also varies at different times and in different situations. For example, body image issues tend to be more prevalent in the summer when we need to wear fewer clothes. Body image issues could also be more important at different stages in life – for example, when young people leave home and meet a lot of new people at work or college.

It is also worth noting that many of the images we are exposed to are not necessarily 'real' people at all. Digital images are usually enhanced to produce an ideal image (some celebrities have complained about this!). Imperfections are airbrushed out, or images from different people are pasted in to create an idea of perfection. The supermodel Kate Moss has referred to glamorous pictures of herself as 'an image – not pictures of me'.

Some people are very vulnerable to these ideal images – and fail to recognize their artificiality. It is also true to say that, as more and more people have cosmetic procedures, the range of variation in society becomes smaller. Over time, there could well be fewer women with either very small or very large breasts – and so those at the extreme end will begin to feel more unusual. It's very important to recognize media images as art and entertainment, not reflections of reality, otherwise cosmetic surgery and digital enhancement will begin to define what we understand as 'normal'.

Other people's opinions

Sometimes it can be helpful to consider other people's opinions on your concerns about your appearance.

JAKE AND PAUL

Jake was very worried about his nose. He felt that it did not look normal and spent considerable time looking at it with a hand mirror, trying to see how it looked in profile. He chose where he sat very carefully when in company so that no one could see him from the side. Objectively, there was nothing remarkable or unusual about Jake's nose. When asked if people commented on it or asked him about it, he said that people did not do so 'because they were too polite'. However, he was convinced that they were looking at him.

Paul was becoming increasingly preoccupied with his nose since breaking it in a football match two years previously. He felt that it looked different from how it had done before, and that there was a clear twist, which was visible when you looked at him straight on. He tried ignoring his nose, but was getting increasingly fed up with people asking him what he had done to it.

The fact that you have a visible difference should never be the sole reason for surgery – many people, as we saw in Chapter 13, do not place as much importance on their appearance as they do on other aspects of their sense of self. They cope positively and are perfectly happy as they are. No one 'should' have cosmetic surgery just to comply with an external ideal. Nor should the opinion of other people be the prime motivation for having surgery. The fact that someone else thinks you 'ought' to do something is not a good reason for surgery if you are happy the way you are.

But the fact that other people can identify what it is that bothers you is helpful. For a start, it means that you and the surgeon can agree on exactly what it is that you dislike and want to change. For Paul, there is a clear twist to his nose. He, his friends and his surgeon can all agree they see it, and they can start to talk about how likely it is that surgery can provide a solution.

The second reason it is helpful if others can see the problem is that it enables you to focus on the results of surgery, the outcomes or what you hope will change. Paul will easily be able to tell if his surgery is successful because people will stop asking him what he has done to his nose. The intrusive comments will stop and that is one very clear reason why he wants to have surgery. (Remember though, he does not have to address this problem through the surgical route – the strategies outlined in Chapter 12 provide very good ways of dealing with other people's curiosity.)

Jake is more complicated. He knows that he is dissatisfied with his nose but he is not absolutely sure he knows why. He wants his surgeon to provide him with a 'nicer' nose, but it is very difficult to pin down exactly what he means by this. He tends to explain his position by saying:

'Anything is better than this'

or

'The surgeon is the one with the experience so I am going to leave it up to him.'

Without a clearer idea of what it is that he wants to change, he is not likely to be satisfied with surgery.

More worryingly, no one else can see a problem. Jake believes his friends are too polite to comment. He is wrong about this. People who have a visible difference can always give examples of specific comments and questions from others. Not everyone intrudes like this, but the absence of any evidence of comments from other people is a good indication that Jake needs to take his time before proceeding to surgery. His ideas of what he wants to change are too vague, and he therefore has no clear basis for knowing whether or not the operation has been a success. Some surgeons may do a plaster cast of your feature and ask you to re-shape it with a knife to determine if your expectations are realistic. In Jake's case, he should think about seeing a specialist psychologist who works in this area to help him to clarify his ideas, and to think about whether surgery is really the answer for his concerns.

'I just want it to be subtle: I don't want anyone else to notice that I have had anything done.'

If you really think about this request, which is a very common one, you can see that it presents a very difficult challenge for a surgeon. On the one hand, you are concerned enough about a particular feature to feel that it warrants surgery with all the associated risks (and financial costs); in other words, you asking for a significant change. But, because you are hoping no one will notice, you are also asking for a very small change. One way or another, you are very likely to be disappointed. Either the change will be too subtle:

'I am really pleased with the results, but I just wish he had taken a little more off, etc.'

or

'I think I look really great, but I wish that it wasn't so obvious to other people. Everyone keeps asking who my surgeon is.'

If this is how you are thinking, then you need to examine your motivation for having surgery. If you are really keen to achieve a change then that is your priority. If you feel so embarrassed about cosmetic surgery that you don't want other people to know, then should you really be having it? Decisions that are not consistent with your values and beliefs can lead to psychological problems in the long run. When this happens, people tend to be preoccupied by feelings of shame and regret and can even become anxious about going out.

Can surgery make you happier?

The examples throughout this chapter are all based on real people. You can see that there are some common themes in their reasons for wanting to change their appearance. Their reasons vary according to the feature that they dislike, and they also vary according to the degree that their feature can be seen by others – the objective difference from the norm. What they have in common is a real sense that they will be happier if they can change the way that they look. Unfortunately, there is no very good evidence of a direct link between surgery and psychological well-being.

Most of the people who come to a cosmetic clinic talk in terms of improving their self-confidence and self-esteem. Although their immediate goal is to have surgery, they hope that this will enable them to achieve something that is currently missing in their lives. This is sometimes very simple – such as the ability to wear a swimsuit. But the impact may be more far-reaching.

MOIRA

Moira had a complication of pregnancy called pre-eclampsia which meant that she retained a lot of water and put on a great deal of weight. Although her weight fell with sensible eating and exercise, she was unable to do anything about a large fold of extra skin. This caused sweating underneath it and rashes, particularly in the summer. Moira was very embarrassed about her husband seeing her and started to make excuses to avoid sex. She also felt very conspicuous in a swimsuit, felt she could not take the children swimming and would not go on holiday. Gradually she began to buy baggy clothes, especially large sweatshirts and jackets, and would not take these off even when it was very hot.

Moira decided to have an abdominoplasty (tummy tuck). Although she knew that this could not make her look exactly as she had done before she had the children, and that she would have very significant scarring, she felt that the removal of the abdominal fold would allow her to do lots of activities that she felt unable to do. Her goals for surgery were very clear.

Goals for surgery goal (0–10)	Chances of achieving
Remove some of skin excess	10
Reduce sweating and rash	9–10
Wear normal clothes	9–10
Wear swimming costume	8–9
Take children swimming	8–9
Go on holiday	7–8
Feel less self-conscious about sex	4–5

She had a very high chance of achieving some of these. Some goals were ranked lower because they depended on how she *felt,* rather than on her *behavior.* An impact on feelings often takes longer and partly depends on the other things on the list, how her husband felt about the surgery, etc. In general, the more she was able to identify and work towards significant changes in her behavior, the more likely that she would feel good about herself in the longer term.

Moira's surgery left her with a large scar from hip to hip. It could not remove her stretch marks and she had some unevenness at the end of the scar. However, she achieved all the goals on her list and was very satisfied with the impact of cosmetic surgery in changing her behavior and improving her self-esteem.

We have seen elsewhere in this book that the way you *think* and *act* can change the extent to which you are preoccupied by your appearance. One way of thinking about Moira's surgery is that it enabled her to change how she behaved; this then lessened her preoccupation with her abdomen and allowed her to relax with her husband. She might describe this as increasing her self-confidence, but it was the change in behavior that came first. People often get this relationship the wrong way round. They talk about making changes in their life in the future, when they feel more confident in themselves. But this self-confidence is far more likely to grow from making the changes, altering your behavior in a gradual way and building self-esteem through gradually succeeding at the things you find difficult. You will find examples of this graded approach to changing behavior throughout this book. Look back at Chapter 12, for example, at the hierarchy of tasks Fran used to begin going out again after her dog bite (see section entitled "Putting it into practice"). Building on the small steps gradually allowed her to achieve all her goals and go back to work, without relying on surgery.

Research evidence on the psychological benefits of cosmetic surgery

Most people who suffer from BDD are not usually satisfied with the outcome of their surgery. Alternatively, if they are satisfied with the procedure then they are likely to become preoccupied with another area of their body. In other words, the procedure does not alter the symptoms of BDD in terms of the preoccupation, distress and disability in their life.

JOSE

Jose was aged 24 and had body dysmorphic disorder. He had had four operations on his nose. About ten years earlier, he had been bullied and he thought that it was because of his appearance. Despite the surgery, he remained very distressed and preoccupied by the shape of his nose. His parents were finding it difficult to make ends meet after paying for the surgery. They thought that they were giving him the best, even though they did not think that he needed it doing. He was virtually housebound and only came out in the dark. He felt that previous surgeons were incompetent and made his nose look worse in some respects. He frequently brooded on why he had chosen the first surgeon and wished he had seen someone else. He continued spending time searching on the Internet for a surgeon who could help him. He felt he could not do anything in life until he was comfortable with his nose.

The evidence for the benefits of cosmetic surgery in people without BDD is poor. The major problem is that scientists have not yet been able to carry out studies that are rigorous enough for us to fully interpret the findings. This means that we are able to explain the findings in too many different ways to allow us to be clear about whether surgery has psychological benefits or not. Being satisfied with surgery is not the same as experiencing a clear psychological benefit, and unfortunately satisfaction is what most research studies have measured. 'Before and after' studies are not good enough on their own. They do not tell us enough without a comparison group who are having another kind of treatment. It might be the case that any kind of treatment is equally effective, or that the attention patients get from the surgical team partly explains why they end up feeling better about themselves.

We also do not know whether the cosmetic procedure works in the long term. We know that most people are usually satisfied immediately after surgery, but that could be due to the fact that they have so much invested in it, or to other psychological reasons. Although the examples given in the media and the people who undergo surgery on TV often report very positive changes, we simply do not know whether the changes they expect in the long term happen or not. Many people come back for repeat procedures. This could be because they are really pleased with the outcome of the first procedure – or because the initial effect was good but wore off very quickly, or because it didn't work but they are desperately hoping that it might work the next time. So we have much more research to do before we can be certain. However, we do know enough to be able to offer some broad guidelines.

Cosmetic surgery appears to be most effective in cases such as Moira's, described above, and least effective in cases such as Jose's, also described above. We have summarized the characteristics of such cases below.

PREDICTORS OF GOOD OUTCOME AFTER SURGERY

• There is a measurable problem (feature too big/small/asymmetric).

• The problem is clearly identifiable by others (friends/family/surgeon).

• The way that behavior is affected can be described.

• There are clear goals for surgery.

• The surgeon and patient agree on the surgical goals and the likelihood of achieving them.

• There are clear, achievable and realistic targets for behavior change after surgery.

• Goals are expressed as 'what I can do', not 'how I will feel'.

All the following have been linked to poor outcome and indicate a need for specialist assessment before considering a procedure:

PREDICTORS OF POOR OUTCOME AFTER SURGERY

• The motivation for surgery comes from someone other than you.

- You cannot describe the problem clearly, or have lots of different features you dislike.
- Other people are unable to see what is wrong.
- You are suffering from body dysmorphic disorder (e.g. you have excessive preoccupation and distress with a feature that others say is not that noticeable or abnormal) as it does not alter the symptoms of BDD.
- You are unclear about how the problem impacts on your life.
- There are vague goals for surgery (e.g. 'I want it to look more attractive').
- The surgeon and you have not agreed specific surgical goals.
- Outcomes are expressed as feelings rather than behavior (e.g. 'I want to feel more confident').
- Outcomes are unrealistic (e.g. 'I want my life to be completely different').
- The behavior to be changed is someone else's (e.g. 'I want my husband to stop seeing other women').

PLUS

• There have been repeated cosmetic procedures, which have had poor outcomes in the past.

We can illustrate this with another example.

SALLY

Sally was referred after having undergone surgery on her nose and being very unhappy with the results. She had asked her surgeon to give her a nicer nose. He suggested that he make her nose narrower and reduce the size of her nostrils. After surgery she said that she still disliked her nose. She had the procedure done again but remained unhappy and even more preoccupied with her nose. When we planned out her goals as they might have been when she first considered surgery, they looked like this:

Goals for surgery	(Therapist-rated chance of achieving goals from 0 to 10)
Make my nose look nicer	1–2
Reduce my preoccupation with my nose	1–2
Make me more confident	0–1
Make me feel better about myself	0–1
Help me get a boyfriend	0–1

You can see from this list that Sally was far more characteristic of someone for whom the outcomes are unsatisfactory. She was vague about what she wanted the surgeon to do and none of the things she hoped to achieve was within her control. She needed to identify specific examples of behavior that she hoped to change, as in the following list:

Goals for surgery	(Therapist–rated chance of achieving goals from 0 to 10)
Make my nose narrower at the base	9–10
Reduce the size of the nostrils	9–10
Reduce the time I spend looking in the mirror	7–8
Help me to socialize with friends	4–5
Help me get a boyfriend	4–5

You can see that Sally can clearly measure the first three things on the list. She can then begin to work on socializing with her friends – in fact she can enlist their support with this. If she is going out with friends she is far more likely to find a boyfriend, so we have raised the probability of this too.

Unfortunately, when surgery is not successful, when it does not meet expectations, many people respond by having more surgery. You might tell yourself that it is nearly right, but a little more is needed. Or you might think that another surgeon would be better, or that a hospital overseas might be a good option. Sometimes we see people having a procedure repeated over and over again. Unfortunately, this has the effect of increasing rather than reducing their preoccupation with the feature in question. It can be very difficult to treat this problem successfully. There is also the risk that repeated surgery and scarring will result in the feature being less satisfactory than it was in the first place. This is clearly a very bad outcome, so it is always a good idea to talk through the reasons for your disappointment with a psychologist, as well as your surgeon, before rushing back for more surgery. Some of the most depressed and suicidal individuals with BDD are those who blame themselves severely for having cosmetic procedures that they feel have made their appearance worse.

Timing of cosmetic surgery

What is the trigger for thinking about surgery? Even if you are someone who has thought about surgery for years, as an option in the future, it is important to work out why now is a good time. It can be very tempting to think about changing your appearance as a response to other significant changes in your life. Psychologists talk about 'life events' or the significant challenges we all face at some point in our lives. These include changes in relationships, jobs, bereavement, children leaving home, moving house, etc. Rushing to make an irreversible change when they are unhappy is something that people often regret. It is better to leave a reasonable gap – a few months – before planning surgery after any of these significant changes in your life. This is particularly important if lots of changes have occurred together.

Cosmetic surgery for children

Cosmetic procedures such as correction of bat ears (pinnaplasty) are regularly carried out for children. Indeed, the NHS will carry out these procedures only on children and not adults. The rationale is to prevent the teasing and bullying that can go on in schools. Other procedures are not ideal in young people, for the very practical reason that they are still growing. It is therefore unusual to offer cosmetic procedures under the age of 18. However, breast reduction or enlargement and nasal surgery are increasingly requested at milestones such as leaving school. Young people are frequently choosing to 'correct' a feature that they feel to be abnormal before meeting a new group of friends. It is important that they are made aware of any possible problems associated with different procedures. For example, there is a considerably reduced chance of being able to breast-feed after bilateral breast reduction (BBR), and many surgeons therefore prefer to offer this procedure to older women who have completed their families.

Pressure from others

There is a growing fashion for giving people gift vouchers for private cosmetic surgery. If surgery is not something you have considered, do not be influenced by the idea of doing it cheaply. Similarly, reputable clinics should not encourage you to have further procedures. Offering a cut price procedure if you sign up to more than one is an indication that you should choose a different provider. People sometimes choose to go in pairs or with a group of friends. This is not a good idea. You need to be able to stand back and make a decision without group pressure. This is not the same as taking a friend with you to a consultation to listen and help you to ask relevant questions. The pressure comes when you are all planning to have the same procedure together. Someone in the group will be the least certain that they want this, and it can be very hard to withdraw when everyone else is going ahead.

Finding a surgeon

All surgeons who carry out cosmetic surgery in the UK should be properly trained in plastic surgery. To ensure that a surgeon meets this standard, make sure that he or she is included on the list produced by the British Association of Aesthetic Plastic Surgeons (see Appendix 1).

As an additional guide, most aesthetic (cosmetic) surgeons in the UK are or have been consultant surgeons in the NHS. It can be tempting to find the cheapest source of surgery, but many people end up spending more in the end. Reputable surgeons recognize that there are potential complications in all surgery. Infection, or the need to revise a scar, are examples. As a rough guide, 5–10 per cent of patients may need further revision or treatments in addition to the usual treatment. To cover this potential cost, reputable surgeons spread the risk across their whole practice and therefore charge slightly more for all patients, so that there is no problem with treating anyone who encounters a problem after their operation. Less reputable surgeons cut the costs but do not provide any safety net if you are not happy with the outcome of surgery. It is very important to check what arrangements are in place if you have a problem, and it is well worth paying a little more for high-quality treatment.

Are there people who should never have cosmetic surgery?

There are some medical conditions that make any kind of surgery more dangerous, for example heart conditions. Undergoing any elective (non-essential) surgery is unwise in this situation.

Other risk factors for surgery include smoking and obesity. Smoking increases the risk associated with anaesthetic and also makes the healing process less efficient by reducing the amount of oxygen available in the blood. Obesity also increases anaesthetic risk and the likelihood of complications such as infection. Cosmetic surgery is not a weight reduction technique. It is sometimes used to reduce surplus skin after weight loss, but procedures such as abdominoplasty are not designed to make you slimmer.

It may seem surprising that surgery is often considered inappropriate for some people with body image concerns. Body dysmorphic disorder is better treated using CBT and/or the medication described in Chapter 14. This is because the central problem in BDD is the *preoccupation* with a feature, rather than the feature itself. Although surgery may change the appearance of the feature, it usually does not alter the extent to which people are worried or preoccupied or continue to check their appearance in the mirror. In this sense then, it fails to change the problem behavior, or alter beliefs or mood. In fact it can make the problem worse if someone becomes trapped in a cycle of repeated surgery. It is therefore wise to get advice from a psychologist or psychiatrist before seeking cosmetic surgery, if your problems with your appearance fit the pattern described in Chapter 2.

There are some other psychiatric conditions for which a cosmetic procedure may not be a good idea. An eating disorder or any body image problem that involves excessive preoccupation with appearance (like BDD) is unlikely to be successfully treated through surgery alone. Indeed, repeated surgery usually leads to increasing dissatisfaction for people with BDD. Conditions such as depression are not necessarily a barrier to surgery but timing is important. Generally, it is not a good idea to undertake surgery without further assessment if you are currently receiving psychological therapy or psychiatric medication or you are under any kind of stress or pressure in your life.

Should I be considering surgery?

Having read this chapter, you should be clearer about whether surgery is going to be appropriate for you, and whether or not now is a good time. Take some time to think about the following questions and complete the questionnaire below.

QUESTIONNAIRE 13.1: IDENTIFYING THE PROBLEM FEATURE

1. Do your body image problems affect one area of your body or one feature?
[Space left intentionally blank in the original book]

2. Is your condition noticeable to other people? Do others currently comment or tease you about your appearance?
[Space left intentionally blank in the original book]

3. Have you tried to manage your condition using the psychological methods outlined in this book?
[Space left intentionally blank in the original book]

4. Have you had cosmetic surgery in the past? If yes, were you satisfied with the outcome?

[Space left intentionally blank in the original book]

5. Do you have a condition such as body dysmorphic disorder, depression or an eating disorder?

[Space left intentionally blank in the original book]

6. Have you had any major changes or additional stress in your life recently?

Or has a relationship recently ended?

[Space left intentionally blank in the original book]

7. Are you under pressure from others to consider surgery?

[Space left intentionally blank in the original book]

8. Are you able to tell people exactly what you dislike about your feature?

[Space left intentionally blank in the original book]

9. Are you able to pinpoint exactly how you would like your feature to change? Write down exactly how you would like to change your appearance. Use very objective language (e.g. longer, shorter, bigger, rounder, rather than value

judgements such as nicer, more attractive, normal)

[Space left intentionally blank in the original book]

10. What are the chances that surgery can achieve this change? (You may not know this without talking to a surgeon.)

[Space left intentionally blank in the original book]

11. How do you expect your life to be different after surgery? Write this down as specifically as you can:

[Space left intentionally blank in the original book]

12. After surgery I will be able to...

[Space left intentionally blank in the original book]

13. If I am able to do the things I have listed above, I hope to achieve some longer-term goals such as...

(Have a look at Moira's case above to give you some ideas.)

[Space left intentionally blank in the original book]

14. Have you been able to identify very clear target behaviors that you hope to achieve?

[Space left intentionally blank in the original book]

15. Can you achieve them without cosmetic surgery?

[Space left intentionally blank in the original book]

If you find it difficult to answer this questionnaire, it would be a good idea to get some advice. Appendix 1 at the back of this book lists some professionals who specialize in body image concerns who may be able to help you. If you are at all uncertain, cosmetic surgery is probably not a good option for you at this particular point in your life.

14

A guide to medication for body image problems

This chapter discusses the potential benefits and disadvantages of medication for body dysmorphic disorder in order to help you make an informed choice about whether or not you wish to take such medication. The discussion could also be relevant for someone who is significantly depressed (for example, as a result of a disfigurement) or if you are suffering from bulimia nervosa. However, if you have doubts and questions about medication after reading this chapter, you should discuss them with your doctor, rather than just ignoring a prescription or stopping your medication.

If you have been recommended medication and decide to take it, it is also important to take it at the correct dose and frequency. The possible side effects of medication, and what you can do to minimize them, are also discussed in this chapter. In addition, we provide advice on how to stop taking antidepressant medication. Being well informed is vital, as some people who have been prescribed medication will not get it dispensed at the pharmacy, and others might take it inappropriately (for example, at a lower dose than recommended or not daily) or not at all.

Medication may be suggested:

- if you have moderate to severe symptoms of BDD, as an alternative to cognitive behavior therapy (CBT) or in addition to CBT
- if you have BDD or bulimia nervosa which has persisted despite CBT being delivered competently
- if you have a body image problem and you are also significantly depressed or suicidal.

You might find it difficult to get CBT treatment because of long waiting lists or other restrictions in public medicine and insurance cover. As a result, you might be offered medication before you receive CBT. More research is needed on how to get the most out of combining treatments for BDD. We think that CBT and medication are equally effective for most people with BDD, though we don't yet have published research evidence to support this. However, it is very important that individuals have a choice. Although CBT could be more costly to provide than drug therapy *in the short term,* psychological treatments are usually more cost-effective in the long term. This is because the cost of the drug continues for several months and there is a higher risk of relapse with medication alone, when the patient stops taking it, compared with an effective psychological therapy.

Some individuals do better on a combination of CBT and medication than either treatment alone. This is usually recommended if you fail to respond adequately to CBT on its own or if your BDD is more severe. The problem is that no one can predict with any certainty who will respond best to what treatment.

Frequently asked questions about medication

Isn't taking medication a sign of weakness?

Taking medication is not a sign of weakness or failure. You probably wouldn't think that taking medication was a weakness if you had heart disease or cancer. Your relatives and friends are more likely to think of your behavior as weak if you *don't* take medication and will find it difficult to understand why you don't do everything you can to get better. If some of them do criticize you for taking medication, they probably don't understand what you are experiencing and their opinion is not worth considering. Mental disorder is no different from other medical problems in this respect, and taking medication is a practical approach.

How quickly does medication work?

Even if medication is of benefit, it will not work right away. Most people notice some improvement in their symptoms after about four to six weeks, while maximum benefit should occur within four to six months. Make sure you continue to take your medication at the highest dose you can tolerate for this period before judging how effective it has been.

How long will I need to take medication for?

Never stop taking medication without discussing it with your doctor first, and always ensure that you have another prescription ready before you run out of drugs. This is because, if you do not take medication regularly or stop it suddenly (for example, you forget to take it on holiday), you can be at risk of experiencing withdrawal symptoms. This is discussed in detail at the end of this chapter (see section entitled "Stopping or reducing your anti-depressant medication").

Once you have recovered from BDD or depression and have stopped taking medication, you could have a relapse if you have had no other therapy. The risk of relapse will partly depend on the natural pattern of your BDD without treatment. For example, for a first episode of BDD, the chance of recurrence is lower if you continue to take an anti-depressant for up to a year after you have recovered. If you have a second episode of BDD, then your chances of relapse are lower if you keep taking an anti-depressant for a couple of years after you have got better. If you are someone whose BDD keeps recurring, then the risk of relapse is much higher and you will probably be advised to remain on the medication for at least five years. A few people might need to be on medication for many years to reduce the risk of relapse.

For many people, the risk of relapse is minimized by combining the medication with CBT. If you are planning to stop medication, ensure you do it after discussion with your doctor and within an agreed timeframe. Be aware that your depressive symptoms could start to return within a few weeks or months, so don't plan to stop before predictable major stresses and life events.

SSRIs

The first choice of medication for most people with BDD or depression is a class of anti-depressants called selective serotonergic reuptake inhibitors or SSRIs for short (see Table 14.1). 'Serotonergic' means that the drugs act on serotonin nerve endings in the brain. 'Selective' refers to the fact that they act on serotonin nerve endings, rather than others such as noradrenaline or histamine nerve endings. 'Reuptake inhibitor' refers to the way the drug acts: it helps to increase the concentration of serotonin in the nerve cells. This in turn helps to increase the messages passing along certain pathways in the brain and to reduce anxiety.

Compared with older anti-depressants, SSRIs are generally safe. An overdose will not usually harm you.

For someone with BDD, an SSRI can reduce your preoccupation and distress with your feature. In BDD, a part of your nervous system might have an excessive load on it as your mind tries to make things better. SSRIs *enhance* this normal activity of the brain and improve its ability to dampen anxiety and reduce your preoccupation. SSRIs are also used for panic attacks, obsessive-compulsive disorder (OCD) and depression, so they are not used specifically for BDD. Afamily doctor can prescribe the drug or refer you to a psychiatrist who can discuss your issues in more detail.

Which SSRI might be prescribed?

In general, all SSRIs are likely to be equally effective for BDD or depression, but individuals respond differently to different drugs. The most evidence for BDD is based on trials conducted with fluoxetine. However, your doctor will help you choose the most appropriate SSRI for you, given your circumstances and history. For example, citalopram or escitalopram are usually a good choice if you are on other drugs at the same time and they are usually well tolerated.

Fluoxetine takes longer to be metabolized by the body, so it doesn't matter so much if you forget a dose one day as it does not vanish from the blood when you stop taking it. It is also now the cheapest of the SSRIs and the easiest to come off. However, some people find fluoxetine slightly more likely to increase anxiety when they first start taking it. Some SSRIs, such as paroxetine, can be more difficult to withdraw from and other things being equal are best avoided (see 'Stopping or reducing your medication anti-depressant',).

If you or someone in your family did well or poorly with a medication in the past, this might influence your choice. If you have medical problems (for example, problems sleeping) or you are taking another medication, these factors will influence your doctor's choice so that side effects and possible drug interactions are minimized. Make sure you tell your doctor if you:

• are pregnant or plan to get pregnant or are breastfeeding
• have any other medical conditions
• are taking any other medication or herbal drugs such as St John's wort.

Can I drink alcohol with an SSRI?

In general, you can drink alcohol as long as you do so in moderation and do not binge-drink. However, people's reactions to alcohol do vary when taking medication and some people can become more aggressive or sedated. See how you respond to one drink initially.

Fluvoxamine and sertraline do not mix very well with alcohol so be aware that this mixture can impair your judgement. Also when you are on one of these medications, you should not drive or operate machinery. Excessive alcohol can also be a factor in depression and will interfere with your recovery.

What dose of an SSRI should I be prescribed?

The normal starting dose and suitable target doses of different SSRIs are listed in Table 14.1 overleaf. When progress is slow, you may need to increase the dose and you should check this with your doctor. If you experience significant side effects, you can always start on a lower dose, after discussion with your doctor. You can then build the dose up slowly. Tablets should be swallowed with some water while sitting or standing to make sure that they do not stick in your throat. If you miss a dose, take it as soon as you remember it. However, if it is almost time for the next dose, skip the missed dose and continue your regular dose. Do not take a double dose to make up for a missed one.

TABLE 14.1: SSRI ANTI-DEPRESSANTS

Chemical name	Common trade names	Usual starting dose (mg)	Target dose (mg)	Liquid preparation
Citalopram	Cipramil, Celexa	20	50	Yes (20mg=5ml)
Escitalopram	Cipralex, Lexapro	10	20	Yes (5mg=5ml)
Fluoxetine	Prozac	20	60	Yes (20mg=5ml)
Fluvoxamine	Faverin, Luvox	50	200	No
Paroxetine	Seroxat, Paxil	20	60	Yes (10mg=5ml)
Sertraline	Lustral, Zoloft	50	200	Yes (100mg=5ml)

Can vegans have SSRIs?

Citalopram elixir, fluoxetine elixir, clomipramine elixir, sertraline tablets and paroxetine tablets or liquid do not contain any animal products.

What about reports of SSRIs causing suicide?

There is some evidence that a few anti-depressants can cause a slight increase in suicidal ideas (not acts) in young people with depression. For young adults, the increased risk of suicidal ideas is extremely small. So long as you monitor such feelings, talk about them openly with your doctor and relatives, and are seen regularly, this is something that can be managed. The thoughts of suicide will then decrease as your depression lifts.

Anti-depressant medication for children and adolescents

Anti-depressant medication for children with BDD or depression is not so well studied, and CBT is recommended as the first line of treatment. This is because scientists don't yet know the long-term effects of anti-depressants on the immature brain of a child and also because anti-depressants are often ineffective in young people or may be associated with a very slight increase in suicidal ideas (see above).

Equally, these risks need to be judged against the risk of a young person with severe BDD or depression not using medication or not responding to CBT (or refusing it). If he or she is continuing to experience severe BDD, this can have a major adverse impact on both development and education. In such cases, an anti-depressant is recommended. Only fluoxetine has been shown in controlled trials to have a favourable balance of risks and benefits for the treatment of depression in the under-18s and this is the SSRI that is usually recommended for BDD. The dose should usually start at a half the adult dose (10mg) and can be increased gradually. Therefore, a psychiatrist should supervise the use of an anti-depressant for a child or adolescent and monitor his or her mental state closely (for example, weekly for the first four weeks).

An SSRI should be offered in combination with an evidence-based psychological treatment. If treatment with fluoxetine is unsuccessful or is not tolerated because of side effects, consideration should be given to the use of another anti-depressant. In this case, sertraline or citalopram might be second-line treatments. Guidelines recommend that venlafaxine (Efexor) and paroxetine (Seroxat, Paxil) and clomipramine anti-depressants should not be used for the treatment of depression in children and young people. The side effects listed below occur in children as they do in adults. In addition, children can become over-excited, irritable or 'silly'; if this type of reaction is severe it could be a reason to stop the medication.

What side effects occur with SSRIs?

Some people experience side effects with SSRIs and those who do normally find them to be minor irritations that decrease after a few weeks. The main side effects are described in this section. Most people find that they are not usually a problem in the long term. They will not alter your personality or 'turn you into a zombie' and they will cease when you stop taking the drug. The worst side effects usually occur in the first few days or weeks after commencing the drug. This is the time when you are most likely to stop taking the drug because you have not experienced any improvement in the symptoms of your depression. (This is because it takes four to six weeks for the full benefits of the medication to become apparent.) There is one side effect that does not tend to improve over time: sexual difficulties (see section entitled "Tremor"). However, side effects that persist, including those of a sexual nature, will decrease when you stop taking the medication.

You are more likely to experience side effects if you are on a large dose or if your dose has been rapidly increased. If you are unable to tolerate the medication, you can try reducing the dose and then increasing it to the previous level more slowly. For example, if you find that you are feeling nauseous after a few days of taking fluoxetine or paroxetine at 20mg, you can reduce the dose to 10mg for a week or two and then increase it to 20mg again when your body has become more accustomed to the drug. This can also be done if it is a liquid and increased very slowly. Another alternative is to switch to a different SSRI altogether. Again, discuss this with your doctor beforehand.

The possible side effects of SSRIs and how to deal with them are given below. The list looks rather daunting but remember that the symptoms only occur in a minority of people. They stop if you discontinue the drug under guidance from your doctor. Alternatively, your doctor will discuss with you how to manage the side effects better. Monitoring of your mood and possible side effects is the key to all treatments – keep track of how you feel with a standardized measure and use it like a temperature chart on a weekly basis. If your mood is not improving, and especially if you are becoming more suicidal, discuss the issue with your therapist or psychiatrist and ask whether you need to change tack.

Nausea

Nausea (feeling sick) is the most common but temporary side effect of an SSRI and affects about 25 per cent of patients taking an SSRI compared with about 10 per cent of those on a placebo (dummy pill). Citalopram and fluvoxamine are slightly more likely than the other SSRIs to cause nausea. The feeling can be significantly reduced by taking the drug after food. Alternatively, halve the dose for a couple of weeks and then increase it slowly back to the normal dose. If the nausea still persists, an anti-nausea drug (for example, metoclobemide) might help.

Diarrhoea or constipation

SSRIs can cause diarrhoea in up to 15 per cent of patients compared with about 5 per cent who take a placebo. Diarrhoea can be significantly reduced by drinking plenty of apple juice (which contains pectin) or the use of a drug, bismuth subsalicylate (Kaopectate). Constipation occurs in 5 per cent of patients taking an SSRI. Diarrhoea or constipation can be improved by taking bulking agents such as Fybogel or psyllium seed husk and eating plenty of bran and roughage. For both diarrhoea and constipation, you should drink at least 2 litres of water a day.

Headache

Up to 20 per cent of patients taking an SSRI find they develop headaches. Headache is a common symptom of tension and occurs in about 15 per cent of patients taking a placebo. Symptoms of headache can usually be helped by simple painkillers such as paracetamol and should decrease after a few weeks of taking an SSRI.

Excessive sweating

Excessive sweating occurs in about 10 per cent of patients taking an SSRI, compared with 5 per cent of those taking a placebo. There is no easy solution to this problem although it should decrease over time.

Dry mouth

Dry mouth affects about 10 per cent of patients taking an SSRI, compared with 5 per cent of those taking a placebo. Sucking on sugarless gum or sugar-free boiled sweets can stimulate production of saliva, or you could try a spray that can be bought over the counter that provides artificial saliva. Again, the symptoms usually decrease over time.

Tremor

Shakiness or tremor occurs in about 10 per cent of patients taking an SSRI and 3 per cent of those on a placebo. A betablocker (for example, propranolol) can be prescribed to help reduce tremor if it is severe.

Sedation or insomnia

Between 10 and 20 per cent of patients on SSRIs feel sedated and between 5 and 15 per cent cannot sleep. With some SSRIs, the problem can sometimes be resolved by changing the time of day you take your medication (take it at night, for example, if it makes you drowsy), temporarily reducing the dose, or taking a different SSRI altogether. Fluoxetine may be activating and should normally be taken in the mornings. Sertraline is less likely to cause sedation. Fluvoxamine and trazodone are more likely to cause sedation and are best prescribed at night. If sedation is a problem, do not drive or use machinery.

Sexual problems

The sexual side effects of SSRIs can take the form of delayed ejaculation in men and an inability to reach an orgasm in women.

They can also occasionally cause both men and women to lose libido although this is complicated to assess in the presence of depression. (However, there is one case report of an SSRI causing orgasms with yawning!)

Some atypical serotinergic anti-depressants do not cause delayed ejaculation. However, their benefit in BDD is not known. Trazodone is one example, which can very rarely cause 'priapism' (a persistent and painful erection) and which should be treated as an emergency at a casualty department. Nefazadone was similar to trazodone but did not cause delayed ejaculation or erectile problems; unfortunately it was withdrawn by the manufacturers for commercial reasons and is now available only on a named-patient basis. Another anti-depressant to consider if sexual dysfunction is a problem is reboxetine or dofepramine, as they act on the noradrenergic nervous system. However, they are likely to be less effective for BDD.

In the case of SSRIs generally, if you are on a relatively high dose, the problem of sexual side effects can sometimes be solved by lowering the dose or taking a 'drug holiday' and missing a dose on the day of sexual activity. However, this needs to be done with caution as you may experience some withdrawal symptoms (see below). Taking a drug holiday is usually safe with fluoxetine, which remains in the body for up to five weeks after stopping taking it. However, later findings suggest there are dangers in suddenly stopping some SSRI medication, so it is important you speak to your doctor before doing this.

In the past there were case reports of people finding it helpful to take cyproheptadine or buspirone (Buspar) several hours before sex. However, later studies found them to be no different from a placebo (or dummy pill). Another possible solution is ginkgo biloba. This is a herbal extract of the maiden hair tree and is sometimes used to enhance memory, particularly in the elderly. It can be purchased in healthfood shops. Ginkgo biloba has been used to treat sexual problems caused by anti-depressant drugs in a series of 14 patients. They had a variety of difficulties including erectile problems, delayed ejaculation, loss of libido and an inability to reach orgasm. The patients took a daily dose of 240mg for six weeks. The only side effect was gastric irritation (reported by two patients). Overall, the group reported improvements. Two out of the 14 patients reported no improvements and two reported that sexual functioning was completely restored. This study needs to be done as a controlled trial, but in the meantime gingko biloba could be worth trying as a natural supplement. It would also be sensible to inform your doctor.

There are also reports concerning the use of Viagra or Cialis for men and women taking SSRIs. Viagra has been reported as successful in reversing the sexual side effects of SSRIs. Again, this needs to be researched carefully. If you wish to take Viagra, try a dose of 50mg one hour before sexual activity, having first discussed it with your doctor. If this does not improve things or gives only a partial response, you could try increasing it to 100mg. Some patients with heart conditions will not be able to take it. Cialis has a possible advantage of a longer-lasting effect. The possible side effects of Viagra or Cialis include headache, flushing and dizziness. Do not buy such drugs from the Internet as you have no guarantee of quality and it could just be a dummy pill or even worse. So always go to your doctor to discuss getting a prescription. However, Viagra or Cialis are not widely regarded as reversing SSRI side effects as not enough research has been done.

Loss of appetite

Loss of appetite and weight loss occur in between 5 and 10 per cent of patients taking SSRIs (especially fluoxetine). Reducing the dose can halt this effect, though the symptoms usually fade away over time anyway. Some SSRIs can sometimes cause slight weight gain in the long term and you might need to adjust your diet and exercise program. Depression and inactivity will also contribute to weight gain.

Nervousness or agitation

Some people feel more anxious or 'wired' or more impulsive when starting an SSRI. This can be more common with fluoxetine, which then causes agitation or insomnia if taken too late in the day. Sertraline is probably less likely to cause anxiety. It is always difficult to tell whether anxiety is associated with the depression or might be caused by the drug. If it is caused by the drug, the problem might be solved by (a) trying a lower dose; (b) switching to a different SSRI; or (c) adding a different drug that may reduce anxiety. The feeling of increased anxiety is usually temporary and will subside over time. Feelings of increased agitation in some SSRIs is *rarely* associated with an increase in violence or suicidal ideas. This is more likely to occur in a young person. If this happens, seek urgent medical advice. The feelings will subside on gradual withdrawal from the medication and you could try a different therapy or type of anti-depressant.

Rashes

Rashes are rare, but if you do get one, you should speak to your doctor and stop taking your medication. This is more likely to occur with fluoxetine.

Mania

Anti-depressants can very occasionally induce mania, especially in someone who is prone to bipolar disorder. You might be overactive, unusually uninhibited, full of energy, irritable and able to go without any sleep. This condition can involve dangerous or risky behaviors. You should seek medical attention quickly. You could be advised to stop taking the medication.

If side effects are a problem

Whenever side effects are a problem, always discuss them with your doctor. The doctor is likely to advise you to do one of the following:

- reduce the dose
- try a different SSRI
- add another medication to counteract side effects such as insomnia or sexual problems, or

- wait and see, as many of the side effects tend to improve over time.

All SSRIs are equally effective overall. However, you might get a better response from a particular SSRI, or your doctor might wish to try you on another one or on a different class of antidepressant according to how well your mood improves or how troublesome your side effects are.

Tricyclics

Tricyclics are an older class of anti-depressants: they were first developed for the treatment of depression and obsessive compulsive disorder in the 1960s. The name 'tricyclic' is used to describe the structure of the chemical.

They may be prescribed as second or third line drug if an SSRI has not helped.

Tricyclics lost favour to SSRIs because the former have more side effects. Clomipramine (trade name Anafranil) is a tricylic that is used for treating BDD because, compared with other tricyclics, it is a potent serotonin reuptake inhibitor. It can also be used for depression. It is normally started at a low dosage (for example, 75mg at night) and gradually increased to a maximum that you can tolerate. The minimum dose required for an effect is usually

125mg. Higher doses are sometimes used, up to 300mg a day, although the usual dose is up to 225mg. Higher doses tend to increase the frequency of side effects. Most of the side effects are related to the dose and tend to reduce over time but some may persist. They will cease if the drug is discontinued.

Clomipramine is more often prescribed at night so that the sedative side effects have worn off by the morning. Some people metabolize a tricyclic very quickly, and so, even when they are taking a high dose, they may have a relatively low level of the drug in the bloodstream. If necessary, the level of a tricyclic and its metabolite can be checked by a blood test to determine if it is safe to increase the dose to a higher level. Alternatively, you may be given a genetic test to see if you are someone who metabolizes such drugs faster than others.

Common side effects of clomipramine

• **Dry mouth:** At least two-thirds of patients taking clomipramine experience a dry mouth. You get a dry mouth when you produce less saliva than normal. Sucking on sugarless gum can stimulate production of saliva or you could try a spray that can be bought over the counter that provides artificial saliva. Good mouth hygiene is important, as are regular visits to your dentist.

- **Dizziness:** Dizziness on standing is a common side effect for about 25 per cent of patients taking clomipramine. You can reduce dizziness by rising slowly or sitting on the side of the bed and squeezing the muscles in your calf as you stand up.
- **Tremor:** About 15 per cent of patients taking clomipramine develop shakiness or a tremor in their arms. There are no simple remedies for tremor, although another drug (a beta blocker, such as propranolol) may reduce a tremor if it is severe.
- **Weight gain:** Weight gain can be a problem with clomipramine and you should therefore be especially careful to eat healthily.
- **Constipation:** You have a 25 per cent chance of becoming constipated if you take a clomipramine. A diet full of roughage from vegetables or bran and prunes or a bulking agent such as Fybogel or psyllium husks will help. Always remember to drink plenty of water. Laxatives that stimulate the bowel should not be used except occasionally.
- **Drowsiness or fatigue:** Clomipramine can cause drowsiness, which can be reduced by taking the dosage at night. Some people

could still experience a hangover in the morning. If this happens with you, spread the dose over the day.

- **Blurred vision, headache:** Clomipramine can also cause blurring of vision or a headache. There is no good solution to this apart from switching to a different antidepressant.
- **Sexual problems:** Clomipramine can be a reason for delayed ejaculation or, less commonly, impotence in men. It can also cause women difficulties in reaching orgasm. For suggested solutions see under side effects of SSRIs (see section entitled "What side effects occur with SSRIs?").
- **Increased sweating:** People taking clomipramine sometimes complain that they sweat more or that their hot flushes have increased. There is no easy solution to this but it should improve over time.
- **Epileptic fits:** There is a small risk (for about 0.5 per cent of individuals taking clomipramine) of having an epileptic fit. In this case, the drug will need to be discontinued or the dose significantly reduced. The majority of fits, however, occur in patients taking more than 250mg of clomipramine.

- **Urinary problems:** Occasionally, clomipramine can cause urinary retention or hesitancy in the elderly, in which case the drug will need to be discontinued.
- **Heart problems:** People with pre-existing heart disease treated with clomipramine should have an ECG (electrocardiogram) before beginning treatment and at regular intervals during treatment, as it could cause some individuals to develop an irregular heartbeat.

Stopping or reducing your anti-depressant medication

If you are already taking anti-depressant medication, then don't stop or change the dose on your own. The reason is that you might experience withdrawal symptoms from the antidepressant and it's best to reduce such medication slowly. Whether you experience withdrawal symptoms or not is unpredictable. Many people do not experience any or only minor ones; a small minority have marked or severe symptoms that require careful reduction of their medication. Note that some doctors may refer to withdrawal symptoms as 'discontinuation', which is partly a euphemism to avoid the association with an addiction or dependence. However, it is now generally recognized that, for a few people, it is a type of addiction, as the stopping of the drug causes withdrawal symptoms and craving. The body finds it difficult to adapt if a drug is removed suddenly and it is therefore sensible to taper the dose gradually over several weeks. Withdrawal symptoms can be minimized or prevented if you are warned beforehand about how to manage the situation. Always discuss what you want with your doctor and plan things together. Do not be afraid to ask for a second opinion where necessary.

In most people, these withdrawal effects are mild. For a small number of people – and no-one can predict who they might be – the effects can be unpleasant if the medication is stopped suddenly. The speed at which the discontinuation of a drug causes withdrawal symptoms is related to how fast the drug is metabolized and leaves your system. Fluoxetine is the least likely of all SSRIs to cause withdrawal symptoms. This is because it breaks down very slowly and is in your body for up to five weeks after your last dose. If it does cause withdrawal symptoms, they tend to come on within two or three weeks of stopping it. The 'worst' drugs linked to withdrawal symptoms are venlafaxine (Efexor) and paroxetine (Seroxat, Paxil), which can cause symptoms on the same day you miss a dose. Sertraline (Zoloft) commonly causes withdrawal symptoms within two to three days.

Possible physical withdrawal symptoms can include the following:

- flu-like symptoms (aches, fever, sweats, chills, muscle cramps)
- gastroenteritis-like symptoms (nausea, vomiting, diarrhoea, abdominal pain or cramps)
- dizziness, spinning, feeling hungover, feeling unsteady
- headache, tremor
- sensory abnormalities (numbness, sensations that feel like electric shocks, abnormal visual sensations or smells, tinnitus).

The second group of symptoms that can occur are mainly psychological:

- depression (crying, deteriorating mood, fatigue, poor concentration, loss of appetite, suicidal thoughts/attempts)
- anxiety-like symptoms (anxious, nervous, panicky mood)

- a preoccupation and distress with your appearance
- irritability (agitation, impulsivity, aggression)
- confusion, memory problems
- mood swings (elation, mania)
- hallucinations (auditory, visual)
- feelings of dissociation (detachment, unreality, nightmares).

Are your symptoms those of withdrawal or a relapse?

Another problem is deciding whether symptoms that emerge on stopping medication are those of *withdrawal* or whether they are a *relapse* of depression. The following differences may help you and your doctor to tell.

DO YOUR SYMPTOMS COME ON SUDDENLY OVER DAYS OR WITHIN A WEEK AFTER STOPPING?

Withdrawal symptoms come on relatively suddenly, within days or weeks of lowering or stopping an anti-depressant. Symptoms of relapse of depression usually occur within one or more months of stopping.

ARE YOUR SYMPTOMS PHYSICAL?

Physical symptoms such as feeling dizzy or light-headed, having flu-like aches, sweating, nausea, numbness, electric shocks and headaches are usually part of the withdrawal state. While some of these physical symptoms can occasionally occur in relapse of depression, they would have been part of the original symptoms you had, and you might recognize them as such.

HOW QUICKLY DO YOUR SYMPTOMS IMPROVE WHEN YOU STOP MEDICATION?

Withdrawal symptoms peak within about seven to ten days and are usually gone within three weeks; by contrast, symptoms of a relapse of depression will persist and may get worse.

HOW QUICKLY DO YOUR SYMPTOMS IMPROVE IF YOU RESTART THE MEDICATION?

Withdrawal symptoms immediately improve when you restart the drug. Symptoms of relapse may continue or get worse and take several weeks to improve when you recommence an antidepressant.

HOW DO MY DOCTOR AND I REDUCE THE DRUG SLOWLY ENOUGH?

The first step is to decide when to reduce the dose. This normally depends on whether you have been well for long enough and whether you are still vulnerable to relapse. Have you had an effective psychological therapy that can now protect you? The optimum rate of reduction of an anti-depressant to a standard dose is related to the type of drug. In general, each reduction should take place over a month.

The rate at which you reduce the drug depends on the nature of the drug, the dose you are taking and the severity of any withdrawal symptoms you experience. For example, paroxetine (Seroxat or Paxil) being prescribed at 20mg daily might be reduced to 10mg for one month. Each reduction would then guide the speed at which the medication is further reduced. If withdrawal symptoms emerge, you may have to slow down. For example:

- if you experience mild or no symptoms then you need not change the rate of reduction (e.g. paroxetine from 10mg to nothing)
- if you experience moderate withdrawal symptoms, the next reduction would be smaller (e.g. paroxetine from 10mg to 5mg)
- if you have severe withdrawal symptoms your doctor will probably restore the original dose and then start smaller dose

reductions (e.g. paroxetine 20mg to 15mg for a month). If this results in no symptoms or mild symptoms, it could then be reduced to 12.5mg

Most withdrawal symptoms can be minimized by reducing the drugs slowly and this should be done under the guidance of your doctor. Some patients have been advised to take the drug on alternate days, but this does not make sense unless it is long-acting like fluoxetine. It is nearly always better to reduce the dose of an anti-depressant by a small amount on a daily basis. Further discussion on withdrawing from anti-depressants can be found in the very helpful book *Coming Off Antidepressants* (see Appendix 1).

Liquid preparations

To obtain smaller doses for a withdrawal program or to start at a lower dose, you can cut the tablets into smaller pieces. Alternatively, if you are simply unable to tolerate a tablet, you may find it easier to have your medication in the form of a liquid (elixir), and it can be easier to reduce the dose of a liquid by successively measuring a smaller amount. The drugs available in liquid form are listed in Table 14.1.

Use of medication in pregnancy and breastfeeding

Most of the SSRIs and clomipramine are generally considered safe for pregnant women. However, as no manufacturer wants to be sued, they all recommend 'caution' and say that their product should not be used in pregnancy or breastfeeding. No mother wants to cause harm to her baby, but in general there are no significant problems. Fluoxetine, paroxetine, sertraline and clomipramine are the most studied in pregnancy or breastfeeding, so these are the most widely prescribed drugs for pregnant women. Animal and human studies suggest a very low risk but they are not fully conclusive. The risk of 'spontaneous abortion' may be very slightly higher than normal but the figures are difficult to interpret. Most doctors prefer to be cautious and therefore treat BDD or depression with a psychological treatment where pregnancy is possible or planned. However, if you or your doctor believe that medication is necessary (and depression commonly gets worse during pregnancy), or if you find a psychological approach difficult, it is nearly always better for you to be functioning as a mother than suffering from depression, whatever the precise risks involved. However, you should discuss this fully with your doctor, as there might be new evidence.

What if an SSRI or clomipramine fails?

There are other options if you do not get better with two or more SSRIs or clomipramine, and these are best discussed with a psychiatrist. For example, there is some evidence for the benefits of combining different anti-depressant drugs (say, an SSRI such as citalopram with clomipramine). Sometimes a very high dose of a SSRI may be used. Alternatively, your doctor might recommend a different class of anti-depressant (for example, venlafaxine) or combining an SSRI with buspirone in BDD. Buspirone is an anti-anxiety drug.

Anti-psychotic drugs

Some doctors prescribe drugs for BDD that block dopamine receptors either alone or as an additional treatment to a SSRI. These are also known as anti-psychotic drugs and include olanzapine (Zyprexa), ziprasidone (Geodon), risperidone (Risperidal), aripiprazole (Abilify), haloperidol (Haldol), quetiapine (Seroquel), sulpiride, trifluoperazine, pimozide and chlorpromazine. Some anti-psychotics (especially olanzapine and to a lesser extent risperidone) are more likely to cause weight gain and sedation.

Dopamine-blocking drugs are normally used for treating psychosis and paranoia. There is no evidence for the benefit of dopamine-blocking drugs either alone or in combination with another drug in BDD. One study suggested that adding pimozide to people who have failed to respond to an SSRI did not make any difference compared with a placebo in BDD. Anti-psychotics may still be prescribed in the short term if you are very agitated or, for example, have tics or have more complex problems with paranoia.

What are the side effects of dopamine-blocking drugs?

In low doses, dopamine-blocking drugs may help to reduce anxiety and do not usually cause problems. The main side effect may be tiredness. Some anti-dopamine drugs cause weight gain and loss of libido. When dopamine blockers are prescribed in higher doses, they can have side effects such as stiffness in the limbs or slurred speech that can be countered by medication such as procyclidine. A small minority of women experience hormonal changes, such as stimulation of prolactin, which stops their periods.

With a very high dose or if you are especially sensitive, such drugs may cause abnormal movements such as a tremor and you might need other tablets to counteract these effects. In general, an anti-psychotic drug is not recommended in the long term for unipolar depression. At a higher dose it can emotionally numb you and prevent you from experiencing pleasure.

If you are already taking such medication, then please don't stop or change the dose on your own. Always discuss your wishes with your doctor and plan things together. Do not be afraid to ask for a second opinion where necessary.

Tranquillizers

Tranquillizers are drugs that aim to reduce anxiety or have a sedative effect. The most common are a group of drugs called benzodiazepines (diazepam or Valium, nitrazepam, lorazepam, clonazepam). Others are prescribed for sleep. There is no evidence for their benefit in treating BDD.

Tranquillizers used to be prescribed very commonly in the past but are less used now because of the risks of addiction. They are used for managing severe agitation in depression in the short term. The main side effects are slower reaction times, so they should not be used if you operate machinery or drive. The main problem is of dependence, so that a sudden withdrawal can lead to a short-term increase in anxiety, insomnia, irritability, headaches and many other possible symptoms. Withdrawal from such drugs therefore needs to be managed carefully.

Other treatments

What about electroconvulsive therapy for BDD?

There is no evidence that ECT helps in BDD. It might very occasionally be recommended where the person with BDD has very severe depression that has not responded to medication or a psychological treatment.

What about brain surgery for BDD?

There is no evidence for the benefit of neurosurgery in BDD. There have been a few cases with mixed reports in BDD but there are no controlled trials comparing surgery with a sham treatment. Neurosurgery is generally safe, but can be followed by some rare complications such as epilepsy, haemorrhage, persistent headaches or infections.

What about deep brain stimulation for BDD?

Other medical techniques are being re-searched but these are still purely experimental. One, known as deep brain stimulation, passes an electric current to electrodes implanted in the brain. Because the stimulator can be switched on and off, the effects are reversible. However, in our experience, when individuals with BDD raise the possibility of neurosurgery and deep brain stimulation, they are avoiding a great deal and this needs to be the focus of the therapy.

15

Finding help

When to consider professional help

A self-help book could be all that is required for some people to overcome a body image problem. After all, even with professional help, it is likely to be your own efforts between sessions that make the biggest difference. You might consider using this book with the aid of a professional; this is called 'guided self-help'. In this case, the book can offer a shared way of understanding your problems, and the strategies to improve the way you feel.

Professional help, with an appropriately trained practitioner, is often the most effective approach. This involves working with a psychologist, psychiatrist, therapist, counsellor or nurse therapist. Cognitive behavioral therapy (CBT) can help most people and will rarely make symptoms worse. We suggest that you seek professional help if your body image problem is in the moderate to severe range, and especially if your attempts at self-help are not bearing fruit after a month or so. If you are feeling hopeless about the future and are having thoughts about ending your life, please seek professional help **immediately.**

Getting the right kind of help

If you are prescribed medication like Prozac, you can virtually guarantee that any pharmacy you go to will give you the right dosage and that the Prozac will be of the same quality. Unfortunately, this is not always true of psychological therapy. Of all the different forms of psychotherapy, only CBT has been shown to work effectively for a body image problem and is likely to be the treatment of choice. When choosing a suitable therapist, the alarm bells should ring when you encounter therapists who:

• do not tell you what type of therapy you are receiving

• just keep asking 'How does that make you feel?'

• spend *most* of the time wanting you to discuss your childhood and the cause of your body image problem

• do not share their understanding of what maintains your problem

• do not problem-solve with you

• do not negotiate relevant homework between sessions

> • do not monitor your progress in overcoming your symptoms.

If you are not sure, ask what type of therapy or counselling you are receiving. There is no evidence that general counselling, psychodynamic therapy, psychoanalytical therapy, hypnotherapy or transactional analysis is of any benefit for moderate to severe body image problems. People can find such approaches supportive or helpful for some issues but they are rarely helpful by themselves in overcoming a body image problem. Supportive psychological therapy might also help people to a degree with mild problems.

Similarly, beware of a doctor who offers only medication without also recommending a psychological treatment. There might also be problems with obtaining psychological therapies on the NHS because of the lack of funding but this is not the fault of the doctor. This is a problem that requires political action and takes a long times to solve. In the meantime seek support, use the principles outlined in this book (or other CBT-based self-help material), and consider asking your doctor for medication or consider private therapy.

Fears about seeking help

You might have a number of worries about seeking help such as:

- 'What if it doesn't help?'
- 'It will be too embarrassing to tell them about my problem.'
- 'They'll think I'm mad and want to keep me in hospital.'
- 'What if they pass the information on to social services or my employer?'

If you find it difficult to talk about some of your worries, it's usually helpful to say you are embarrassed or ashamed. Remember that worrying is normal and any health professional who has the slightest experience with body image problems will be sensitive to your difficulties. He or she will not consider you mad or want to keep you in hospital against your will. Individuals are assessed for detention only in extreme circumstances: if you are a danger to yourself or others (for example, if you are actively suicidal, neglecting yourself badly or are very underweight). Such information is kept confidential and cannot be shared with other agencies or your employer without your permission. It does not go on any employment records or to social services. Only in *extreme* circumstances would a therapist ask someone to assess the impact of a person's body image problem on his/her family and children. Treatment may not help initially, as it can take a few weeks to take effect, but if nothing is risked, nothing is gained and your problem is likely to persist for some time. Furthermore, CBT or medication very rarely makes your problem worse.

In teaching centres, you may be asked if a student or trainee may sit in. It is important to continue training others in psychological treatment but you are entitled to refuse without it affecting your treatment.

Remember, as with all other thoughts, try to treat your thoughts about seeking help as 'just thoughts,' which are likely to be quite common under the circumstances. Rather than trying to ignore them, or debating them in your mind, take your thoughts with a pinch of salt and act consistently towards pursuing your goal of overcoming your body image problem.

Getting the most from a psychological therapy

You will get most from a psychological therapy if you:

- keep your appointments
- are honest and open with your therapist
- tell your therapist if you do feel very embarrassed or ashamed about your symptoms
- attempt the homework agreed between you and your therapist during therapy sessions (having a good relationship with your therapist is important, but adherence to daily testing out of alternatives is the biggest predictor of success in therapy)
- challenge your usual way of responding to your problem (e.g. the way you check, compare, brood, avoid) and act *as if* you don't have an emotional problem (even if you don't believe it)
- act against the way you feel and do it 'unconfidently' and 'uncomfortably' even if you are not sure it will work
- have clear goals that you want to achieve and you can agree on with your therapist
- regularly monitor your progress with your therapist, using progress charts or scales
- tape-record the sessions so you can listen to them again
- give the therapist feedback.

You might find that you are not ready for CBT and it might be better to return when you feel more committed to change and able to do the homework regularly. Don't believe you are a 'hopeless case' – change is nearly always possible. Even a small change is worth making, and then you can build on it. Don't be afraid to seek a second opinion or a referral to a specialist centre.

Types of professionals offering help

There is a range of mental health professionals who will offer help for a body image problem. Most mental health teams are multidisciplinary, which means that they include people from different professional backgrounds.

- Psychiatrists are medical doctors who specialize in mental disorder. They can prescribe medication for BDD or bulimia and will probably be more knowledgeable about dosage and other issues required for BDD and bulimia than your family doctor. Only a few psychiatrists are trained in CBT.
- Clinical psychologists have a basic training in psychology and have then trained in the clinical application of psychological

assessment and therapies. They do not prescribe medication. Many will offer CBT but might not have had the specialist training and supervision required.

- Counselling psychologists have a basic training in psychology and are then trained in counselling and therapy. They do not prescribe medication. Some offer CBT but might not have had the specialist training required.

- Nurse therapists are originally trained in psychiatric nursing, and in the UK most have specialized in CBT.

- Psychotherapists and counsellors come from a broad range of therapy backgrounds. Most will listen to you and help you to work through issues in your life. They do not prescribe medication. They are not usually trained in CBT.

- All of the above may be suitably trained and supervised in CBT but will not have a lot of experience with body image problems!

It is important to realize that, at the time of writing, there is nothing to stop anyone calling themselves a counsellor or psychotherapist, whether or not they are properly trained. No therapist with a recognized professional qualification is going to mind you asking about his or her relevant training and qualifications.

It is very important to satisfy yourself about these things as well as the type of therapy used. Here are some questions that you may want to ask:

> • What experience has he or she got of treating body image problems (for example, how many patients or clients has he or she treated)?
> • What therapy does he or she use?
> • If providing CBT, is he or she accredited or accreditable as having a minimum training in CBT?
> • What are his or her expectations for change at the end of therapy and do these match your goals?
> • Do you get on with the therapist?

Of course you will want someone who is experienced with body image problems, but if he or she is not, try to judge whether he or she is willing to learn more. Details of finding an accredited therapist are given below.

If you have problems with your therapist

If you want to complain about any professional, think clearly about the nature of the problem – for example, is it the type of treatment, the therapist, the location, or something else?

Are there contributing factors (e.g. the personality of your therapist or you feeling more depressed)? Can you sort it out with the therapist or another member of the team? Can you think of possible solutions to discuss with the professional? If the professional is refusing further therapy, listen to his or her reasons and write them down. If the reasons are financial (for example, it costs too much), don't give up, as you could have to persist to get another opinion.

Finding professional help in the UK

If you would like professional treatment in the UK, your family doctor or general practitioner is the best place to start. He or she will usually be aware of what services are available locally. If you are worried about seeing your GP, take a relative or friend with you. If you find it difficult to talk to your GP, write a letter and give it to him or her. At your consultation, write down the key points that you want answered. You can always change your GP if you think you might be better understood or treated by another.

The information that you tell your GP is confidential and cannot be shared without your permission. If your local mental health service is unable to assist, they might refer you to a national service. Unfortunately, getting referred to a specialist service is not always easy (due to funding shortages) and will usually depend upon the support of your local mental health team. Make it clear that you will need cognitive behavioral therapy from a trained practitioner. For therapy services in the NHS, you can usually be referred only to a department and not to a particular individual. Despite this, you could find it helpful to do your own research and find out the names of recommended therapists from a support group or national charity (see the list of addresses given in Appendix 1).

In their treatment guidelines for OCD and BDD, the National Institute of Health and Clinical Excellence (NICE) recommend that patients should have access to an OCD/BDD multidisciplinary healthcare team which will focus on the more severe cases and decide who should be referred onwards to a national service. One of the authors of this book (David Veale) runs a national service in the UK for BDD at the South London and Maudsley Trust. This is for out-patient treatment or for a more intensive treatment program on a residential unit. There is also a separate stream of funding from the Department of Health for a treatment refractory service – further details can be found on the website www.iop.kcl.ac.uk/ncg.

In the UK, it is usually *quicker* to obtain help privately but this does not necessarily mean that the treatment will be any better. Good and bad treatment can occur both in the public and the private sector. It is best to ask for recommendations from your local support group or a national charity, which may keep a directory of practitioners. In the UK, you can also try searching for a private accredited therapist on the website of the British Association for Behavioural and Cognitive Psychotherapies (www.babcp.com) in the 'Find a Therapist' section. Not all cognitive behavioral therapists bother to become accredited and there are many from psychiatry, psychology or nursing backgrounds who are excellent cognitive behavioral therapists.

Finding help in the USA

In the USA, finding a cognitive behavioral therapist may be difficult depending on where you live. You could ask for a referral from your family doctor or recommendation from an academic psychiatry or psychology department. The best recommendation could come from your local support group or charity. It is likely to be a member of the Association for Behavioral and

Cognitive Therapies, which maintains a directory of therapists who can be contacted (www.aabt .org). As in the UK, it is usually quicker to obtain help privately but this does not mean you will necessarily get any better treatment. Good and bad treatment can occur both in the public and the private sector.

Finding help in the rest of the world

The European Association for Behavioural Cognitive Therapies lists member associations on its website http://www.eabct.com. Details of the Australian Association for Cognitive and Behavioural Therapy can be found on its website at http://www.aacbt.org/.

Charities and support groups

In addition to professional help, national charities and local support groups can be invaluable. In the UK if you have BDD, support the BDD Foundation, BDD Help or OCD Action. If you have a disfigurement, support Changing Faces. For an eating disorder, support BEAT (formerly known as the Eating Disorders Association). In the USA, if you have BDD, you can support the Neysa Jane BDD fund and the OCD Foundation.

These charities will offer you information on local resources and support groups, which provide a forum for mutual acceptance, understanding and setting of goals. They will also be able to recommend local therapists or psychiatrists. People new to the area can talk to others who have learnt successful ways of coping. Reading books and Internet articles about body image problems are useful ways of getting further information or support. The more you know about the problem and the more you can become your own therapist, the better equipped you will be to overcome it. And when you recover from your body image problem, you can help raise funds for research into better treatments, and campaign for better services and for training for more cognitive behavioral therapists in public medicine. Unfortunately, many of these charities are too small to be able to focus enough energy on raising funds for research, especially compared with the big charities dealing with cancer or heart disease.

Appendix 1

Useful contacts and information

UNITED KINGDOM

Acne Support Group
1st Floor
Howard House
The Runway
South Ruislip
Middlesex HA4 6SE
Helpline Tel: 0044-20-8841-4747 (24hrs)
Administration Tel: 0044-20-8841-8400

The Acne Support Group gives support and help to people with acne and rosacea.

The BDD Foundation
Website: www.thebddfoundation.org
Email: admin@thebddfoundation.com

The BDD Foundation aims to increase awareness and understanding of body dysmorphic disorder.

BDD Help
Website: www.bddhelp.com

Email: emma@bddhelp.com

Information about overcoming BDD. The website is maintained by someone who has recovered from BDD.

BEAT (Previously known as the Eating Disorders
 Association)
103 Prince of Wales Road
Norwich NR1 1DW
Tel: 0845-634-1414
Youthline: 0845-634-7650
Email: help@b-eat.co.uk
Website: www.b-eat.co.uk

Beat is a national charity based in the UK, providing information, help and support for people affected by eating disorders.

**British Association of Aesthetic Plastic
 Surgeons**
The Royal College of Surgeons of England
35–43 Lincoln's Inn Fields
London WC2A 3PE
Advice Line Tel:
020-7405-2234
Administration Tel:
020-7430-1840
Fax: 020-7242-4922
Email: info@baaps.org.uk

Website: www.baaps.org.uk

**British Association for Behavioural and
 Cognitive Psychotherapists (BABCP)**
Victoria Buildings
9–13 Silver Street
Bury BL9 0EU
Tel: 0161-797-4484
Fax: 0161-797-2670
Email: babcp@babcp.com
Website: www.babcp.com

Changing Faces
The Squire Centre
33–37 University Street
London WCIE 6JN
Tel GB: 0845-4500-275
Tel Wales: 0845-4500-240
Tel Northern Ireland: 0845-4500-732
Tel Scotland: 0845-4500-640
Email:
info@changingfaces.org.uk
Website:
www.changingfaces.org.uk

Changing Faces provides support to people
with disfigurements by publishing information
and running workshops to help them improve
their social skills and develop their self-confidence and self-esteem.

National Institute for Health and Clinical Excellence (NICE)

Mid City Place
71 High Holborn
London WCIV 6NA
Tel: 0845-003-7780
Fax: 0845-003-7784
Email:
nice@nice.org.uk
Website:
www.nice.org.uk

OCD Action

Davina House
Suites 506–507
137–149 Goswell Road
London EC1V 7ET
Office Tel: 0870-360-6232
Helpline: 0845-390-6232
Fax: 020-7288-0828
Email:
info@ocdaction.org.uk
Website:
www.ocdaction.org.uk

OCD Action is a user-led charity for individuals with OCD and BDD.

OCD Youth

Young People's OCD Clinic

Michael Rutter Centre
Maudsley Hospital
Denmark Hill
London SE5 8AZ
Email:
ocdyoutheditor@iop.kcl.ac.uk
Website:
www.ocdyouth.iop.kcl.ac.uk

OCD Youth is an organization especially designed to help children and adolescents with OCD and other related disorders.

Samaritans
Central London Branch
46 Marshall St
London W1F 9BF
Tel: 0207-734-2800
(London branch)
Tel: 08457-90-90-90 (UK)
Email:
jo@samaritans.org
Website:
www.samaritans.org.uk

Samaritans is a registered charity, which offers confidential support to anyone experiencing a crisis or thinking of taking their own life.

Sane & Saneline

1st Floor
Cityside House
40 Adler Street
London E1 1EE
Helpline Tel: 0845-678-000
Email:
info@sane.org.uk
Website:
www.sane.org.uk

SANELINE is a national mental health helpline providing information and support with a database of local and national services.

The Scar Information Service
Website:
www.scarinfo.org/addresses.html

This website provides further links to organizations dealing with facial disfigurement in the UK.

UNITED STATES OF AMERICA

About Face
PO Box 969
Batavia, IL 60510
Tel: 1-888-486-1209
Fax: 1-630-761-2985
Email: info@aboutfaceusa.org

Website: www.aboutfaceusa.org

About Face provides information and emotional support to individuals with facial differences.

The Alliance for Eating Disorders Awareness
PO Box 13155
North Palm Beach
Florida 33408–3155
Tel: 561-841-0900
Fax: 561-841-0972
Email:
info@eatingdisorderinfo.org
Website:
www.eatingdisorderinfo.org

This website seeks to give accessible programs across the USA that allow children and young adults to be educated about eating disorders.

Association for Behavioral and Cognitive Therapies
305 7th Avenue
16th Floor
New York NY 10001
Tel: 212-647-1890
Fax: 212-647-1865

Website: www.aabt.org

The Neysa Jane BDD Fund, Inc.
679 92nd Avenue North
Naples, Florida 34108
Tel: 239-594-5421
Email: nesyabdd@comcast.net

The Neysa Jane BDD Fund provides telephone support and information to BDD sufferers around the world.

OC Foundation
337 Notch Hill Road
North Branford, CT 06471
Tel: 203-315-2190
Fax: 203-315-2196
Email:
info@ocfoundation.org
Website:
www.ocfoundation.org/

The OC Foundation is a nonprofit organization for people with OCD and related disorders such as BDD.

Trichotillomania Learning Center, Inc.
207 McPherson Street,
Suite H, Santa Cruz,
CA 95060–5863–5863

Tel: 831-457-1004
Fax: 831-426-4383
Email: info@trich.org
Website: www.trich.org

This site provides information for people suffering from trichotillomania.

AUSTRALIA

Anxiety Recovery Centre Victoria
42 High Street Road
Ashwood
Victoria 3147
OCD & Anxiety Helpline
Tel: 03-9886-9377
Office Tel: 03-9886-9233
Fax: 03-9886-9411
Email: arcmail@arcvic.com.au
Website: www.arcvic.com.au

The Anxiety Recovery Centre Victoria is an organization for people living with anxiety disorders.

Eating Disorders Association Inc.
12 Chatsworth Road,
Greenslopes 4120
Queensland
Tel: 07-3394-3661
Fax: 07-3394-3663

Email: admin@eda.org.au
Website:
www.eda.org.au

The Eating Disorders Association provides support and information for people with an eating disorder.

CANADA

Obsessive Compulsive Information and Support Centre, Inc.

R. 204–825 Sherbrook Street
Winnipeg MB R3A 1M5
Tel: 204-942-3331
Fax: 204-975-3027
Email: occmanitoba@shaw.ca
Website:
www.members.shaw.ca/occmanitoba/

This website provides assistance and education for people affected by OCD and related disorders such as BDD.

Ontario Obsessive Compulsive Disorder Network

PO Box 151
Markham
Ontario L3P 3J7
Tel: 416-410-4772
Fax: 905-472-4473

Email: info@ocdontario.org
Website: www.ocdontario.org

OCD Ontario is a non-profit charity focused on providing help and information to children and adults with OCD and their families in Ontario.

NEW ZEALAND

OCD Support Group
Floor 2
Securities House
221 Gloucester Street
Christchurch 8011
Tel: 13-366-0560
Fax: 13-365-5345
Email: info@OCD.org.nz
Website: www.OCD.org.nz/

The website provides a place for people with OCD and their families to share common ground, information and support.

South Africa

OCD Association of South Africa
PO Box 87127
Houghton 2041
Tel: 27-0-786-7030
Email: pserebro@iafrica.com

Further reading

These are all user-friendly self-help books.

Body image

Cash, T., *The Body Image Workbook* (Oakland, California: New Harbinger Publications).

Body dysmorphic disorder

Phillips, K., *The Broken Mirror: Understanding and Treating Body Dysmorphic Disorder* (Oxford: Oxford University Press).

Wilhelm, S., *Feeling Good About the Way You Look* (New York: Guilford Publications).

Claiborn, J. and Pedrick, C., *The BDD Workbook* (Oakland, California: New Harbinger Publications).

Pope, H., Phillips, K and Olivardia, R., *The Adonis Complex – How to Identify, Treat, and Prevent Body Obsession in Men and Boys* (New York: Simon and Schuster).

Cognitive behavioral therapy

Willson, R. and Branch, R., *Cognitive Behavioural Therapy for Dummies* (Wiley).

Depression

Veale, D. and Willson, R., *Manage Your Mood* (London: Robinson).

Gilbert, P., *Overcoming Depression* (London: Robinson).

Fennell, M., *Overcoming Low Self-Esteem* (London: Robinson).

Addis, M. and Martell, C., *Overcoming Depression One Step at a Time* (Oakland, California: New Harbinger Publications).

Burns, D., *Feeling Good* (New York: Avon Books).

Dryden, W., *How to Accept Yourself* (London: Sheldon Press).

Glenmullen, J., *Coming Off Antidepressants* (London: Robinson).

Disfigurement

Partridge, J., *Changing Faces: the Challenge of Facial Disfigurement* (London: Penguin).

Eating disorders

Freeman, C., *Overcoming Anorexia Nervosa* (London: Robinson).

Cooper, P., *Bulimia Nervosa and Binge-Eating* (London: Robinson).

Fairburn, C., *Overcoming Binge-Eating* (New York: Guilford).

Obsessive compulsive disorder

Veale, D. and Willson, R., *Overcoming Obsessive Compulsive Disorder* (London: Robinson).

Social phobia

Butler, G., *Overcoming Social Anxiety and Shyness* (London: Robinson).

Trichotillomania and skin-picking

Penzel, F., *The Hair Pulling Problem: A Complete Guide to Trichotillomania* (Oxford: Oxford University Press).

Claiborn, J. and Pedrick, C., *The Habit Change Workbook* (Oakland, California: New Harbinger Publications).

Appendix 2

Assessment forms and progress charts

Chapter 2

THE HOSPITAL ANXIETY AND DEPRESSION (HAD) SCALE

Please read each group of statements carefully, and then pick the one (by writing the number in the box) that comes closest to how you have been feeling in the past week and write that number in the box. Don't take too long over your replies: your immediate reaction to each item will probably be more accurate than a long-thought-out response.

	Anxiety	Depression

1. I feel tense or 'wound up':

    3 Most of the time

    2 A lot of the time

    1 From time to time, occasionally

    0 Not at all

	Anxiety	Depression

2. I still enjoy the things I used to enjoy:

    0 Definitely as much
    1 Not quite so much
    2 Only a little
    3 Hardly at all

                                                                 ☐

3. I get a sort of frightened feeling
as if something awful is about
to happen:

    3 Very definitely and quite badly
    2 Yes, but not too badly
    1 A little, but it doesn't worry me ☐
    0 Not at all

4. I can laugh and see the funny side
of things:

    0 As much as I always could
    1 Not quite so much now
    2 Definitely not so much now
    3 Not at all

                                                                 ☐

5. Worrying thoughts go through my mind:

    3 A great deal of the time
    2 A lot of the time
    1 From time to time but not too
       often
    0 Only occasionally

	Anxiety	Depression

6. I feel cheerful:

   3 Not at all
   2 Not often
   1 Sometimes
   0 Most of the time

7. I can sit at ease and feel relaxed:

   0 Definitely
   1 Usually
   2 Not often
   3 Not at all

8. I feel as if I am slowed down:

   3 Nearly all the time
   2 Very often
   1 Sometimes
   0 Not at all

9. I get a sort of frightened feeling
like 'butterflies' in the stomach:

   0 Not at all
   1 Occasionally
   2 Quite often
   3 Very often

	Anxiety	Depression

10. I have lost interest in my
   appearance:
   3 Definitely
   2 I don't take so much care as I
      should
   1 I may not take quite as much care
   0 I take just as much care as ever

11. I feel restless as if I have to
    be on the move:
    3 Very much indeed
    2 Quite a lot
    1 Not very much
    0 Not at all

12. I look forward with enjoyment
    to things:
    0 As much as I ever did
    1 Rather less than I used to
    2 Definitely less than I used to
    3 Hardly at all

13. I get sudden feelings of panic:

    3 Very often indeed
    2 Quite often
    1 Not very often
    0 Not at all

	Anxiety	Depression
14. I can enjoy a good book or radio or TV programme: 0 Often 1 Sometimes 2 Not often 3 Very seldom		☐

	Anxiety	Depression
TOTAL	☐	☐

Add up your scores for anxiety (in the left-hand column) and depression (in right-hand column).

The scores can be summarized on a chart completed at regular intervals so that you can monitor progress.

If you score 9 or more on the depression sub-scale, you are probably experiencing depression. Similarly, if you score more than 9 or more on the anxiety sub-scale, you are probably experiencing an anxiety disorder. Higher scores (15 or more on the depression sub-scale) could mean that a self-help book might not be suitable for you, and you might need to seek additional professional help.

Chapter 4

Safety behavior monitoring form

My preoccupation	Example of safety behavior	Unintended consequence

Chapter 6

THOUGHT MONITORING CHART

WEEK BEGINNING _____

Write in your most common intrusive thoughts and images about your appearance, and tick the relevant column each time you have that thought, or add the total from your tally counter.

	Mon	Tues	Wed	Thurs	Fri	Sat	Sun
I have an intrusive thought that:							
I have an intrusive thought that:							
I have an intrusive thought that:							
I have an intrusive thought that:							
I have an intrusive image of:							
I have an intrusive image of:							

Chapter 10

COST-BENEFIT ANALYSIS OF _____

Costs – for you and other people. Consider short- and long-term costs.

Benefits – for you and other people. Consider short- and long-term benefits.

References

Questionnaire 2.3

'The SCOFF questionnaire: Assessment of a new screening tool for eating disorders', *BMJ*, 1999 (7223): 1467–1468. Compiled by J.F. Morgan, F. Reid, and J.H. Lacey Reproduced with the kind permission of the authors and St George's Hospital Medical School.

Questionnaire 2.4

'Detecting alcoholism: The CAGE questionnaire'. *Journal of the American Medical Association,* 1984, 252, 1905–1907. Developed by Ewing, J.A.

More psychology titles from Constable & Robinson
Please visit www.overcoming.co.uk **for more information**

Title
An Introduction to Coping with Anxiety
An Introduction to Coping with Depression
An Introduction to Coping with Health Anxiety
An Introduction to Coping with Obsessive Compulsive Disorder
An Introduction to Coping with Panic
An Introduction to Coping with Phobias
Overcoming Anger and Irritability
Overcoming Anorexia Nervosa
Overcoming Anxiety
Overcoming Anxiety Self-Help Course (3 parts)
Overcoming Body Image Problems
Bulimia Nervosa and Binge-Eating
Overcoming Bulimia Nervosa and Binge-Eating Self-Help Course (3 parts)
Overcoming Childhood Trauma
Overcoming Chronic Fatigue
Overcoming Chronic Pain
Overcoming Compulsive Gambling
Overcoming Depersonalizaton and Feelings of Unreality
Overcoming Depression
Overcoming Depression: Talks With Your Therapist (audio)
Overcoming Grief
Overcoming Insomnia and Sleep Problems

Title
Overcoming Low Self-Esteem
Overcoming Low Self-Esteem Self-Help Course (3 parts)
Overcoming Mood Swings
Overcoming Obsessive Compulsive Disorder
Overcoming Panic and Agoraphobia
Overcoming Panic and Agoraphobia Self-Help Course (3 parts)
Overcoming Paranoid and Suspicious Thoughts
Overcoming Problem Drinking
Overcoming Relationship Problems
Overcoming Sexual Problems
Overcoming Social Anxiety and Shyness
Overcoming Social Anxiety and Shyness Self-Help Course (3 parts)
Overcoming Traumatic Stress
Overcoming Weight Problems
Overcoming Worry
Overcoming Your Child's Fears and Worries
Overcoming Your Child's Shyness and Social Anxiety
Overcoming Your Smoking Habit
The Happiness Trap
The Glass Half-Full
I Had a Black Dog
Living with a Black Dog
Manage Your Mood: How to use Behavioral Activation Techniques to Overcome Depression

Name (block letters): _____
Address: _____
Postcode: _____

Email: _____

Tel No: _____

How to Pay:

1. **By telephone:** call the TBS order line on **01206-255-800** and quote **BIP.** Phone lines are open between Monday–Friday, 8.30am–5.30pm.

2. **By post:** send a cheque for the full amount payable to TBS Ltd, and send form to:

Freepost RLUL-SJGC-SGKJ. Cash Sales/Direct Mail Dept, The Book Service, Colchester Road, Frating, Colchester, CO7 7DW

Is/are the book(s) intended for personal use _ or professional use _?

Please note this information will not be passed on to third parties.

Constable & Robinson Ltd (directly or via its agents) may mail or phone you about promotions or products Tick if you do not want these from us _ or our subsidiaries _

New from Constable & Robinson in 2009

The Compassionate Mind
A New Approach to Life's Challenges

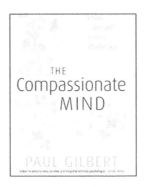

PAUL GILBERT

'As one of Britain's most insightful psychologists,
Gilbert illuminates the power of compassion in our lives.'
Oliver James, author of *Affluenza*

Compassion and particularly compassion towards oneself can have a significant impact on our wellbeing and mental health. Developing our sense of compassion can affect many areas of our lives, in particular our relationships with other people.

In this book, Professor Paul Gilbert explores how our minds have developed to survive in dangerous and threatening environments by becoming sensitive and quick to react to perceived threats. This can sometimes lead to problems in how we respond to life's challenges, and scientific evidence has demonstrated that compassion towards oneself and others can lead to an increased sense of happiness and wellbeing – particularly valuable when we are feeling stressed.

Based on evolutionary research and scientific studies of how the brain processes emotional information, this compassionate approach offers an appealing alternative to the traditional western view of compassion, which sometimes sees it as a sign of weakness and can encourage self-criticism and a hard-nosed drive to achieve.

Professor Paul Gilbert is the author of *Overcoming Depression,* which has sold more than 110,000 copies, and is Professor of Clinical Psychology at the University of Derby and Director of the Mental Health Research Unit, Kingsway Hospital, Derby.

Visit www.constablerobinson.com for more information

Books For ALL Kinds of Readers

At ReadHowYouWant we understand that one size does not fit all types of readers. Our innovative, patent pending technology allows us to design new formats to make reading easier and more enjoyable for you. This helps improve your speed of reading and your comprehension. Our EasyRead printed books have been optimized to improve word recognition, ease eye tracking by adjusting word and line spacing as well as minimizing hyphenation. Our EasyRead SuperLarge editions have been developed to make reading easier and more accessible for vision-impaired readers. We offer Braille and DAISY formats of our books and all popular E-Book formats.

We are continually introducing new formats based upon research and reader preferences. Visit our web-site to see all of our formats and learn how you can Personalize our books for yourself or as gifts. Sign up to Become A RHYW Registered Reader.

www.readhowyouwant.com

Lightning Source UK Ltd.
Milton Keynes UK
UKOW06f0216050914

238061UK00007B/100/P

9 781459 658745